Appropriate, Negotiate, Challenge

The publisher and the University of California Press Foundation gratefully acknowledge the generous support of the Barbara S. Isgur Endowment Fund in Public Affairs.

Appropriate, Negotiate, Challenge

ACTIVIST IMAGINARIES
AND THE POLITICS OF
DIGITAL TECHNOLOGIES

Elisabetta Ferrari

UNIVERSITY OF CALIFORNIA PRESS

University of California Press
Oakland, California

© 2025 by Elisabetta Ferrari

Library of Congress Cataloging-in-Publication Data

Names: Ferrari, Elisabetta, author.
Title: Appropriate, negotiate, challenge : activist imaginaries and the
    politics of digital technologies / Elisabetta Ferrari.
Description: Oakland, California : University of California Press, [2025] |
    Includes bibliographical references and index.
Identifiers: LCCN 2024018190 (print) | LCCN 2024018191 (ebook) |
    ISBN 9780520402034 (cloth) | ISBN 9780520402027 (paperback) |
    ISBN 9780520402041 (epub)
Subjects: LCSH: Internet and activism—United States—21st century. |
    Internet and activism—Hungary—21st century. | Internet and
    activism—Italy—21st century. | Social movements—United States—
    21st century. | Social movements—Hungary—21st century. | Social
    movements—Italy—21st century.
Classification: LCC HM851 .F484 2025 (print) | LCC HM851 (ebook) |
    DDC 361.2097309/05—dc23/eng/20240514
LC record available at https://lccn.loc.gov/2024018190
LC ebook record available at https://lccn.loc.gov/2024018191

34 33 32 31 30 29 28 27 26 25
10 9 8 7 6 5 4 3 2 1

A Laila e a tutte le altre

* * *

To Laila and all the others,
partisan women,
the communication infrastructure
of the Italian Resistance

Contents

Illustrations

Acknowledgments

This book began as a PhD dissertation at the Annenberg School for Communication at the University of Pennsylvania. The more time passes, the more grateful I become for the extraordinary sense of community I felt while I was there. I am particularly thankful for the friendship and support I received, inside and outside of the basement of 3620, from Elisa Baek, Isabelle Langrock, John Remensperger, María Celeste Wagner, Natacha Yazbeck, Natalie Herbert, and Paul Popiel. My thanks also go to the members of the Media Activism Research Collective, especially Rosie Clark-Parsons and Jasmine Erdener.

I am thankful for Guobin Yang's encouraging, kind, and thoughtful guidance throughout the PhD. Jessa Lingel has been an incredible mentor, and I am very grateful for her continued support. Michael X Delli Carpini provided excellent feedback in the early stages of this work. I am also grateful to Barbie Zelizer for her mentorship.

Post-PhD, this book was written and rewritten, largely during the COVID-19 pandemic, as I moved between Philadelphia, Ann Arbor, and Glasgow. The Center on Digital Culture and Society at the University of Pennsylvania provided invaluable support for the development of this project. At the University of Michigan, Christian Sandvig and 2020/21 members of the InfraLab—Youngrim Kim, Yuchen Chen, Natalie Ngai, Li Cornfeld, Gabriel Grill, Allegra Fonda-Bonardi, Jennifer Hsieh—read a draft of chapter 4 and provided feedback and encouragement, as well as meaningful interactions during the height of COVID-19. Lisa Nakamura showed me what true leadership and community building can look like, even in difficult times such as a global pandemic. At the University of Glasgow, Ida Nordberg, Lito Tsitsou, and Lluis de Nadal Alsina offered much-needed camaraderie and migrant solidarity. While scattered across the United States and the world, Samantha Oliver, Sean Fischer, and Monica Bolelli were wonderful digital writing buddies and kept me coming back to my writing against all odds.

Colleagues and friends have also generously read portions of this work. Revati Prasad, Allie Levin, Sandra Ristovska, and Marina Popescu read many drafts over the years and always found the right words to support me. I am incredibly lucky to have them in my life. Brendan Mahoney gave useful feedback on a draft of chapter 5; Gábor Tóka helped in the revisions of the appendix.

Portions of this book appeared as journal articles in *Media, Culture & Society* and *Communication, Culture & Critique*. I thank these journals for allowing me to reprint previously published work here. I also thank Stefan Roch for allowing me to use his photos of the Hungarian internet tax protests.

The University of California Press has been wonderfully supportive. Special thanks go to Michelle Lipinski for all her encouragement and to Jyoti Arvey for her help. I am also very grateful to the anonymous reviewers who offered constructive feedback. Throughout the process, Laura Portwood-Stacer's advice on book publishing was indispensable.

I am thankful for the funding I received for this research, which came from the Waterhouse Family Institute for the Study of Communication and Society at Villanova University, as well as the Internet Policy Observatory at the University of Pennsylvania; I am especially grateful to Laura Schwarz-Henderson for her continued confidence in me and my work. OSSCOM at the Catholic University of Milan hosted me in 2017 and gave me a base from which to explore Milan's activist scene.

Friends offered support of all kinds while I researched and wrote this book. Thank you to Elisa Iori, Annamaria Mazzoni, Paolo Dallasta,

Francesco Sassi, Martina Castigliani, and Robert Vamos. Sorry for the rants.

Thank you to my family: to my Mom and Dad for all their support and to Paola and Daniele (the best in-laws a girl could ask for). To my husband, Marco Bolognesi, whom I first met many, many years ago in an activist meeting not dissimilar from the ones described in this book: thanks for being there, then and now.

Finally, to the activists who have generously talked to me about their activism and their lives: thank you for sharing what you do and for doing what you do. Go change the world.

1 Introduction

"We will need a website when they come for us."

—LUMe activist

The day I first met with the young activists of the Metropolitan University Laboratory (LUMe), I was elated that they had invited me to talk to them about my research for this book. I joined them during one of their assemblies, at which they make decisions about the activities of the movement. It was a sunny afternoon in May 2018, and the activists were sitting in a circle, smoking, talking, and drinking beer, just outside of their occupied space, in the small strip of grass between the entrance to their building and the tram tracks, right in the center of Milan, Italy.

When they invited me to stick around for the rest of the meeting, I could not anticipate that I would end up witnessing a discussion about their long-defunct website, a blog that the activists had opened in 2015, when LUMe was just getting started. As I would later learn, the website had become a hot-button issue for the collective. LUMe saw the value of having a self-created, well-maintained website that would accurately represent them and their activities, but the activists also felt that the effort needed to build and maintain that kind of website was too great, especially because that effort would have to come on top of the intense labor that the activists already put into managing their communication, both with each other and with the public, via Facebook.

In the discussion I stumbled upon, some of the activists passionately argued for the need to have a functioning and appealing website. Their arguments all revolved around the idea that having a website had a political meaning. Some of the activists simply said that "having your own website is a political practice," that there is a difference between creating a website that can support creative experimentation and using social network sites like Facebook, which constrain what activists can say and do through them. One of LUMe's main activities is to promote grassroots cultural production. A website, some of the activists argued, would be exactly the kind of infrastructure that could support grassroots activist culture. Others provided a slightly different argument, which seemed to resonate with the assembly: that LUMe needs a way to archive and showcase the concerts, the plays, the demonstrations, the reading groups, the meetings, the cultural events—all the things that the movement has organized, hosted, and sponsored over the years of its existence. The necessity to show what the movement has done is salient for the activists of LUMe, because at the core of their activism is a practice that is rooted in the history of Italian social movements but remains illegal, risky, and ultimately precarious: the occupation of unused buildings for political activity. LUMe has occupied three buildings since its foundation in 2015, using them to hold meetings and concerts and host political debates and theater performances—reclaiming political space in the heart of the city of Milan. The threat of eviction by law enforcement is always present in the activists' minds: "We will need a website when they come for us," as one of the activists said in the meeting—when "they" come to evict LUMe, to erase all they've done. A website would be a way for LUMe to show its value in the face of an eviction or other attempt to shut down the occupation. For the activists, documenting, archiving, and showcasing their activities are all important political practices, which they feel cannot be adequately accomplished without a website. And yet they are not prepared to commit resources to creating their own website, because so much of their labor, time, and attention is already devoted to other websites: social network sites, particularly Facebook. It is through Facebook that LUMe activists communicate with each other and their public. It is to Facebook that LUMe activists turn when they want to say something about their political ideas or publicize their activities. And while they regret not having a website, Facebook remains their priority.

This book is about how contemporary leftist social movements in different countries envision the role of digital media in their struggles for social change. It is about conversations like the ones that the activists of LUMe have been having about their website: conversations that show how social movements perceive digital technologies to be political and how activists understand their technological practices through a political lens. It is also about how the digital technologies originating from Silicon Valley, which are often portrayed as global and universal, are the expression of specific political orientations, which may be at odds with the politics of the movements for social justice. And it is about how activists in different countries experience the politics of mainstream digital technologies and respond to them.

Activists all over the world have long turned to corporate digital technologies, such as Facebook and Twitter, to organize, coordinate, and communicate with the public. While digital technologies have often been promoted by mainstream media and Silicon Valley enthusiasts as enablers of change, activists have questioned the effectiveness of such digital tools, as well as their potential for surveillance and abuse. Over the span of a decade, from the Arab Spring to the Black Lives Matter protests, internet technologies have become both crucial and problematic for activists. While Occupy Wall Street protesters in 2011 livestreamed their actions to show the world what they were doing, anti-racist and abolitionist activists in 2022 were more likely to use social media to warn fellow protesters to turn off their phones during demonstrations to avoid being tracked by law enforcement. These different approaches to the internet do not just reflect changes in the technologies themselves, which are better and better at tracking us, or an ongoing discussion among activists on how best to use digital platforms. They are indicative of the different ways in which activists think and talk about the politics of digital technologies. They present different visions of the role of digital technologies in activism.

The growing scholarly literature on digitally mediated activism has sought to explain how activists use digital platforms and whether and how these digital technologies have changed activism. Scholars have raised questions about the organizational dynamics and the changing political logics that are emerging in digitally mediated movements (e.g., Bennett & Segerberg, 2013; Tufekci, 2017), as well as about how personal and collective identities come to play a role in these forms of technologically enabled collective action (Jackson et al., 2020; Kavada, 2015). However, this scholarship has mostly considered how movements approach technologies as tools: how they use technologies for protest. It has only recently begun to consider how movements approach technologies as political objects, whose political orientation can and should be examined. We need ways of accounting for how the activists of LUMe discuss whether and how to run a website as part of their political choices and ways to make sense of the politics of mainstream technologies.

Scholars of science and technology studies (STS) and media historians have told us, over and over again, that discourses are an integral component of what we call "technologies"; in other words, that technologies are not just material artifacts, they are also sets of practices and discourses. These discourses are inherently political: they envision specific types of relations between the self, society, the state, and the economy. Following STS authors Patrice Flichy (2007a) and Sheila Jasanoff (2015), I call these discourses technological imaginaries. Imaginaries are not only political; they are also plural and conflicting in society and are constructed by a variety of actors, including activists.

However, we can also clearly recognize technological imaginaries that have become mainstream, dominant ways of discursively constructing digital technologies. I argue that over the past two or three decades, the dominant technological imaginary has been actively constructed and spread by Silicon Valley actors. This dominant imaginary has established a powerful connection between digital technologies and social change, popularizing the idea of technology as inherently supportive of freedom and personal autonomy, privileging technical solutions over political reform, and endorsing neoliberalism. This imaginary also comes through in the technologies that have been created by Silicon Valley actors; many of the problems plaguing digital technologies today can be traced back to the peculiar blend of technocratic ambitions and populist justifications that characterizes this imaginary.

The dominant technological imaginary of Silicon Valley is familiar to us; we have been exposed to it for a long time. Social movements have been exposed to it as well. Further, as seen in the cases of the Arab Spring and the Occupy movement, movements have also been explained through the lens of this imaginary; they have been reduced to manifestations of networked technologies, conjured by the free flow of information and the supposedly horizontal structures of social network sites. Yet in their day-to-day struggles for social change, activists all over the world make sense of the dominant technological imaginary of Silicon Valley in different ways, as I show in this book.

I argue that social movements respond to the dominant, techno-utopian and neoliberal imaginary of Silicon Valley by constructing their own technological imaginaries, which appropriate, negotiate, or challenge Silicon Valley's imaginary. Imaginaries of appropriation accept both the dominant technological imaginary and the technologies of Silicon Valley. Imaginaries of negotiation reject the dominant imaginary but allow for the use of Silicon Valley's technologies, generating political tensions and frictions. Imaginaries of challenge reject both the imaginary and the technologies of Silicon Valley. Appropriation, negotiation, and challenge are influenced by three political factors: the ideology of the social movement, the political context, and the presence of other technological imaginaries that are prominent in the movement's political landscape and to which movements also respond.

These activist technological imaginaries both reflect and shape the politics of the movements. They reflect the politics of the movements because they are grounded in their ideologies and their political contexts; this means that different social movements may envision, and utilize, the same digital technologies in different political ways. But imaginaries also shape the politics of the movements, in the sense that they have a role in influencing how these movements perceive their political possibilities. In particular, the power of Silicon Valley's imaginary and movements' reliance on Silicon Valley technologies can limit activists' ability to imagine technological and political alternatives, which are crucial for social change.

Through the notion of technological imaginary, this book offers a framework to understand the relationship between activism and digital technologies, which centers the political importance of mainstream and activist discourses about technologies. By focusing on technological imaginaries constructed and deployed by both dominant actors—such as Silicon Valley—and social movements, the book gives us a way to understand the politics of digital technologies and just how contested they are.

It contributes to the growing literature on activism and digital technologies by showing the importance of considering how social movements approach technology in a political way through discursive and imaginative processes. It also adds to long-standing interdisciplinary debates on the politics of technology by bringing together a critique of Silicon Valley with attention to how activists conceptualize and experience digital technology.

SOCIAL MOVEMENTS AND DIGITAL TECHNOLOGIES

Recent scholarship on social movements and activism has given us important, sometimes contradictory, insights into the relationship between social movements and digital technologies. While it would be impossible to account for the ever-growing literature on activism, protest, and internet technologies in its entirety, it is worthwhile to identify a few key trends in this research. Early accounts of the relationship between social movements and the internet, which focused chiefly on the global justice movement of the late 1990s and early 2000s, coalesced around two approaches: an organizational one, which explained how digital technologies reduced barriers for collective action, making organizing more affordable and more effective across national borders (e.g. Della Porta & Tarrow, 2005; Earl & Kimport, 2011); and an approach that centered the need for self-expression and saw digital technologies as crucial in the creation of an alternative public sphere (Atton, 2002; Downing, 2008), fueled by independent "open" projects such as Indymedia (Juris, 2005; Pickard, 2006).

While valuable, both of these approaches were too tied to the idiosyncrasies of the global justice movement to be able to make sense of the social movements that came afterward. By the time activists occupied Zuccotti Park in Lower Manhattan in September 2011, it had become clear that older explanations about the role played by the internet for activists no longer fully applied, despite the clear legacy of the global justice movement in contemporary movements (see Wolfson, 2014). The events of the Arab Spring, the Indignados encampments, and Occupy Wall Street gave rise to an explosion of scholarship on social movements and the internet, which specifically focused on mainstream, corporate-owned social network sites, chiefly Twitter and Facebook. By and large, this scholarship on the movements of 2011 coalesced around examining the changing "logics" of organizing at play in these movements. The most popular concept to emerge from this scholarship is that of "connective action," coined by Lance Bennett and Alexandra Segerberg (2013) to theorize the logic that characterized the movements of 2011 (as opposed to traditional collective action). In practice, this focus on the new logics of activism was translated into an overwhelming attention to how different movements have used corporate social network sites and how the use of such platforms might be changing how movements come to exist and operate.

This overwhelming attention to social network sites, their properties, and their effects on social movements has been challenged in the subsequent scholarship, which sought to qualify, contextualize, and deuniversalize the role of digital technologies in contemporary movements. Scholars have highlighted how the use of Twitter and Facebook coexists with other media practices, both online and offline (Zayani, 2015; Barassi, 2015; Treré, 2018; Mattoni, 2012); collective identity, organization, and leadership still matter (Gerbaudo, 2012; Kavada, 2015; Tufekci, 2017); digital technologies do not solve questions related to class and access to socioeconomic resources, even for digital activists (Schradie, 2019); and even seemingly digital-born revolutions seldomly emerge spontaneously due to technological innovations (Lim, 2012; Kraidy, 2016; Lee & Chan, 2018). Reflecting on newer movements that have emerged since the mid-2010s, such as the extraordinary and multifaceted global feminist mobilization (Chenou & Cepeda-Másmela, 2019; Loney-Howes et al., 2021) and the Black Lives Matter movement in North America (Bonilla & Rosa, 2015), scholars also considered how digital technologies interact with systems of oppression, showing how social networks can change the game for marginalized groups but also constrain what they can do online (Jackson et al., 2020; Clark-Parsons, 2022; Kuo, 2018).

This vibrant scholarship has promoted an interdisciplinary discussion on many facets of the relationship between digital technologies and activism. However, it has yet to fully address one important aspect: how discourses about the role of the internet in activism and social change, as constructed both by mainstream actors and by activists, play a role in all of this. Our societies are fascinated by technologies. Technological innovations often feature prominently in how journalists and commentators explain what is happening around us. Around the time of the Arab Spring, when images and footage from Tunis and Cairo started making their way into international news after circulating on social network sites, the twin monikers "Facebook revolution" and "Twitter revolution" became unavoidable; they popped up in media coverage and everyday conversations, linking the extraordinary insurgency across the Middle East and North Africa to those mainstream social network sites. Academics have long disproven the notion of "[insert social media] revolution," and I have no intention of relitigating this debate here. But it is important to say that however disqualified by abundant academic research, these discourses about the centrality of technology to social change continue to play a role in how a variety of actors talk about activism. These discourses are deterministic, prescriptive, and political. And activists are constantly exposed to them.

We need a way to understand these discourses about social change and digital technology, a framework that allows us to uncover both their power and appeal and how much they are problematic. These discourses have been circulating for years in the media, percolating into everyday conversations and political debates. They are so common that they become difficult to question. How do activists respond to these discourses about digital technology and social change? Do they matter in the life of social movements? While we know that the Arab Uprisings were brought about by much more than the use of Facebook or Twitter, we cannot ignore that there were protest signs during the occupation of Tahrir, for instance, that used the language of "Facebook revolution." Why did activists seize on those labels? What did they mean for them?

At the same time, as LUMe's discussion of the political importance of its website shows, activists also develop their own discourses about digital technologies. They also imagine how technology might be part of their struggles for social change. They think about technology in a critical, political way. This is an aspect that is often missing in the scholarship on activism and digital technologies, because scholars often take for granted that activists will embrace Facebook or Twitter, focusing on the use of these platforms. One important exception has been the scholarship that has drawn on the anthropological notion of "media imaginaries" to interrogate how activists understand digital media technologies and their own media practices (e.g., Barassi, 2015; Treré, 2018). As I discuss in chapter 2, these scholars have shown how fruitful it is to map the meaning-making processes that surround activists' media practices and to focus on the discourses that social movements develop around digital media. Their contribution is critical to expanding how the literature on social movements addresses what digital technologies mean for activists. Their work highlights the need to account for how movements might think critically about these digital technologies and to understand how they relate to mainstream discourses about activism and technology. In conversation with these scholars, this book offers a framework that allows us to look at both how activists make sense of mainstream discourses about technology and social change and how they construct their own.

CONCEPTUALIZING ACTIVIST TECHNOLOGICAL IMAGINARIES

In this book I develop a theoretical framework to investigate how social movements relate to technologies and envision them in their struggles for social change, taking into account how activists respond to mainstream ideas about technology. This framework is based on the notion of technological imaginary, which I define as a set of practice-based beliefs, individual and collective, implicit and explicit, about the role of technology in social life and social change.

My theorization of technological imaginaries brings together insights from different scholarly traditions. My work is inspired by Alberto Melucci's (1989) approach to social movement studies, which sees movements as processes of collective self-definition; for me, this means investigating how movements construct themselves as collective actors and how their relationship with technology might play a role in these collective processes. Thinking about movements and digital technologies through the lens of Melucci's work allows us to recognize that discursive processes are crucial in the life of social movements. As a broad range of work on media history reminds us, discourses about technology, society, and change are central to technology itself (e.g., Marvin, 1988; Marx, 1964; Nye, 1996; Turner, 2006; Williams, 1975); these scholars have pointed out, over and over again, the social and political significance of how technology is conceptualized. The centrality of discourses to technology has also been explored in STS, particularly via the notion of imaginaries, whether technological (Flichy, 2007a) or sociotechnical (Jasanoff, 2015). For STS scholars, imaginaries are meant to account for the collective visions that guide the process of shaping and adopting technologies (Flichy, 2007a) and for how a variety of different actors, including nation-states, link "visions of the desirable futures" to technological development (Jasanoff, 2015). Adopting the idea of "imaginaries" is useful because it allows us to bring together discourses and practices, as sociologist Charles Taylor (2004) did with his notion of the social imaginary. Imaginaries are not free-floating, high-level theories; they are grounded in the practices of different social actors, including ordinary people.

As I define them, technological imaginaries are not only relevant because they influence how technology is designed, adopted, and utilized; they are also important because they envision specific social, political, and economic relationships to technology. In fact, technological imaginaries include visions of social change that need to be critically investigated. Technological imaginaries are political and can be deployed for political purposes by a variety of social actors. They are based on both practices and discourses. They are held by ordinary people, not just by elites or institutions. And crucially for our understanding of the relationship between activism and technology, technological imaginaries are multiple and conflicting in society. However, some imaginaries are so widespread and powerful that they can become dominant within a given space and time. While many actors can develop technological imaginaries, this book is dedicated to investigating activist technological imaginaries, how they are constructed, and how they interact with and respond to other dominant technological imaginaries.

The technological imaginary that is now dominant across most of the world has emerged from Silicon Valley actors, who have promoted it to legitimize themselves and their technologies. This dominant imaginary is an evolution of the "Californian Ideology" theorized by Richard Barbrook and Andy Cameron (1996). As I explain in chapter 2, it is a political vision that holds together technocratic ideas and populist impetus, proclaiming that digital technologies equate freedom and autonomy, that technology can and should solve sociopolitical problems and that neoliberalism is the only political economic arrangement that can allow an optimal level of technological—and thus social—development. While thriving on its supposed global, universal nature, this imaginary is also deeply US American; this also means that it is based on—and reproduces—the structures of intersecting oppression along lines of race, gender, sexual orientation, and disability that underpin US social relations, as can be clearly seen in the recent scholarship that has addressed this issue (e.g., Benjamin, 2019; Broussard, 2018; Costanza-Chock, 2020; Noble, 2018).

Many mainstream, deterministic discourses about the centrality of technology to activism depend on the power of this complex dominant technological imaginary. But activists all over the world encounter the dominant technological imaginary in multiple ways: through media coverage, political discourse, pop culture, and the technologies of Silicon Valley themselves, since they often reflect this imaginary in their affordances. When activists approach the digital technologies of Silicon Valley, they also approach its dominant technological imaginary. How do they make sense of it? How do they respond to it? I argue that activists construct their own activist technological imaginaries, which appropriate, negotiate, or challenge the dominant technological imaginary of Silicon Valley. What these activist technological imaginaries look like depends on the ideology of the social movement that constructs them, the political context in which they operate, and what other types of technological imaginaries are relevant in their political context.

ANALYZING ACTIVIST TECHNOLOGICAL IMAGINARIES

This book analyzes the activist technological imaginaries constructed by three leftist activist groups in Hungary, Italy, and the United States through a qualitative approach. My methodological choices were informed by my theoretical orientation toward studying "movements as processes" (Melucci, 1989) and exploring the discursive constructions that enable the action of social movements. However, as scholars of activism know very well, one of the challenges of studying movements is the invisibility of certain fundamental processes that define them. But this also applies to studying activists' (and, in general, people's) relationship to technology, which is often left unspoken. In many ways the widespread technologies that we use every day may seem trivial and commonsensical, hardly something that can be approached directly in academic research. Studying the technological imaginaries of social movements is difficult exactly because they can be invisible and therefore difficult to reconstruct directly. The challenge is thus to find methods that can interrogate the commonsensical, taken-for-granted aspect of technology, engender a reflection in the research participants, and create a conversation between researchers and participants about the meaning of everyday technologies and their symbolic power. This is why I have explored different activist technological imaginaries through a multimethod qualitative approach that combined observation of activists' meetings, events, and online interaction; in-depth qualitative interviews with activists; and a novel creative method, developed for this project: the visual focus group.

I also chose to examine activist technological imaginaries by looking at social movements in different political contexts. I wanted to see the similarities and differences in how activists thought and talked about technology. Would the dominant technological imaginary of Silicon Valley mean the same to all of them? Would the corporate digital platforms of Silicon Valley mean the same to all of them? It is not my intention to suggest that we can identify specific national activist technological imaginaries that would apply to, say, all leftist Italian movements or all leftist US movements. Rather, my approach is to dive into how each individual social movement constructs its own technological imaginary and how this discursive construction is influenced by the politics of that movement, in its specific context. In practice, this means that the following chapters contain much information about the political ideas, practices, and political context in which the activists I examine operate; this rich description is needed to account for how the politics of these movements come into play in how the activists conceptualize the role of technology. Through this in-depth exploration, I give space to activists' own conceptualizations of their political relationship with digital technologies and contextualize them within broader political dynamics. It is through the juxtaposition of these different cases, in their similarities and differences, that I arrived at my categorization of activist technological imaginaries, which distinguishes between imaginaries of appropriation, negotiation, and challenge.

As I explain in more detail in the appendix, this book is based on more than three years of multimethod qualitative research in Italy, Hungary, and the United States. While my work on this book has continued well after 2020, the empirical material that informs this book was collected and analyzed before the COVID-19 pandemic. While I believe that the insights I provide are relevant for our study of activism and digital technology even in/after the pandemic, the empirical analysis offers a snapshot of the political, social, and cultural context of the period between 2017 and 2020.

This book is about leftist movements: movements that in different ways organize and mobilize for futures of social justice. However, the framework I develop to study the relationship between activists and digital technologies can also be applied to study different types of movements. For instance, one could consider how movements of the extreme Right, in different national contexts, relate to the dominant imaginary of Silicon Valley. In fact, given the influence that extreme right-wing forces have had on national governments across the world and on their regulatory action, it is urgent for academic research to also consider how these actors conceptualize the role of technology in our societies.

Cases

The book is based on the in-depth study of the technological imaginaries of three social movement actors: the Hungarian internet tax protests of 2014, the Italian student collective LUMe (Laboratorio Universitario Metropolitano; Metropolitan University Laboratory), and the US-based Philly Socialists.

The Hungarian internet tax protests were organized in October 2014 to oppose the Hungarian government's decision to impose a tax on internet consumption. A group of left-liberal activists, previously involved in different movements, organized two successful demonstrations in Hungary's capital. The first one drew ten thousand people to the streets of the capital, Budapest; the second gave rise to the largest demonstration that the country had seen post-1989, with one hundred thousand people marching in the city. After this mobilization, the internet tax was withdrawn indefinitely. The core group of organizers decided to refrain from creating a new political organization but continued to be active in different causes through other collectives. They have since been part of a broad civil society mobilization that has emerged to oppose the governments of Prime Minister Viktor Orbán and his self-proclaimed vision of "illiberal democracy" (Orbán, 2014).

LUMe is based in Milan, Italy. It is an anticapitalist, antiracist, antisexist, antifascist collective, composed of students and recent graduates of the universities and art academies in Milan. It is an "occupied social center," that is, a social movement that occupies unused buildings for political purposes; it is currently occupying a municipality-owned maintenance deposit, where it hosts concerts, theater performances, and public discussions, as well as its own meetings. The collective was founded in April 2015 during the occupation of a different building, located next to the University of Milan.

Philly Socialists (PS) is a socialist organization based in Philadelphia, with dues-paying members and a commitment to building working class power outside of the electoral system. It was founded in 2011. Besides being active in city-wide protests, the members run a number of projects, including a community garden, free English as a second language (ESL) classes, and a workers' collective. Like other socialist groups, it grew significantly during the presidency of Donald Trump (2016–2020); unlike groups such as the Democratic Socialists of America (DSA), the Philly Socialists steers clear of electoral politics, preferring to organize at the grassroots level (a strategy known as "base-building"). It has been particularly involved with the fight for better housing conditions; in 2016 the group created the Philadelphia Tenants Union.

As I discuss more in depth in the appendix, the three case studies were selected to allow me to assess how activist technological imaginaries could be constructed by activists embedded in different political environments. These three cases present some similarities. Most importantly, I argue that these three cases are part of a wave of movements that has mobilized against right-wing populist governments worldwide (Orbán in Hungary, Trump in the United States, and the alliance between Matteo Salvini's League and the Five Star Movement in Italy). These groups are also all situated to the left of the mainstream in their respective countries and eschew parliamentary representation. In Hungary, the activists who organized the Hungarian internet tax protests are part of a left-liberal activist area that occupies the most leftist position in the truncated

Hungarian political spectrum; these activists are not only opposed to Orbán's authoritarian fantasies but are also culturally progressive and generally concerned with socioeconomic injustice. LUMe's politics and political practices firmly place the collective within the Italian "radical leftist" area, commonly considered far to the left of the institutional Left in Italy; LUMe opposes capitalism, but also racism, sexism, populism, and neofascism. As a socialist organization committed to revolutionary politics, PS is also far to the left of the mainstream Left in the United States; its opposition to neoliberal capitalism goes hand in hand with a critique of the two-party system and of sexism and racism. Last, these groups all employ similar protest repertoires, such as nonviolent demonstrations and protest actions, and value participatory mechanisms in their organizations.

However, there are strong differences in the political orientations of these movements and in the political contexts in which they are embedded. First, as I explain in detail in the chapters that follow, the leftist political orientations of these groups are different; these differences, I argue, play a crucial role in the construction of their different activist technological imaginaries. Further, the political contexts in which these actors operate, as influenced by diverse historical trajectories, differ greatly. Hungary's socialist legacy and the consequences of the transition to democracy chart a complicated relationship to Western democracy, which is likely to affect how movements interpret Silicon Valley's technologies, as well as the dominant technological imaginary. Italy's political instability and its history of heightened political conflict have contributed to the development of a lively leftist social movement scene, where movements are able to learn from each other and build on shared political repertoires, including in relation to technologies. Looking at these Hungarian and Italian cases brings into stark relief the peculiarities of the American political system, in terms of both its marginalization and repression of radical and socialist forces and its long-standing fascination with technological development. The different political orientations and political contexts of the Hungarian internet tax protests, LUMe, and PS thus play a crucial role in my analysis of their technological imaginaries.

As is evident from this description of my case selection, this book does not intend to offer a strictly comparative design. While this can be seen as a limitation of the research, it is also important to consider that, as Veronica Barassi (2015) underlined, it might be impossible to neatly compare different cultures, nations, and indeed activist groups. However, as she argued, it is useful to juxtapose different case studies, with the understanding that highlighting the differences and similarities between the cases can help us make sense of how the specificities of each individual case can follow more general patterns. It is in this spirit that I selected these cases and conducted my analysis.

Multimethod Qualitative Research

My analysis is based on in-depth qualitative interviews with activists; observation of activists' meetings, events, and online interactions; and a novel creative method, developed for this project: the visual focus group. I explain my methodological approach in more detail in the appendix.

I conducted individual in-depth interviews, either in person or via videoconferencing software, with activists from each of the three movements. When interviewing activists, I asked them questions about their experience in the movement and their relationship with technology. Following Susan Leigh Star (1999), who wrote that infrastructures become visible upon breakdown, and Taina Bucher (2016), who studied how people react to the perceived faults of algorithms, I incorporated questions that guided interviewees toward discussing moments in which they had become aware of the role of technology in their activist lives or in which they perceived digital technologies to have caused problems in their personal lives or within the movements they are involved with. I spoke in English with the activists of PS and of the Hungarian internet protests, while I interviewed LUMe members in Italian.

Over the course of three years, I also observed meetings and public events hosted by LUMe and PS; this included protests, organizational assemblies, book presentations, and working group meetings. I was not able to take part in any meetings or protest events of the Hungarian internet tax protests, which took place in 2014, before I began the fieldwork for this book. I took notes and collected any written materials that were available in the meetings and events I was able to attend in Milan and Philadelphia. My observation of the movements provided insights into the dynamics of discussion and organization that characterize PS and LUMe. I also observed the online presence and media production of the three groups, analyzing their websites and their posts across Facebook, Twitter, and Instagram. I read the existing media coverage on these groups. What I learned was particularly useful in reconstructing the histories, political positions, and organizational structures of the three groups, allowing me to supplement what I discovered through the interviews.

I also designed a creative method to better address how the activists relate to digital technologies; I found it difficult to address this issue solely via qualitative interviews, given that it often feels so mundane and taken for granted. To tackle this difficulty, I drew inspiration from the literature on graphic elicitation tasks (Bagnoli, 2009; Gieseking, 2013) and as mentioned, developed a new creative method for this research, the visual focus group (Ferrari, 2022). The visual focus group embeds a collective drawing task in the structure of a focus group, helping to support reflexive conversations among participants; for this book, activists participated in the visual focus group to discuss their visions about digital technology and were asked to draw what the internet is like for them. The process of collectively agreeing on a picture of the internet helped to uncover some of the unspoken assumptions about digital technologies that participants held, thus allowing them to reflect on these assumptions collectively. While I planned to conduct visual focus groups with both LUMe and PS, I was only able to hold them with the Italian activists.

The empirical data were analyzed through thematic (Braun & Clarke, 2006) and open (Corbin & Strauss, 2008) coding. Because the analysis was directed at reconstructing the specific technological imaginary of each activist group, the material pertaining to each case was analyzed separately, one movement at a time.

Taken together, data from my observations, interviews, and visual focus groups provide a detailed account of activists' technological imaginaries, which I present alongside in-depth explanations of the politics of these activist groups and of the political contexts they inhabit. Far from being just background information, this deep contextual discussion of the politics of the movements is integral to my interpretation of these activist technological imaginaries.

Ethics

Activists are often in vulnerable positions, even in democratic contexts. They can be targeted by law enforcement, lose their jobs for their political positions, and be subject to immense amounts of abuse on social media platforms. Academic research should not add any risks to the already complicated lives of leftist activists. In my research process, I tried to minimize the collection of personally identifiable information. I offered activists the possibility to communicate with me using encrypted messaging services and email providers, in addition to my institutional contact details. I used pseudonyms for all the participants involved in this study, choosing common Hungarian, Italian, and American names, respectively. Activists were often curious about the need to be assigned pseudonyms. They did not always feel the need to be anonymized, and this generated interesting discussions about the use of research participants' data and the availability of personal information online. While I use pseudonyms for individual activists, I sought and obtained the consent of both LUMe and PS to use the real names of their groups; this did not apply to the Hungarian organizers, who never formed, let alone named, a stable collective or organization.

However, I also believe that social movement researchers have a responsibility regarding their research data that goes beyond the pseudonymity of individual participants. Arne Hintz and Stefania Milan (2010) have written convincingly about the mismatch between the sensibilities of radical activists and the institutional arrangements and incentives that characterize academic research. They highlighted that for radical activists all social science is "police science," because it can reveal internal mechanisms, practices, and motivations that could potentially be used by other actors to undermine or sabotage the movements. Especially with the rise of big data approaches to studying activism, we have seen an increased scholarly attention to documenting how movements make decisions and even to predicting the "tipping points of collective action; while scholars are driven by a desire to understand these processes and not influence them, it's important to consider what could be the afterlives of that research. I kept this constantly in mind while writing this book.

Finally, this book is written from the perspective of someone who was an activist in Italy long before becoming interested in academic research. I've also been in endless organizational meetings, distributed leaflets, and organized protests. While I approach this research rigorously both theoretically and methodologically, I don't do it as a neutral spectator. I care about these activists. In their actions I see glimmers of a more just future.

And I study their technological imaginaries because I believe that how they think about the role of technology in social change matters greatly to how they can achieve it.

OUTLINE OF THE CHAPTERS

Following this introductory chapter, chapter 2 lays out the theoretical framework that I develop and use throughout the book. First, I show how my conceptualization of activist technological imaginaries builds on lessons derived from different literatures: media history and cultural studies (e.g., Marvin, 1988; Mosco, 2004; Turner, 2006), STS (Flichy, 2007a; Jasanoff & Kim, 2015), and cultural sociology (Taylor, 2004). Based on these lessons, I expand on my definition of technological imaginaries by explaining their key characteristics. I then identify the current dominant technological imaginary, which I theorize as arising from Silicon Valley actors and as hinging on three key tenets: the equation of technology with freedom and autonomy, technosolutionism, and the subordination to neoliberalism. In so doing, this imaginary brings together populist and technocratic ideas. While arising out of the peculiarities of Silicon Valley and of the US political scene of the 1990s (Barbrook & Cameron, 1996), it has posited its universality by presenting its tenets as if they were global, unbiased, and equally suitable for everyone, regardless of gender, race, or nationality. I also discuss what it means to consider this imaginary as dominant in the ongoing backlash against Silicon Valley (i.e., the "techlash). Having established how I conceptualize technological imaginaries and identified Silicon Valley's as the dominant technological imaginary, I then argue that social movements construct their own activist technological imaginaries, which interpret Silicon Valley's imaginary and respond to it in different ways. I present the categorization of activist technological imaginaries that I develop in the subsequent empirical chapters. These categories are imaginaries of appropriation, which endorse both the dominant imaginary and the technologies of Silicon Valley; imaginaries of negotiation, which reject Silicon Valley's imaginary but allow for the use of its technologies; and imaginaries of challenge, which reject both the imaginary and the technologies of Silicon Valley. As I show through my empirical analysis in chapters 3–5, three crucial factors influence how social movements construct their technological imaginaries in response to Silicon Valley's: the ideology of the social movement, the political context in which it is embedded, and the salience of other prominent technological imaginaries to which activists also respond.

Chapter 3 examines the technological imaginary of the Hungarian internet protests. I name it *mundane modernity*: an imaginary that grounds long-standing tropes of Western modernity in the everyday practices of internet use. Activists, in fact, associated the internet with equality and development, the future, and rationality; in so doing, they reproduced discourses about the role of technology in Western modernity. However, they also insisted on the mundanity of the internet, its importance for everyday life. I argue that this imaginary of mundane modernity is one of appropriation, which endorses both the technologies and the imaginary of Silicon Valley, reimagining them for a postcommunist context. Mundane modernity reinterprets the pillars of Silicon Valley's imaginary by equating the internet with freedom (both political freedom and market freedom) and with Western democracy. It appropriates Silicon Valley's imaginary to make it resonant in a postcommunist context, in which ideas of Western modernity, democracy, and freedom are contentious.

Chapter 4 turns to the technological imaginary of the Italian student collective LUMe. LUMe activists fiercely critique how the power of corporations structures the internet and are deeply skeptical about the purported democratic nature of online communication. However, they also feel that corporate digital technologies are inescapable and indispensable for organizing; in fact, they rely extensively on Facebook, WhatsApp, and Instagram. Using the words of the activists, I conceptualize their technological imaginary as "using the tools of the system to fight the system." This is an imaginary of negotiation, which consciously holds together a strong critique of the dominant technological imaginary of Silicon Valley as an expression of neoliberalism, with a reliance on corporate digital platforms in service of the fight against neoliberalism.

Chapter 5 analyzes the technological imaginary of PS. For these US-based socialist organizers, digital technologies are far from being an ideal space for radical politics, because of law enforcement surveillance, because they can be toxic environments, and because digital technologies don't offer the same possibility for interaction as offline spaces. But while not ideal, these digital technologies are good enough, for now, to recruit people to the socialist cause. I condense this imaginary in the phrase "organizing where people are," which highlights how PS organizers make sense of their use of corporate digital platforms as a way to recruit people where they already are, even if that means social media. This technological imaginary is one of negotiation, because the organization rejects the dominant imaginary of Silicon Valley while relying on its technologies. This negotiation is based on a strategic use of the notion of *organizing*, which allows the group to frame its technological practices as just one piece of a more complex online and offline strategy.

In the final chapter, I reflect on what the different activist technological imaginaries examined in the book can tell us about the relationship between social movements and digital technologies. Taken together, the imaginary of appropriation of the Hungarian internet tax protests and the imaginaries of negotiation of LUMe and PS show us that activists are keenly aware of the politics of the digital technologies they employ and that their decisions about which technologies to use are, in fact, more political than they appear. I argue that the technological imaginaries that guide these choices are profoundly influenced by the politics and the political contexts of social movements, but that they also play a role in how social movements think about political action.

The different activist imaginaries analyzed in the book highlight that despite the dreams of universality embedded in Silicon Valley's imaginary, we are confronted with the existence of multiple, situated, political internets; digital technologies mean different things for different social movements because of their different political ideologies and political contexts. This multiplicity, however, does not diminish the power of Silicon Valley technologies and of the dominant technological imaginary. On the contrary, these activist imaginaries show us how difficult it is for activists to imagine alternatives to Silicon Valley; even movements that reject its imaginary end up putting a lot of labor into trying to make Silicon Valley's technologies work with their politics. This tension can have a long-lasting impact on the capacity of social movements to mobilize effectively and to promote sustainable technological practices. While Silicon Valley has come under scrutiny and is facing increasing regulatory pressure, the power of its technological imaginary in shaping how activists (and the public) think about social change is still as strong as ever.

The continuing dominance of Silicon Valley can also be seen in the scarcity, among activist movements, of imaginaries of challenge, the third category of activist technological imaginaries I identify, which either envision the abstention from Silicon Valley technologies or promote the development of alternative digital technologies.[1] The fact that these imaginaries are less present among contemporary social movements further underscores the power of Silicon Valley and how difficult it is for activists to move away from mainstream corporate technologies.

This difficulty of imagining different technologies is, I argue, part of a more general crisis of the imagination: an inability of contemporary social movements to imagine alternatives to the systems of exploitation and domination that mark our time. However, as the interlocking global environmental, economic, and health crises demonstrate, this collective imaginative work is urgently needed if we hope to bring about not only better technologies, but also better futures.

2 Technological Imaginaries and the Universal Ambitions of Silicon Valley

How we think and talk about technology matters.[1] To truly understand the place of technology in our societies, in our politics, in our lives, we cannot only think about its material aspects. We also need to consider technologies as sets of practices and discourses, to which we are exposed and with which we have to contend. These discourses about technology are political: not because they are aligned with one political actor over the other, but because they envision specific kinds of social and political arrangements, which are connected to specific technologies. This book focuses on how these political discourses about technology play out in the life of social movements that are organizing for social justice.

The goal of this chapter is to lay out my theoretical framework, which makes sense of the complex political relationship between social movements and technology through the notion of (activist) technological imaginary. I accomplish this goal in three steps. First, I define what I mean by technological imaginaries, building on the lessons arising from three different literatures: media history and cultural studies, broadly defined (Marvin, 1988; Mosco, 2004; Turner, 2006); STS (Flichy, 2007a; Jasanoff & Kim, 2015); and cultural sociology (Taylor, 2004).[2] Drawing on the insights from these strands of scholarship, I explain the key characteristics of technological imaginaries, as I see them: they are political, they have a political economy, they are based on both practices and discourses, they are constructed by ordinary people, and they incorporate visions of the future and the past. Further, while technological imaginaries are plural and conflicting in society, there should be at least one clearly identifiable imaginary that is dominant at a given time.

Second, I examine in detail what I identify as the current dominant technological imaginary. Arising as it does from Silicon Valley actors, I theorize it as hinging on three key tenets: the equation of technology with freedom and autonomy, technosolutionism, and the subordination to neoliberalism. Through these three tenets, this imaginary brings together populist and technocratic ideas. Although arising out of the peculiarities of Silicon Valley and of the US political scene of the 1990s (Barbrook & Cameron, 1996), it has also posited its universality by presenting its tenets as if they were global, unbiased, and equally suitable for everyone, regardless of gender, race, or nationality. I also discuss what it means to consider this imaginary as dominant in the ongoing backlash against Silicon Valley (i.e., the "techlash").

Third, I explain how social movements all over the world are confronted with this dominant technological imaginary and its universalist tendencies; they encounter this imaginary through the technologies developed by Silicon Valley actors, but also through media coverage and media representations of digital technologies. I then argue that social movements construct their own activist technological imaginaries, which interpret Silicon Valley's imaginary and respond to it in different ways. I offer a categorization of social movements' technological imaginaries, which is developed through the empirical analysis contained in the book. I distinguish between imaginaries of appropriation, imaginaries of negotiation, and imaginaries of challenge. Three crucial factors influence how social movements construct their technological imaginaries in response to Silicon Valley's: the ideology of the social movement, the political context in which it is embedded, and the salience of other prominent technological imaginaries to which activists also respond.

SITUATING TECHNOLOGICAL IMAGINARIES

Over the years, a number of scholars have made important contributions to our understanding of the relationship of technologies—and communication technologies in particular—to society. Without trying to fully account for all of the insights emerging from this literature, I highlight here the key lessons that I have drawn upon in my theorization of technological imaginaries. From the highly heterogeneous scholarship on media history and cultural studies, broadly conceived, I take the idea that discourses are a crucial component of technology itself and that discourses surrounding "new" technologies can have a particularly powerful political connotation. I build on STS work that explicitly theorizes and deploys the notion of imaginaries (Flichy, 2007a; Jasanoff, 2015) to account for how collectives imagine the role of technology. Through the sociological work of Charles Taylor (2004), whose modern social imaginaries are unrelated to technologies, I acknowledge how imaginaries bring together practices and discourses, guiding the understanding of a variety of social actors beyond technical or political élites.

Discourses Are Integral to Technologies

From the telegraph to electricity to the internet, scholars have shown how discourses about technology can be considered a part of technology itself and how such discourses tend to give new meaning to existing social struggles, anxieties, and hopes. They also have considered how discourses about technology tend to recur in almost identical ways for each "new technology" and have thus demystified the hype surrounding the introduction of new technologies. Furthermore, they have pointed out how this discursive construction of technology is profoundly political.

This scholarship has shown that societal discourses are as integral a component of technology as its technical design (Marvin, 1988; Mosco, 2004; Winner, 1986). This contention stands in stark opposition to technologically deterministic approaches, but also challenges its opposite, the idea that technology is wholly predetermined by extant socioeconomic processes. In contrast, what this heterogeneous group of scholars has pointed to is the fact that the decisions that happen in the course of technological development (and adoption) "occur within a discursive framework" (Lister et al., 2009, p. 73). According to Raymond Williams (1975), the development of technology, in fact, is "not only a matter of some autonomous process directed by remote engineers" but also "a matter of social and cultural definition" (p. 137).

Discourses about technologies—especially recently introduced ones—are conflicting and nonlinear (Flichy, 1995). They are not only conflicting because they can be divergent, but also because they are usually the expression of interests and ambitions that might be difficult to reconcile. As Williams (1975) reminded us, speaking about television, changes in technologies do not depend "on the fixed properties of the medium nor the necessary character of its institutions, but on a continually renewable social action and struggle" (p. 138). And in fact, the discursive and nondiscursive struggles surrounding the meaning of technologies have been at the core of this body of literature.

Scholars have focused a lot on the moments when technologies are introduced, because it is around these initial moments that conflicts and anxieties unfold. Martin Lister and colleagues (2009) suggested that "new technologies are taken up within a culture and are hooked into, or have projected onto them, its wider social and psychological desires and fears" (p. 70). On the one hand, new technologies provide a renewed avenue for the unfolding of preexisting struggles of power between societal groups. As Carolyn Marvin (1988) explained in her analysis of electricity, "Old habits of transacting between groups are projected onto new technologies that alter, or seem to alter, critical social distance" (p. 5). On the other hand, new technologies are also looked at through the lenses of existing societal anxieties and aspirations. New technologies can thus come to be seen as "a solution to social and cultural ills" (Lister et al., 2009, p. 429) or as the materialization of fears and instabilities.

However, the newness of technology is itself a discursive construction, accompanied by promises of "a new cultural, and even existential, order to come" (Robins, 1996, p. 11). This is not just a temporal realization; it is not just that, to borrow Marvin's (1988) book title, all old technologies have been new at some point. Discourses about the newness of technology are important because they often reassert the power of technology to change societal processes (for better or worse). But as Vincent Mosco (2004) argued, these discourses of newness repeat similar claims throughout time: "Practically every substantial technological change has been accompanied by similar claims. The chant goes on: This changes everything. Nothing will ever be the same again" (p. 119). Discourses of newness are nothing new; they have already been around for other technologies, such as the telegraph, electricity, radio, and TV.

Crucially, these discourses of newness perform a political function. For instance, in his analysis of the relationship between the pastoral idea and the image of the machine in American culture, Leo Marx (1964) unearthed the rhetoric of progress surrounding new technologies: "To see a powerful, efficient machine in the landscape is to know the superiority of the present to the past" (p. 192). This association between progress and new technologies is pervasive and difficult to question: "It is the obviousness and simplicity of the machine as a symbol of progress that accounts for its astonishing power" (Marx, 1964, p. 192).

These powerful discourses of technological newness can also take on an even more explicitly political character. This is clearly evident in the context of the United States. Mosco (2004) highlighted how one of the historically recurring promises of new technologies is that of transforming politics, by bringing "power closer to the people" (p. 98). Langdon Winner (1986) stated that the railroad and the telegraph were "greeted as the very essence of democratic freedom" (p. 45). Speaking of the same technologies, Leo Marx (1964) contended that US public figures saw them as "a token of possibility for democracy" (p. 190), which later turned technology into "a transcendent symbol: a physical object invested with political and metaphysical identity" (p. 206). David Nye (1996) agreed and explained how technologies came to be tied to US democracy: "The citizen who contemplated such public improvements became aware of the power of democracy and saw himself as part of the moral vanguard, leading the world towards universal democracy" (p. 36). Technologies can thus become political symbols and promote specific political values; in turn, discourses of "newness" can spill over, turning promises about new technologies into promises of sociopolitical change.

The political connotations of these discourses about technologies are even more evident when we consider the digital. Though coming to different conclusions, Fred Turner (2006) and Mosco (2004) both considered the symbolic political valence of the internet, as shaped by discourses produced by a heterogeneous group of actors that brought together countercultural sensibilities and market libertarianism. Turner (2006) highlighted how by the 1990s the internet had become both a symbol of political liberation through collaborative, nonhierarchical processes and a tool for making liberation happen; internet technologies thus came to be seen as an emblem of the countercultural revolution (Turner, 2006, p. 238). In critiquing the mythical discourses surrounding the early internet—"myths of cyberspace"—Mosco (2004) also talked about the 1990s as a turning point in our symbolic conception of the internet. In particular, he highlighted the political valence of these mythical discourses of technology, which, among other things, suggested that the internet had brought about "the end of politics" (p. 105). This is a discourse about the replacement of old political relations with new practices based on technology, under the understanding that "the internet is not just a corrective to democracy; it is democracy" (Mosco, 2004, p. 115). The myths that Mosco (2004) deconstructed cast the internet as a symbol of a different type of political relations. If we think about them in the long historical trajectory of technological developments, these myths do not make entirely new claims. And yet they are powerful claims, which although repeated throughout history can exert a symbolic power, shaping conversations not just about technologies but also about political and social processes and how they should adapt to new technologies.

Discourses are thus a crucial part of what we call technology: they shape how people think about technology and incorporate it in their daily lives. But they also connect technologies to the big picture, to ideas about society, politics, and the future. So where do these discourses come from? Who constructs them, and how?

Technologies Are Imagined Collectively

In STS, scholars have grappled with the importance of how technologies are conceptualized through the notion of "imaginaries," in particular Patrice Flichy's (1995, 2007a) "technological imaginary" and Sheila Jasanoff's (2015) "sociotechnical imaginary." Both authors guide us in thinking about the processes through which technologies are envisioned collectively; they focus on how different groups, different collective actors, imagine technology in relation to society.

For Flichy the technological imaginary is a key component in the process of innovation, both in terms of the development and the diffusion of a technology; it is a "collective vision or imaginaire," "common to an entire profession or sector, rather than to a team or work collective" (Flichy, 2007a, p. 4). Through this concept, Flichy rejected teleological approaches to technology; he embraced the messiness and conflict that can arise with technological inventions and used the concept of technological imaginary to account for their nonlinear development. Flichy's technological imaginary is a discursive space that can "mobilize both designers and users" (2007a, p. 6), accounting for both the development and the adoption of technology.

Despite the acknowledgment of users, Flichy's work mainly focused on the inventors, adopters, or funders of technologies. In contrast, Jasanoff (2015) chose the term "sociotechnical imaginary" to fully include "the imaginative work of varied social actors" (p. 11). She defined sociotechnical imaginaries as "collectively held, institutionally stabilized, and publicly performed visions of desirable futures, animated by shared understandings of forms of social life and social order attainable through, and supportive of, advances in science and technology" (Jasanoff, 2015, p. 4). There are a number of noteworthy and productive components in Jasanoff's definition, which highlight the political implications of sociotechnical imaginaries: not just their collective, public, and performed character, but also the fact that they link technology to social change, to "visions of the collective good" (Jasanoff, 2015, p. 11). Jasanoff put sociotechnical imaginaries squarely in the context of modern ambitions concerning the role of science and technology, specifically linking the imaginaries to "advances" in such domains. She also highlighted the legitimating role that science and technology can play and the difference between the imaginaries developed in different national contexts (Jasanoff, 2015, p. 13).

Both Flichy and Jasanoff acknowledged that multiple imaginaries can coexist and compete in a given society, producing "contrasting visions of the future" (Flichy, 2007b, p. 133). However, the ways in which both of these authors conceptualized imaginaries is predominantly tied to technology-related or institutional actors.[3] While including different types of social actors, including social movements, among those who hold sociotechnical imaginaries, Jasanoff nevertheless spoke of imaginaries as "institutionally stabilized." Even if we loosen up the meaning of *institution*, I think that in this Jasanoff ended up retracing the original formulation of the concept of sociotechnical imaginary (Jasanoff & Kim, 2009), which centered nation-states and their political institutions. But I would say that it is particularly important to study imaginaries at times when different, conflicting imaginaries are still up for grabs and not yet institutionally sanctioned. And it is also important to study imaginaries as they are constructed and deployed by actors outside institutions and outside the tech sector. How do regular people fit into how we think about imaginaries of technology?

Imaginaries Are Based on Discourses and Practices

To help us think about how regular people come into play in the construction of imaginaries, I turn to sociology, and specifically Taylor's (2004) work on social imaginaries.

Taylor's social imaginaries, it is important to say, completely disregard technologies. Robin Mansell (2012) filled this gap and showed how Taylor's concept can be used to trace differing visions of "those engaged with developments in the information society" across academic and policy debates (p. 6). Following Taylor and Mansell, I want to highlight the productive insights that the notion of "social imaginaries" can nevertheless offer us and that we can use to flesh out how technological imaginaries operate (see Treré, 2018 for another examination of this issue).

Taylor defined social imaginaries as "the ways people imagine their social existence, how they fit together with others, how things go on between them and their fellows, the expectations that are normally met, and the deeper normative notions and images that underlie these expectations" (Taylor, 2004, p. 23). He developed this idea in the context of a theory of Western modernity, which maps the emergence of modern nation-states. He identified three such imaginaries: the market economy, the public sphere, and the self-governing people (Taylor, 2004, p. 2). In his formulation, these modern social imaginaries coexist within modernity, but each of them is also dominant within a national polity (although he mainly considers the United States, France, and the United Kingdom) during the establishment and consolidation of that polity into a modern nation-state. Indeed, Taylor's is not a theory that accounts for changes in the modern social imaginaries or for a challenge to them. The imaginaries he identified are static and dominant in their respective societies. In fact, Taylor remarked that "once we are well installed in the modern social imaginary, it seems the only possible one" (2004, p. 17), foreclosing the possibility of contesting it.

Taylor took great care in emphasizing that modern social imaginaries are not social theories. In distinguishing imaginaries from social theories, he offered two insights that are particularly useful to consider when thinking about technological imaginaries. First, he argued that the social imaginary is not an abstract idea held by élites, nor is it an ideology; rather, it is how "ordinary people 'imagine' their social surroundings" and is thus "shared by large groups of people, if not the whole society" (Taylor, 2004, p. 23). It is this widespread, collective acceptance of a social imaginary that generates its legitimacy. Second, Taylor underlined that practices are crucial to the imaginary: "If the understanding makes the practice possible, it is also true that it is the practice that largely carries the understanding" (Taylor, 2004, p. 23). In moving us away from abstract, élite-focused notions toward imaginaries that include practices and are developed by ordinary people, Taylor adds two important lessons that we can draw upon to think about technological imaginaries.

TECHNOLOGICAL IMAGINARIES AND THEIR CHARACTERISTICS

Building on the lessons from media history, cultural studies, STS, and sociology, I define *technological imaginary* as a set of practice-based beliefs, individual and collective, implicit and explicit, about the role of technology in social life and social change. Technological imaginaries capture how people conceptualize the relationship between technology and society, and how this relationship informs processes of social change. These imaginaries are rooted in practices; while they can be individually held, they are generally constructed by collectives. They can be explicit, communicated, and performed (for instance through public actions), but they also have an implicit, taken-for-granted character. Technological imaginaries are marked by six characteristics: they are political; they have a political economy; they are based on both practices and discourses; they are constructed by ordinary people; they are plural and conflicting, with the potential for one imaginary to become dominant in a given society; and they incorporate visions of the future and of the past.

First, technological imaginaries are profoundly political. They are connected to different visions of social change (Jasanoff, 2015); they can be contentious and publicly performed. They are normative visions about society (Jasanoff, 2015). But drawing on the lessons from media historians that I sketched out earlier, we can also see that technological imaginaries are political because they can be deployed for political purposes by a variety of social actors. Think, for instance, of the ways in which "the machine" (Marx, 1964), the "technological sublime" (Nye, 1996), and the "digital sublime" (Mosco, 2004) are implicated in the construction of a national US identity, but also specific political and economic interests. While the political nature of the technological imaginaries is not the central element in Flichy (2007a) and Jasanoff (2015), I suggest that highlighting its political component is key to deconstructing and critically interrogating the ways in which our visions of technologies become enmeshed in how we think about social change.

Second, technological imaginaries have material consequences. Speaking of the ways in which technologies are political, Winner (1986) argued that they are " ways of building order" in the world and that "consciously or unconsciously, deliberately or inadvertently, societies choose structures for technologies that influence how people are going to work, communicate, travel, consume, and so forth over a very long time" (p. 28). Keeping with Winner, the ways in which we choose structures for technologies, including their regulation, are clearly influenced by the imaginaries that surround said technologies. In this sense, imaginaries have very material consequences that need to be investigated. At the same time, imaginaries are also embedded in material arrangements: technological imaginaries have a political-economic dimension to them. For instance, Mosco (2004) argued that the "myths of cyberspace" he critiqued are profoundly interconnected with the economic forces of neoliberal globalization; they "embody, or mutual[ly] constitute, political economic interests" (Mosco, 2004, p. 142). Technological imaginaries are embedded in specific visions of the relationship between technology, society, and the economy; they envision specific political economic conditions.

Third, a technological imaginary is constructed by both discourses and practices.[4] Applying Taylor's (2004) emphasis on the interconnected role of "practices" and "understanding" in the social imaginary to technological imaginaries means recognizing that technological practices give actors a sense of what could be done with the affordances of technology, what technology's role could be; yet actors also put into practice the visions of technology that they have developed. People develop visions of technologies through their use of technology, but their use of technology is shaped by how they envision it. This connection between practices and discourses also helps explain the implicit character of technological imaginaries: discourses about technologies might become so embedded in people's technological practices that they disappear from view and become difficult to understand and question. This way of thinking about practices and discourses also carries an important methodological consequence: in order to fully understand technological imaginaries, we need to go beyond analyzing texts in which technological discourses are made explicit and embrace qualitative approaches that allow us to account for the role of practices.

Fourth, technological imaginaries are held by ordinary people; they are not solely the purview of the actors that have the power to directly influence the development, deployment, or regulation of technology. Like Taylor's (2004) social imaginaries, technological imaginaries are powerful because they are widely shared and make sense to a large variety of "regular" people. This means that different social groups in society can construct their own technological imaginaries. However, it is also clear that, if imaginaries have a material, political economic component to them, some imaginaries might become more widespread because they are held by— and likely advantage—powerful actors.

Fifth, I envision technological imaginaries to be plural and conflicting within a certain society. The notion of technological imaginary must allow room for multiple imaginaries to coexist and even clash with each other. Yet we can assume that we should be able to identify a technological imaginary that can become dominant at a given time. But it need not be the only one, and we should be able to find that alternative imaginaries are always being developed by other actors. Flichy (2007a) and Jasanoff (2015) both recognized that imaginaries can be multiple and "produce contrasting visions of the future" (Flichy, 2007b, p. 133), but we should also ask what role divergent, clashing imaginaries can play in political mobilization.

Sixth, while technological imaginaries are visions of the future, they are also constructed in implicit or explicit opposition to a more or less accurate image of the past. Since the technological imaginary is related to political culture, it has a historical dimension related to political history. But it is also related to history because, as we learn from the scholars who have sought to demystify the hype surrounding new technologies (e.g., Marvin, 1988; Mosco, 2004), discourses about technology emphasize technology in relation and in opposition to the past. This history, implicated in the way we speak of new technologies, can also be inaccurate; it can lead us to erase certain technological advancements in favor of others. In other words, considering the ways in which different technological imaginaries have been constructed and used over time allows us to not only chart the changes in society's political relationship to technology, but also interrogate the ways in which visions of the past inform discourses about the future.

Given my reliance on some aspects of Taylor's (2004) theorization of the social imaginary, I want to address its relationship to technological imaginaries. While Taylor's social imaginary is crucial in centering "ordinary people" and the role of practices, I do not find it suitable to address how people conceptualize the role of technology in society. It would be tempting to associate the modern social imaginaries identified by Taylor with corresponding technological imaginaries. In fact, it is evident that the three main social imaginaries identified by Taylor (2004) have become three ways of talking about digital technologies, and the internet in particular: the internet as an enormous market, based on exchanges of data; the internet as the public sphere; and the internet as direct democracy. It would thus seem that the technological imaginary is an applied, circumscribed version of the social imaginaries. However, I believe that the relationship is more complicated than that. I would like to suggest that different technological imaginaries can produce different visions of technology while aligning themselves to the same social imaginary. Take, for instance, Fred Turner's (2006) account of the clash between different approaches to technology in the social and political movements of the US 1960s. Turner looked at the New Communalists, who merged their communalist values with the vision of technology emerging out of Cold War society, and contrasted them with the Free Speech Movement at Berkeley and other movements of the New Left, which had a rather critical vision of technology, which they associated with the military-industrial-academic complex (Turner, 2006, pp. 11–12). These are two very different visions of technology that coexisted not only within the American society of the 1960s but also within the movements of that time. Yet both technological imaginaries are perfectly in line with the same social imaginary of individual freedom, autonomy, and independence that Taylor recognized as crucial to the (modern) United States (Taylor, 2004, p. 149). One technological imaginary sees personal independence as best realized through the use of technologies; the other sees this independence as threatened by the technology employed by the impersonal bureaucracies of the state and by the "war machine." Both technological imaginaries, although conflicting, draw on the same raw elements of the same US social imaginary, that is, the value of personal independence. There is thus no one-to-one correspondence between Taylor's social imaginaries and technological imaginaries.

THE DOMINANT TECHNOLOGICAL IMAGINARY OF SILICON VALLEY

While fleshing out my definition and the characteristics of the technological imaginaries, I have argued that although imaginaries are plural and conflicting, there should be a clearly identifiable technological imaginary that is dominant in a particular place and time. But what is the current dominant technological imaginary? It is a set of discourses that have been popularized by US technology companies, a group of actors commonly called "Silicon Valley" because most of them are located in that area of Northern California. The current dominant technological imaginary is an evolution of what Barbrook and Cameron (1996) called the "Californian Ideology," which, they asserted, "simultaneously reflects the disciplines of market economics and the freedoms of hippie artisanship. This bizarre hybrid is only made possible through a nearly universal belief in technological determinism" (p. 50). In turn, this belief is based on "a profound faith in the emancipatory potential of the new information technologies" (Barbrook & Cameron, 1996, p. 45). Turner (2006) traced the emergence of this discourse back to the countercultural movements of the 1960s in California; Mosco (2004), Eran Fisher (2008), and Thomas Streeter (2005) all highlighted the importance of the 1990s as a critical juncture for the consolidation and mainstreaming of these ideas, in conjunction with the end of the Cold War and the rise to prominence of new forms of right-wing libertarianism in the United States. They also underscored how the tech magazine *Wired* contributed to making these discourses about technology both popular and glamorous (Barbrook & Cameron, 1996; Fisher, 2008; Flichy, 2007a; Streeter, 2005; Turner, 2006).

Although we might dislike, criticize, and oppose the dominant technological imaginary of Silicon Valley, we are nevertheless immersed in it. It is thus imperative to investigate what it posits; what the visions of technology, society and social change it puts forward are; and what its political underpinnings are. Understanding this dominant imaginary is crucial to recognizing, and challenging, its power.

Freedom, Technosolutionism, Neoliberalism

The key tenets of this imaginary are powerful. First, this imaginary connects the digital to freedom, personal autonomy, and democracy, which are imagined to be accessible to everyone through the use of technologies (Barbrook & Cameron, 1996; Streeter, 2005; Turner, 2006). This empowering and liberatory vision of digital technologies is a core promise of Silicon Valley and one of the main sources of its allure. It is a promise to tech workers, who can see themselves as working toward desirable sociopolitical goals, contributing to overthrowing hierarchies, and enabling democratic self-expression. But it is also a promise for regular people, who—the imaginary suggests—can fulfill themselves as individuals and as citizens through the use of digital technologies, which are inherently free, freeing, and democratic. This equation of technology with freedom, democracy, and autonomy has proven incredibly powerful and difficult to question. However, it is important to underscore, as many have done, that this association is based on a fundamentally individualistic and market-driven view of what freedom, democracy, and autonomy are: a liberation not through collective action and political change, but through the individualized use of the technologies available on the market.

Second, the dominant technological imaginary of Silicon Valley suggests that people's problems and challenges can and should be addressed through the development and deployment of technologies, as opposed to, say, through the implementation of different policies (Fisher, 2008;

Morozov, 2013; Robins, 1996). Meredith Broussard (2018) called this idea "technochauvinism": "the belief that tech is always the solution" (p. 7–8). Evgeny Morozov (2013) used the term "technosolutionism" to criticize this line of thinking, arguing that by privileging technological fixes, it also ends up redefining what counts as a problem; according to Morozov, techno-solutionism recasts "all complex social situations either as neatly defined problems with definite, computable solutions or as transparent and self-evident processes that can be easily optimized" (2013, p. 5). This focus on technological solutions forecloses the possibility of tackling social and political issues through social and political processes, pitching digital technology as the only, inevitable avenue through which problems can be addressed.

Third, despite being a vision that celebrates the revolutionary power of technological innovation, this imaginary is fully embedded into and functional to dominant political-economic arrangements, that is, neo-liberalism. This means that there is a political-economic dimension to the dominant technological imaginary (Dean, 2005; Fisher, 2010; Mansell, 2012; but mostly, Mosco, 2004). Turner (2006) and Mosco (2004) convincingly explained how this affinity between Silicon Valley and neoliberal ideas came into being during the 1990s and how it was naturalized by *Wired* magazine. In the following decades, this connection between digital technologies, Silicon Valley, and neoliberalism has become a symbiotic relationship, as Jen Schradie (2015) highlighted. In *Abolish Silicon Valley*, which is part memoir and part manifesto, former start-up founder Wendy Liu recounted her experience as a software engineer and powerfully criticized this uncritical perpetuation of neoliberal ideas: "The dominant narrative within Silicon Valley is that technology is inseparable from capitalism, and so innovation requires letting the free market run roughshod over every aspect of our lives" (Liu, 2020, p. 4). It is also clear that this imaginary helps to further legitimize neoliberal capitalism: it portrays society as classless and free of socioeconomic struggles (Fisher, 2008) and sociopolitical inequalities (Schradie, 2015) and promotes the idea that the market, with its endless supply of technology, is the place for the resolution of problems and the improvement of people's lives—not politics (Mosco, 2004). This neoliberal erasure of the role of the state and belief in the boundless power of the free market is particularly striking given the crucial role of US public spending and federal policy in fostering Silicon Valley's growth (O'Mara, 2019).

Individualized freedom, technosolutionism, and neoliberalism are thus the three core tenets of Silicon Valley's dominant technological imaginary. They reinforce each other. Spelling them out helps us understand their political character: the fact that these ideas are as much about foundational ideas about politics as they are about digital technologies.

Dreams of Universality

The dominant technological imaginary has long been characterized by dreams of universality. It posits its universality by presenting its tenets as if they were global, unbiased, and equally suitable for everyone. However, this imaginary is actually a projection of a biased, bounded, regional set of ideas embedded in a specific political-economic arrangement, which is envisioned to have the same meaning and relevance everywhere in the world.

The technological imaginary of Silicon Valley is, first of all, deeply US American. On the one hand, these ideas originate in a specific space and time: the Silicon Valley of the 1990s, with its "eclectic and contradictory blend of conservative economics and hippie radicalism" (Barbrook & Cameron, 1996, p. 63), but also the US political scene of the 1990s writ large (Mosco, 2004). On the other hand, this dominant technological imaginary should also be understood within a long US history of fascination with "new" technologies. For instance, Nye (1996) argued that the fascination with technological developments—the "technological sublime"—is "a defining ideal for American society" (p. xiii-xiv) and "one of America's central 'ideas about itself'" (p. xiv).[5]

However, this dominant imaginary is also far from being universal because it is the projection of the experience of US-based white men onto everybody else. It is a vision of society that largely obscures differences of race, gender, and class; when it (rarely) acknowledges them, it simply assumes that technology will take care of them. This profoundly biased and limited vision has long characterized Silicon Valley, as can be seen in the venue that most contributed to celebrating it, *Wired* magazine. In my work on the first five years of *Wired*, between 1993 and 1997, I showed how the magazine put forth a discourse that celebrated digital technologies for their ability to do away with gender and race distinctions, by allowing people to experience the world as the "default" white man (Ferrari, 2020a). I called this discourse "selective disembodiment" and argued that it served to reinforce sexist, racist arrangements, while making them seem more palatable, even progressive and emancipatory. While it originated in the cultural milieu of the American 1990s, this discourse did not stay in the 1990s.[6] It clearly informs the dominant technological imaginary even today. As many scholars have shown, we are still faced with technologies that discriminate and oppress (see Benjamin, 2019; Noble, 2018; Ticona, 2022). And yet the dominant technological imaginary conveniently ignores not only how racism, sexism, heteronormativity, ableism, and classism still matter, but also how the technologies of Silicon Valley reinforce these systems of oppression. It is thus essential to deconstruct the implicit standpoint on which Silicon Valley's imaginary rests to fully understand its political connotations.

Technocratic and Populist

Is Silicon Valley progressive? Is it conservative? Or in even more US terms, isn't Silicon Valley squarely Democratic? It seems that, from time to time, the political alignment of Silicon Valley becomes the object of public scrutiny. This was certainly the case in the wake of the 2016 US presidential election, which prompted many discussions on whether certain companies or certain digital platforms could be considered liberal or conservative. However, if we want to assess the politics of Silicon Valley, we need to move beyond its electoral allegiances in the US context, which, by the way, are not as straightforward as they might seem, as O'Mara (2019) explained. We need to look at the foundational visions of politics, society, and the state that are built into the dominant technological imaginary of Silicon Valley.

I argue that this imaginary is underpinned by a blend of technocratic ambitions and populist justifications. Silicon Valley sees itself as a sociotechnical order (Winner, 1986), which is global in scale and capable of influencing democratic politics, but above the remit of any democratic institution.[7] At the same time, Silicon Valley also pitches itself as the true locus of democracy: because it portrays itself as a quirky meritocracy in which the underdogs can stick it to the man and everyone has an equal shot at becoming the next big thing, and because, as we have seen, it portrays its technologies as liberating, empowering, and based on users' "democratic" participation. These populist ideas justify Silicon Valley's technocratic ambitions, legitimizing its global sociotechnical order as an inevitable triumph of the hard-working little guy against the elites of yore.

I have examined how populism and technocracy coexist in the dominant technological imaginary through an analysis of Mark Zuckerberg's "manifesto" (2017), an open letter to the Facebook "global community" penned by its founder and CEO in the midst of the challenges the company encountered after the 2016 US presidential election (Ferrari, 2020b). I pointed to the explicitly political remarks made by Zuckerberg, who borrowed from the language of democratic politics ("democratic process," "referendum," "collective decision-making") to depict Facebook as a democracy of sorts, in which a mix of personalized settings and majoritarian principles shapes the content that users are shown in their Facebook Feeds. I showed how he positioned Facebook as a blueprint for a global polity, calling for political institutions to model themselves after Facebook, asserting it as a model for democratic politics at scale. I highlighted how, in the document, Zuckerberg drew on Facebook's global scale to position it as uniquely suited to address the global challenges that nation-states cannot, such as terrorism or climate change; he asserted that it is indeed Facebook's role to address the global challenges of our time. No nation-state can solve the world's problems, but Facebook can, he seemed to be saying.

Zuckerberg's manifesto made explicit the meeting of technocratic ambitions and populist justifications that fuel the dominant technological imaginary of Silicon Valley. While we might be tempted to dismiss Zuckerberg's self-aggrandizing narrative, he is not alone in portraying technologies as a substitute for political decisions and as a model for politics. This idea is the logical extension of the second tenet of the dominant technological imaginary, technosolutionism: if, indeed, technology is how political issues are solved, why can't politics just become more like technology? This is also, of course, in line with how neoliberalism has eroded the legitimacy of nation-states vis-à-vis the markets (Harvey, 2007). What we are left with is the sense that the political arena is wholly delegitimized as a venue for the improvement of people's lives and that politics should just let tech actors take care of society through market-driven technological development, while preferably also trying to operate more like a tech company.

If Zuckerberg can openly voice his technocratic ambitions, it is because of the populist justifications that are built into the dominant technological imaginary. Scholars have already pointed out the existence of populist elements in the way that digital technologies are portrayed and popularized. Mosco (2004) called it "an individualistic populism suffused with elite ideals" (p. 112), which emerged from the convergence of countercultural and New Right libertarian ideals (Turner, 2006). For me these populist justifications originate in the belief that digital technologies are inherently free, democratic, and supportive of personal autonomy (the first tenet of the dominant technological imaginary). This tenet is what sustains Zuckerberg's use of the language of democratic politics that I highlight here, the way he spoke about Facebook as a community and freely used terms like "democratic process" or "referendum." The populist tendencies of the dominant technological imaginary legitimize Silicon Valley's technocratic ambitions, making it more difficult to question its power. Zuckerberg (2017) even offered his own populist notion of "the people": the Facebook community, or rather "people's intrinsic goodness aggregated across our community," which is imagined in contrast to nation-states and elites. In so doing, he tapped into populist readings of digital technologies that promise rebellion and redemption for the users of these technologies (Streeter, 2005).

The dominant technological imaginary of Silicon Valley is thus at the same time technocratic and populist. It is technocratic because it sketches out the contours of a global sociotechnical order that goes beyond states and governance bodies—an order defined by the dominance of key technological players in an "open" market that is the locus for the resolution of social problems. And yet it is also populist because it builds on the anti-elite ethos of the Californian Ideology and provides a new definition of "the people," solely predicated on the access to and use of digital technologies. This blend of technocracy and populism also makes it clear how much the dominant technological imaginary has evolved, becoming more explicit in its technocratic ambitions. While the Californian Ideology of the 1990s was an insurgent message, Silicon Valley's technological imaginary of the 2010s is a discourse that legitimizes an established dominant industry, capable of influencing politics across the globe.

By examining its technocratic and populist tendencies, we can better single out the politics of the dominant technological imaginary. Beyond its temporary political allegiances or the voting patterns of its rank and file, Silicon Valley asserts a specific imaginary that is political: it promotes specific visions of the relationship between the market, the state, and society. The dominant technological imaginary is a political project, and it should be scrutinized as such.

How Dominant?

When I speak about the technological imaginary of Silicon Valley as dominant, I am often asked if I think this dominance still holds or how long I think it will last. Usually, people ask me about the impact of the Cambridge Analytica scandal, which generated a wave of scrutiny directed not only at Facebook, but at technology companies more generally. Is this "techlash" the beginning of the end of the current technological imaginary? The short answer is maybe. The longer answer is that it seems to me that the criticism that is being moved against Facebook and the other tech giants does not fundamentally question the dominant technological imaginary, but rather in some ways reaffirms it.

Since 2017, Silicon Valley has come under increased scrutiny following the Facebook-Cambridge Analytica scandal (Cadwalladr & Graham-Harrison, 2018; Granville, 2019). Facebook itself was the object of congressional hearings in the United States, while the European Union (EU) has used both its General Data Protection Regulation and antitrust norms to challenge the business model of Silicon Valley's giants, including Facebook and Google (Scott et al., 2019). For a time, even the 2020 US election campaign considered the issue, with Senator Elizabeth Warren talking about her plans to "break up big tech" (Roose, 2019) during the Democratic primaries. Is this the beginning of the end of the dominant technological imaginary of Silicon Valley? Again, maybe.

It might be the beginning of Facebook's downfall, but this does not necessarily mean it is the end of the current dominant technological imaginary. While Silicon Valley might be losing its power to shield itself from regulatory intervention, I argue that the key tenets of its technological imaginary still remain largely unchallenged. It is difficult to regulate a technological imaginary. Policy makers can, and indeed should, impose limits on the market share enjoyed by Silicon Valley companies. They can limit the amount of data that platforms can acquire, share, and sell. But they cannot really stop companies from proclaiming their platforms to be conduits of democracy and freedom. Who would want to do that? The dominant technological imaginary is not about the specific technologies; it is about the relation of those technologies to fundamental political processes. When Silicon Valley comes under scrutiny in the political and policy arena, there is often a concern with its political biases: Are Silicon Valley and its technologies favoring one political party over the other? But as we have seen in my discussion of the dominant technological imaginary, we should be concerned with other biases in Silicon Valley, which hit at a fundamental level of politics and go beyond party affiliation.

To assess the "health" of the dominant technological imaginary of Silicon Valley, we need not look further than to Mark Zuckerberg.[8] With Facebook's dominance being openly contested and subject to regulatory pressures, he has continued to propose different technological fixes to solve people's growing lack of confidence in Facebook (and the company's stock market woes). In 2019 he released another open letter (Zuckerberg, 2019). While its tone is definitely less celebratory than his 2017 manifesto, it nevertheless enthusiastically proposed to reinforce how encryption works across Facebook and shifting the perception of Facebook from a "public social network," as Zuckerberg (2019) called it, to the facilitator of private conversations through Messenger and WhatsApp. Further, Facebook's 2021 rebranding into Meta brought with it the announcement of the development of the metaverse, an all-encompassing platform based on virtual and augmented reality, accompanied by promises that feel like a throwback to the discourses of embodiment and disembodiment of the 1990s (Ferrari, 2020a). What is interesting in these developments is that they reaffirm the dominant technological imaginary of Silicon Valley: its technosolutionism, clearly, but also, particularly with the metaverse, its ambitions to reshape the world in its image. If the imaginary still offers a way out of the troubles that Facebook encountered, we might need to wait to declare its downfall.[9]

The other question I am often asked about the dominance of Silicon Valley's technological imaginary is whether it is truly global. I think it is increasingly global in its reach, both because of its ambitions and because of the global spread of its technologies. This does not mean that it will be as dominant in all areas of the world as it is in the Global North/West. For instance, one might imagine that the technological imaginary of the Chinese government might be the dominant one to consider when trying to assess how different visions of technology play out in China. But I argue that even in cases where there are strong state-driven technological imaginaries, the imaginary of Silicon Valley can still be recognizable and recognized as dominant across the world. Revati Prasad (2020), for example, showed how a state-sponsored internet fiber service in Andhra Pradesh, in Southeast India, imagined itself as a start-up, echoing many key tropes commonly deployed by Silicon Valley actors to talk about their technologies; seeing itself as a start-up allowed this state-backed project to legitimize its operations and business model by drawing on key elements of Silicon Valley's technological imaginary.

ACTIVIST TECHNOLOGICAL IMAGINARIES: A FRAMEWORK

The dominant technological imaginary of Silicon Valley, while far from universal, is no longer confined to the West Coast of the United States. It has made its way, through mass media, pop cultural representations, and even digital technologies themselves (Flichy, 2007a), to other areas of the world. The reach of this technological imaginary was particularly evident during the early commentary on the movements of 2011, especially the Arab Spring. Emblematic of that period was the debate that unfolded between (and around) Clay Shirky and Malcom Gladwell (Gladwell, 2010; Shirky, 2011; Gladwell & Shirky, 2011) over the role played by internet technologies in social movements, which oriented the entire mainstream public discussion on the movements of 2011 around a techno-utopian (Shirky) versus techno-skeptic (Gladwell) binary. Regardless of the different positions expressed, the sheer existence of that specific debate illustrates some of the key aspects of the dominant technological imaginary: that digital technologies are the natural, central, and inevitable lens through which social movements should be discussed, and that the debate over the use of technologies is the only one worth having, because technology is how social change can be achieved. While we might be tempted to dismiss the terms of this debate—and academic scholarship certainly has moved us past this polarizing dichotomy (see Dennis, 2019)—we nevertheless need to acknowledge that it reflects a discursive environment in which movements are immersed. In other words, while activists might construct their own activist technological imaginaries, they are nevertheless confronted with a very powerful mainstream imaginary, which sees technology as the ultimate avenue for social change. How they make sense of this imaginary is at the core of this book.

Through the cases I examine in the following chapters, I analyze how specific activist technological imaginaries are constructed and deployed by different activist groups. In broad terms, my work on activist technological imaginaries is inspired by the constructivist, cultural approach of social movement theorist Alberto Melucci (1989, 1996). Following Melucci, I consider social movements as processes of collective self-definition; this means that I consider the ways in which activists construct their systems of beliefs, negotiate meanings, and make decisions to be the core elements of any analysis of social movements. Activist technological imaginaries are part of these processes of collective self-definition, since, as we will see in the following chapters, they are strictly connected to the more immediately political aspects of these activist groups, such as their ideologies.

I thus see the study of activist technological imaginaries as contributing to the literature on social movements and digital media by moving beyond the analysis of how social movements simply use digital technologies to center the political and imaginative work that activists need to perform in order to navigate the politics of mainstream digital technologies. I am not alone in this effort. Scholars working with the anthropological notion of "media imaginary" (e.g., Barassi, 2015; Treré, 2018; Treré et al., 2017) have also considered how activists make sense of digital technologies. Veronica Barassi (2015) analyzed the media imaginaries of different social movements, linking them to their media practices; this allowed her to argue that different movements "often develop 'different understandings' of what they wanted to achieve from media technologies, which was largely inspired by their political projects and which determined the way that their media practices were organized" (Barassi, 2015, p. 41). Emiliano Treré (2018) positioned media imaginaries as one of the theoretical lenses, alongside media ecologies and algorithmic power, for the study of contemporary digital activism. He then examined in detail the media imaginary of the Italian Five Star Movement (5SM), which he defined as "authoritarian sublime" and of the Spanish Indignados, which he called "technopolitical sublime" (Treré, 2018). Treré, Sandra Jeppesen, and Alice Mattoni (2017) sought to identify the different media imaginaries of the anti-austerity movements in Italy, Spain, and Greece, finding that they have three different "digital protest media imaginaries" (p. 416), which they suggested are largely based on different national activist cultures. My work is in conversation with and has been inspired by these authors. However, I depart from these scholars in two ways. I chose to use (and redefine) the concept of technological imaginary, over that of media imaginary, to allow for a broader application of my theoretical framework, in dialogue with STS approaches.[10] In addition, by explicitly connecting activists' technological imaginaries to the broader discursive environment that surrounds contemporary digital technologies, my framework allows us to map how dominant and activist imaginaries interact and what might be influencing these interactions.

What do social movements' technological imaginaries look like, then? Based on the cases I examine in this book, I propose a categorization of activist technological imaginaries based on how they respond to the dominant technological imaginary of Silicon Valley. The categories consider whether social movements' technological imaginaries accept or dismiss the dominant technological imaginary and whether or not they choose to employ Silicon Valley's digital technologies in their activism. This results in three types of activist technological imaginaries: appropriation, negotiation, and challenge. Imaginaries of appropriation embrace the dominant technological imaginary and endorse the use of Silicon Valley's digital technologies; as shown in chapter 3, the Hungarian internet tax protests constructed such an imaginary of appropriation. Technological imaginaries of negotiation reject the dominant technological imaginary of Silicon Valley, yet they allow for the use of Silicon Valley's digital technologies. LUMe and Philly Socialists both construct imaginaries of negotiation, which are however different from each other. Last, technological imaginaries of challenge reject both the dominant technological imaginary of Silicon Valley and Silicon Valley's digital technologies. In the concluding chapter, I sketch out what imaginaries of challenge might look like; I further distinguish between imaginaries of challenge that are based on the refusal to use Silicon Valley's technologies and those that envision the development of alternative activist technologies.

As I show in the following chapters, I find that three crucial political factors shape how activists construct their technological imaginaries in response to Silicon Valley's dominant imaginary. I account for these factors through my theoretical framework, which leads me to first examine how the ideology of each group guides how activists think about digital technology. Second, I consider how the political context in which movements are embedded contributes to how activists relate to technology: What are the historical or contemporary political conditions that come into play? Third, I highlight how the presence of other technological imaginaries, in addition to Silicon Valley's imaginary, might have an impact on how activists construct their own: How do activists assess and respond to the technological imaginaries deployed by other political actors, such as governments, political parties, and other social movements? Ideology, political context, and other political actors: activist technological imaginaries are shaped by the politics of the social movements that construct them. They show us how activists approach technology in a political way, identifying a relationship between the dominant technological imaginary and corporate digital technologies and carefully considering how their technological practices relate to their political commitments.

This theoretical framework accounts for both the power of the dominant visions about technology and the political and imaginative work that activists perform to make sense of their relationship with digital technologies. It gives us a way to understand the symbolic power of digital technologies: how tech comes to be associated with ideas such as freedom and democracy, and how these associations can be deployed by different political actors. And it allows us to take a more comprehensive and nuanced look at how movements view different technological practices through a political lens: how they see technology as political and how they evaluate its politics in the context of their own political ideas. In short, this framework links a critique of Silicon Valley's neoliberal underpinnings with an understanding of how activists experience and reimagine technology in their day-to-day practices.

CONCLUSION

In this chapter I have emphasized the importance of considering the discourses about technology that different societal groups construct and deploy. Drawing on lessons from scholarly work across disciplines, I articulated how the concept of technological imaginary can help us understand the importance of technological discourses, their collective nature, and their political connotations. I expanded my definition of technological imaginaries, accounting for their six key characteristics.

Building on this conceptualization, I then explored what I identify as the current dominant technological imaginary, one created and propagated by Silicon Valley actors, which brings together technocratic ambitions and populist justifications, based on a vision that equates technology with freedom and democracy, pitches technology as the solution to all possible problems, and is subordinate to and supportive of neoliberalism. I also discussed the evident biases of this dominant technological imaginary, which believes itself to be universal, while being grounded in systems of oppression. I also showed that while Silicon Valley might have come under increased scrutiny recently, the power of its technological imaginary and of its technologies is still very real.

I then explained that in order to understand the relationship between social movements and digital technologies, we need to look at how they make sense of these mainstream ideas about technology. I argued that activists respond to the dominant technological imaginary by constructing their own technological imaginaries, which might appropriate, negotiate, or challenge the visions arising from Silicon Valley. I further explained how the construction of these activist imaginaries is influenced by the politics of each social movement: their ideology, their political context, and how they also respond to other technological imaginaries that are salient in their context. I deploy this categorization in the chapters that follow.

This chapter makes clear what is at stake when we are examining technological imaginaries, especially dominant ones: imaginaries are visions not just about specific technologies, but also about the kinds of social, political, and economic relations that such technologies support and encourage. It is thus particularly important to critically interrogate the biases of the technological imaginaries that become dominant at a given time. The imaginary popularized by Silicon Valley should be investigated to tease out its political connotations and its dreams of universality, particularly as it travels around the world and becomes enmeshed in conversations about mobilization and social change. As I demonstrate in the rest of this book, the underlying politics of the dominant technological imaginary and of the technologies of Silicon Valley is very clear to activists, who respond to it by constructing technological imaginaries that are tied to their own political ideas and political conditions.

3 The Symbolic Power of Mundane Modernity

THE IMAGINARY OF APPROPRIATION OF
THE HUNGARIAN INTERNET TAX PROTESTS

"People throwing routers to the Fidesz hq."[1] That was the update I received via Facebook Messenger from a Hungarian friend on the evening of October 26, 2014. I had just moved to the United States for graduate school and I tried to keep updated on the ever-evolving (usually enraging) political situation in Hungary, where I had lived for three years. My friend was messaging me from a protest in Budapest, Hungary's capital, in which ten thousand people took to the streets to voice their opposition to an "internet tax" that the government wanted to introduce. And at some point, some of them had started to throw routers toward the building that houses the headquarters of the political party that had been in power since 2010, Fidesz. "Priceless," I replied.

This update had been preceded by a blurry panoramic photo that depicted a huge number of protesters lifting their phones, with their screens illuminated, toward the dark evening sky. Better photographs of this same protest action—lit up phones held up high—became the key images of the protests. A couple of days later, in the second demonstration, protesters staged the most impactful version of the iconic image: a photograph captured one hundred thousand people crossing the Danube River on the Elizabeth Bridge in an aerial shot, as they lifted their illuminated phones to the night.

Only a month before these protests in Hungary, the same protest action had been used in the massive demonstrations of Occupy Central, Hong Kong's prodemocracy movement. Pictures showed thousands of protesters in front of the headquarters of the Hong Kong government, holding their cell phones up high, illuminating the night with their screen lights. The image was immediately picked up by both mainstream media and social network sites and circulated worldwide. CNN described the image, saying: "Photographed from above, the glowing screens of mobile phones held aloft by the sea of protesters have created an enduring image of the demonstrators' solidarity" (Hume & Park, 2014). The iconic image of protesters raising their phones to the sky survived the demise of the Umbrella Revolution and traveled far away.

After first reappearing in Budapest in 2014, this image became a symbol of different Hungarian anti-government protests in 2017, this time against legislation targeting civil society organizations and academic institutions. Protesters once again took out their phones and raised them to the sky (*Large Protest*, 2017). After that, in 2017 and 2018, images of protesters raising their glowing cell phones circulated throughout the Central Eastern European (CEE) region: first during the Romanian anti-corruption protests (Gillet, 2017), then in the Slovakian demonstrations that led to the resignation of the prime minister (Santora, 2018). And again in Hungary, illuminated smartphones reappeared during protests after the re-election of Viktor Orbán in 2018 (*Hungary*, 2018) and after the firing of the chief editor of the biggest independent news outlet, *Index*, in 2020 (*Thousands of Hungarians*, 2020).

Routers and smartphones, thrown against buildings or held up high, tell the story of the Hungarian internet protests of 2014 and of how opposition activists were able to mobilize a specific technological imaginary in opposition to the Orbán government. This story begins in October 2014, when the Hungarian government announced the introduction of an "internet tax" that would apply to internet consumption on both mobile and landlines. This proposal was met with protests in the streets of Budapest—the largest mobilization against the right-wing Fidesz government since its election in 2010 and (at the time) the biggest demonstration in Hungary since 1989. Confronted with the size of the protest, Prime Minister Orbán decided to set aside the proposed legislation, which has

since not been reintroduced. This chapter examines the internet tax protests by reconstructing the technological imaginary that was deployed
during the protests.

The internet tax protests were organized by a loosely coordinated group
of experienced liberal-leftist activists based in Budapest. Activists have
been mobilizing for years in opposition to Hungary's "illiberal turn" (Kornai, 2015; Pap, 2018), the deterioration of civil liberties and the rule of law
progressively enacted by the Orbán-led right-wing governments since 2010.
The extraordinary mobilization of the internet tax protests marked a rare
victory for the civil society–based opposition. I argue that this success can
be attributed to the fact that these protests were able to draw on a powerful technological imaginary that turned dissatisfaction with the tax into a
general contestation of the Orbán government.

This chapter theorizes the technological imaginary deployed in the
Hungarian internet tax protests as mundane modernity: an imaginary
that grounds long-standing tropes of Western modernity in the everyday
practices of internet use. Interviewees, in fact, associate the internet with
equality and development, the future, and rationality; in so doing, they
reproduce discourses about the role of technology in Western modernity.
However, they also insist on the mundanity of the internet: its importance
for everyday life. This imaginary thus brings together the political aspirations of Western modernity with the mundanity of internet practices.
It is an imaginary that portrays a fusion of market freedom and political
freedom, which takes on a specific relevance in a postcommunist context.
This imaginary of mundane modernity was powerfully conveyed through
slogans such as "free country, free internet," the improbable throwing
of routers against buildings, and the most recognizable symbol of these
demonstrations: the illuminated phones.

This technological imaginary is one of appropriation, in that mundane
modernity embraces both the technologies of Silicon Valley and its dominant technological imaginary. It reinterprets the pillars of Silicon Valley's
imaginary by equating the internet with freedom (both political freedom
and market freedom) and Western democracy. More than a simple rep-
etition, mundane modernity appropriates Silicon Valley's imaginary to
make it resonant in a postcommunist context, in which ideas of Western
modernity, democracy, and freedom are contentious. This imaginary of

appropriation is, in fact, shaped by the Hungarian political context and the revamping of the modernity-tradition cleavage under Orbán. It is also influenced by the context-dependent ideological positions of Hungarian opposition activists, whose relationship to neoliberalism is less contentious than in other countries, due to the peculiarities of the postcommunist ideological space. Finally, mundane modernity is also clearly shaped by an opposition to the technological imaginary of Orbán's political project: "illiberal democracy" (Orbán, 2014), which is embodied by the internet tax itself.

THE HUNGARIAN INTERNET TAX PROTESTS

In October 2014 the Orbán government clumsily announced that they were contemplating a tax on internet usage for both mobile phones and landlines. This internet tax would have applied to all internet consumption after a first untaxed gigabyte, with a levy of 150 Hungarian forints (at the time about $0.50) for each additional gigabyte. As a first response to the tax, a Facebook page was created: *Százezren az internetadó ellen*, literally "100,000 against the Internet tax," which became the informal organizing hub for the demonstrations.[2] On October 26, ten thousand people marched in the center of Budapest (*Hungary: Internet Tax Angers*, 2014). The government responded by announcing that the tax would be limited to a monthly cap of 700 forints ($2.40) for individual users (Feher, 2014b).

Unsatisfied with the government's amendments to the proposed tax, activists organized a second demonstration for October 28, which gathered an estimated one hundred thousand protesters. It was the largest protest since Hungary's transition to democracy in 1989, and thus also the biggest demonstration against Orbán's government (Dunai, 2014).[3] In stark contrast with previous anti-government protests, which were predominantly concentrated in the capital, Budapest, demonstrations against the internet tax also happened in smaller towns, such as Pécs, Miskolc, and Veszprem on October 26 (Feher, 2014a) and Debrecen, Györ, Pécs, Szeged, and Nyíregyháza on October 28 ("Bürgerbewegung Oder Putschversuch?," 2014). These protests were not coordinated by Budapest-based activists, but rather emerged spontaneously in the different towns.

The mobilization of the Hungarian countryside, usually considered the electoral stronghold of Fidesz, undoubtedly contributed to making the internet tax a highly contentious issue for the government.

The protests received a lot of domestic and international media coverage. While the domestic coverage in pro-government media was predictably skewed against the protests, the fact that the demonstrations were covered *at all* actually helped the activists to break out of the left-liberal circles, as they explained in the interviews. The international media coverage sought, on the one hand, to contextualize the protests within Hungary's authoritarian trajectory (Eder, 2014; Lyman, 2014a); on the other hand, it tried to frame the protests as about "internet freedom," likely because of the struggle over net neutrality that was simultaneously unfolding in the United States and at the EU level (Franceschi-Bicchierai, 2014).

The proposed internet tax was met with criticism by the European authorities. Neelie Kroes, who at the time was serving as European commissioner for digital agenda, harshly criticized the tax on October 22, tweeting: "Proposed internet tax in #Hungary is a shame: a shame for users and a shame on the Hungarian government. I do not support!" (Kroes, 2014). Kroes's spokesperson, Ryan Heath, delivered an even stronger statement on behalf of the EU Commission on October 28, openly siding with the ongoing protests and saying that Kroes "was determined not to allow the tax to become a precedent in Hungary, because it could become a problem for Europe's wider economic growth" ("Commission Slams Hungary's 'Internet Tax,'" 2014). The harshness of the EU Commission's declarations should not surprise us, given the long string of confrontations between the EU and the Orbán government; however, since conflict with European institutions has often been welcomed by Orbán, who has sought to position himself as a defender of the Hungarian nation against foreign intervention, we might question whether such a strong condemnation by the EU would even have an effect on the situation.

While activists were getting ready to hold a third demonstration, on October 31, Orbán said in a radio interview that the tax proposal had been misunderstood by the population and that it would not be introduced in its current form (*Hungary Internet Tax Cancelled*, 2014). Orbán's speech was somewhat puzzling: while maintaining that the proposal had been misunderstood, he nevertheless appealed to his long-standing criticism of the pre-1989 regime to cast this decision in a more positive light, saying that his government would not go against the will of the people because they are "not communist" (*Hungary Internet Tax Cancelled*, 2014). The organizers of the protests saw this as an unequivocal victory against the government and celebrated it with a third demonstration (Lyman, 2014b). This celebratory demonstration drew a much smaller crowd, of about five thousand people, but marked an important moment, one of the few victories of Hungarian activists against the Orbán governments. Since the protests of 2014 and Orbán's radio address, there have been no further attempts by the Hungarian government to tax internet usage.

Before the government backed out of the internet tax, the protests had begun to move beyond the initial demand to not have the internet taxed (see also Gagyi, 2014). As a participant in the protests noted, slogans changed from "free country, free internet!" to "Orbán piss off! We want democracy! Europe, Europe! Russians go home! Filthy Fidesz, corrupt Fidesz!" (observer, personal communication). Opposition movements that had been organizing—mostly unsuccessfully—for years found in the internet tax an issue they could use to gather support around a broader platform of opposition to the Orbán government. It seemed paradoxical that the threat of a few hundred forints per month in extra taxes would lead Hungarians to protest so massively against the government, while the same government had already changed the Constitution (Human Rights Watch, 2013) and curtailed the freedom of the media (Brouillette, 2012). What was so special about the internet tax that could make so many Hungarians take to the streets?

HUNGARY'S ILLIBERAL TURN AND THE MOBILIZATION OF AN ACTIVIST OPPOSITION

The last fifteen years of Hungarian politics has been marked by the rise to power of Orbán and his right-wing Fidesz party. Orbán was elected prime minister in 2010 and then reelected in 2014, 2018, and 2022. During his terms as prime minister, based on the strong parliamentary majorities enjoyed by Fidesz, he has pushed forward a conservative agenda that he describes as "illiberal democracy" (Orbán, 2014). Orbán first explicitly deployed that label in a 2014 speech, in which he argued that his recent electoral success gave him a mandate to "break with liberal principles and methods of social organization, and in general with the liberal understanding of society" (Orbán, 2014). He continued: "A democracy does not necessarily have to be liberal. Just because a state is not liberal, it can still be a democracy. And in fact we also had to and did state that societies that are built on the state organization principle of liberal democracy will probably be incapable of maintaining their global competitiveness in the upcoming decades and will instead probably be scaled down unless they are capable of changing themselves significantly" (Orbán, 2014). Orbán thus stated that liberal democracies are bound to fail over the next few decades, while Hungary, having chosen to become an illiberal state, will regain competitiveness on the world stage. He affirmed that Hungary's was "a different, special, national approach" to democracy, claiming a Hungarian specificity that can be deployed to resist the liberal principles (and regulations) of the EU. In the same speech, he also asserted that the reorganization of the Hungarian state should be constructed around the idea of a "national community," which in his view is, of course, an ethnonational community of white Christian Hungarians, and which should be "organized, reinforced and in fact constructed" (Orbán, 2014).

This illiberal project relied on amending the Fundamental Law (i.e., the Hungarian Constitution) to tilt the balance of power in favor of the executive branch and weaken the power and independence of the court system (Bozoki, 2015; Human Rights Watch, 2013), enacting sweeping changes to media policy that undermined independent media (Brouillette, 2012; Pap, 2018, pp. 22–23), and increasing taxes while cutting budgets related to health care, education, and pensions (Bozoki, 2015). The Fidesz government also changed the electoral system in a way that provided an advantage to the party (Pap, 2018, pp. 24–25), leading some to call Hungarian elections "free and unfair" (Bozoki, 2015). In addition to the Media Laws, Orbán relied on allied businessmen to consolidate the market share of pro-government media in the country (Bienvenu, 2016; Kingsley, 2018). Further, Orbán has used a rhetoric that creates "enemies" of the Hungarian nation on whom any shortcoming of the government can be blamed (Csaky, 2017). These scapegoats include the EU; refugees;

"liberal" nongovernmental organizations (NGOs); and any actor that can be connected, directly or indirectly, to Hungarian American billionaire George Soros (Eotvos Karoly Policy Institute et al., 2014).

These sweeping changes were made possible by the fact that Fidesz (and its ally, the KDNP, the Christian Democratic People's Party) won a majority of over 66 percent of parliamentary seats in the 2010 elections, giving Orbán the supermajority needed to alter the Constitution. Since 2010 the Fidesz governments, which have all enjoyed parliamentary supermajorities, have amended the Constitution five times. The constitutional changes have been the object of scrutiny and controversy between the Hungarian government and European institutions. However, as András Pap (2018) has argued, the way in which Fidesz built the new constitutional regime, that is, by mixing and matching elements from different European constitutions, has made it difficult to uncover "the destructive features of the regime, let alone being able to raise specific, reasoned criticism" (p. 4); while taken individually, each of the elements have a place in a liberal order, their assemblage in what Kim Lane Scheppele (2013) has called a "Frankenstate" threatens individual freedom and the rule of law. Pap also has defined the illiberal turn as "defying rule of law principles, dismantling core institutional guarantees for government control and adopting an ideologically biased constitution that cements these developments" (2018, p. 5). Peter Wilkin (2018) similarly has argued that the aim of the new constitutional regime created by Fidesz was to create "a permanent bias in support of Fidesz so that if they were to lose an election their appointees would still be in positions of power over whatever actions alternative governments might take" (p. 23). In this "democratic backsliding," the membership of Hungary in the EU contributes to both constraining and stabilizing the new illiberal state (Wilkin, 2018).

The illiberal turn did not stop after the momentary defeat of the government on the internet tax. In fact, Orbán's illiberal democracy has become a model for other right-wing and populist forces in the CEE region and in the rest of the world (Buzogány & Varga, 2018). Since 2014, the Orbán governments have continued to attack the media (Bienvenu, 2016) and civil society (Csaky, 2017). In 2017, new legislation targeted Hungarian NGOs by instituting more cumbersome reporting procedures and by requiring the disclosure of foreign donations (Csaky, 2017). It waged a prolonged battle with an unusual enemy, Central European University (CEU), the university based in Budapest and founded by billionaire George Soros, forcing the institution out of the country (Mudde, 2017). Both the legislation against CEU and against NGOs should be understood as targeting Soros, who has been construed by the Hungarian government as a symbol of anti-Hungarian cosmopolitanism. In 2018 the newly re-elected government approved a controversial labor reform, dubbed "slave law" by its opponents, which amended the labor code to allow companies to demand more overtime work hours from their employees and to delay payment for said overtime (Graham-Harrison, 2019).

But the event that brought illiberal democracy to the attention of the world was the refugee crisis of the mid-2010s, when the Hungarian government showed its xenophobic tendencies in an even clearer way (Csaky, 2017). Although brewing for quite some time (Dessewffy & Nagy, 2016), tensions over migration came to prominence in Hungary in the fall of 2015, when hundreds of thousands of refugees attempted to enter the EU through Hungary; while many ended up in camps across the country, thousands were stranded in Budapest around Keleti train station, where they were denied access to the trains going to Western Europe (Kallius et al., 2016). The violent rhetoric deployed against migrants constructed a non-Christian Other that threatened the Hungarian nation; at the same time, this rhetoric also targeted the Roma and the homeless population (Kallius et al., 2016). Hungary opposed the EU relocation scheme, the "migrant quotas," which aimed to more fairly distribute refugees among member states. In 2016 the government called for a farcical national referendum on the EU scheme (Pállinger, 2019); it ultimately did not reach its necessary quorum and was declared invalid. However, the government has continued to campaign on the issue of migration; in particular, it used a national consultation to ask voters about an alleged "Soros plan" to encourage immigration to Hungary and passed a "Stop Soros" bill, which criminalized a good deal of migration-related work or volunteering (Zerofsky, 2019), while simultaneously attacking George Soros.

While the internet tax itself should thus be contextualized in the larger turn toward illiberal democracy that is at the heart of Fidesz's politics, the internet tax protests should be examined within the broader civil society opposition to the Fidesz governments. By the time the internet tax was proposed, Hungary had seen the emergence of several protests, largely concentrated in the capital, which were the expression of leftist and liberal concerns surrounding the right-wing politics of Fidesz (for a general introduction see Glied, 2014). It is this grassroots activist scene that has been the most vocal opposition to Orbàn in the country, not traditional political parties. In fact, the dominance of Fidesz has been heightened by the immense difficulties and popular delegitimation of the opposition parties, such as the Hungarian Socialist Party (Magyar Szocialista Párt or MSZP) and the green-liberals of Politics Can Be Different (Lehet *Más a* Politika or LMP). While an analysis of the shortcomings of the Hungarian opposition parties is beyond the scope of this chapter, it is useful to point out that their lack of popular legitimacy has opened the door for activist groups and various types of associations, including NGOs, to play a crucial role in opposing Fidesz.[4] At the same time, the unreliability of the opposition parties has also left social movements without institutional allies.

The two most successful social movements to emerge between 2012 and 2014 were One Million for the Freedom of the Press in Hungary (better known as Milla) and Hallgatói Hálózat or HaHa (i.e., "student network"). They sponsored demonstrations that criticized the Orbán government for its curtailing of media freedom and fundamental rights and for its educational reforms, respectively. Like the internet tax protests, Milla also started as a Facebook-based mobilization, and its use of digital media has been crucial for creating new spaces of protest (Wilkin et al., 2015); while it focused on the issue of press freedom, it aimed to mobilize civil society against the general illiberal direction in which Fidesz had begun to lead the country. The HaHa student movement protested against the austerity cuts to public university funding, but its contestation also became a criticism of the Hungarian political system, which it believed should be changed from the bottom up (Zontea, 2015). While these movements, and many other smaller protests, contested the Fidesz government, they never posed a significant challenge to its electoral dominance. Both Milla and HaHa are important points of reference for the internet tax protests, whose organizers were all at least marginally involved in one or both movements. The internet tax protests, however, were larger than the any of the protest actions ever organized by either Milla or HaHa.

Anti-Orbán protests continued after the success of the internet tax protests. The refugee crisis of 2015 brought new activist groups to the fore, such as Migszol and Migration Aid (Dessewffy & Nagy, 2016; Kallius et al., 2016). However, it was in 2017 that Hungary saw demonstrations as large as or larger than the internet tax protests of 2014. The protests were catalyzed by the simultaneous introduction of legislation targeting NGOs and CEU, as explained earlier (Gorondi, 2017). These protests, which continued for weeks, saw the mobilization of similar constituencies to those that had participated in the internet tax protests; some of the activists who were involved in the organization of the internet tax protests also played a crucial role in the 2017 protests. In 2018 large protests broke out in Budapest after Orbán's reelection (Bienvenu & Santora, 2018). Later in the year, the introduction of the labor code reform, which the opposition renamed "slave law," gave rise to a prolonged contestation of the government, which brought together left-liberal activists, opposition parties, and trade unions (Graham-Harrison, 2019). Despite the continued mobilization of this activist opposition to Orbán, Fidesz was able to win more than 51 percent of the votes in the European elections of 2019 and gain a fourth consecutive majority in the general elections of 2022.

ORGANIZATION OF THE PROTESTS

The first protest against the internet tax, which took place on October 26, was organized in less than a week. As mentioned, the initial impetus was provided by the Facebook page "100,000 against the Internet tax" and the Facebook event it created to invite Hungarians to take part in a demonstration against the tax. Both the page and the event rapidly received a lot of social media attention and gathered likes and event "attendees." This unexpectedly high volume of attention led the creator of the Facebook page and event to reach out to other activists on the Budapest civil society scene.[5] While the creator of the page was very proficient in managing Facebook content, the other activists had indispensable organizational and planning skills, an extensive network of contacts and experience in organizing demonstrations. This allowed the freshly formed group of activists—who knew each other (or at least knew of each other), due to the small size of the activist scene in Budapest, where everyone seems to know everyone—to mobilize rapidly and secure the necessary permits and equipment (e.g., amplification) for the demonstration. These field preparations included negotiating with the police and organizing field marshals to guarantee the security of the demonstrators. The organizers jumped into planning mode without knowing what to expect, as Péter recalled:

> We didn't have any plans, any strategic goals with what to do with this. So we didn't have any lineup, okay, speakers, or any other kind of performance. We had nothing. The only thing we had was a Facebook page with an enormous amount of people attending. So that's where we started.

The second demonstration, held on October 28, was also organized quickly; however, this time the organizers had a better idea of what the demonstration would look like. They also had more resources available, since they were able to raise funds both online and during the first demonstration.

While the external communication about the demonstration happened largely through the Facebook page and YouTube (through the channel "100,000 against the Internet tax," available at https://www.youtube.com /channel/UCW6N-NXIQ-BEloZWYMOV5Dw), activists met face to face several times over the course of the protests, in spaces offered by various NGOs, in addition to communicating via Facebook Messenger. The organizers also maintained a Twitter account (@NoNetTax_HU; no longer available); however, none of the interviewees even mentioned the account, which appears to have played a minor role in the mobilization, especially given the limited adoption of Twitter in Hungary.

Who were the activists that organized the internet tax protests? They were Budapest-based, liberal leftists, with university degrees. At the time of the protests, most of them were in their late twenties and early thirties. Many had several years of previous experience in political parties, social movements, or NGOs. The Budapest-based activist scene is relatively tight-knit, and people move almost seamlessly between different causes and organizations. Eszter described the Hungarian activist community thus: "We are like, I don't know, like 100 people or more . . . 300–400 sometimes and we are activists here in Hungary, and we get involved in a lot of things like this." Bálint laughed as he told me that he got involved in the internet tax protests through the "same people" who get him to join "every protest in Hungary."

Despite the success of the internet tax protests, the organizers could not (or chose not to) form a more stable social movement or activist organization. This is partially explained by the fact that most of them were already involved in other activist organizations of different kinds. Some interviewees pointed to the fact that the political conditions did not seem suitable for the creation of a more permanent movement. Daniel expressed his regret about the failure to establish a movement: "We did not put down the basis of the movement, and actually those people involved in, which were at some point more than 20 people, were not . . . an organized movement, but just people randomly getting together." Laszlo explained that it seemed difficult to bring other issues into the internet tax protests. He reported having heated conversations with people who wanted to use the internet tax protests to quickly build a more comprehensive political platform, to which he replied:

> Yes, we also want to have complete and coherent reform, but then we have to build a movement and we have to, you know, come together. So it's more work, it's not just, you know happening, in a second.

Laszlo's words highlight how Hungarian activists would need a sustained, structured mobilization to really push forth a platform of social change. But he did not think that the internet tax protests could or should be that. Interviewees also reported being pressured by other activists and by left-liberal media commentators, who insisted that the protest organizers should get together to form a new political party. Daniel dismissed those suggestions, but added that he felt "this empty space, which we did not fill."

Even if the activists did not create a more stable movement organization or a party, the internet tax protests are considered one of the rare successes of the Hungarian opposition to Orbán. László explained that the protests are used in public discussions to demonstrate that it is possible to score a success against Orbán. Eszter reported that the internet tax protests made it easier to mobilize Hungarians afterward, as it showed that large-scale protests could in fact take place and have an impact.

A SUCCESSFUL SINGLE-ISSUE PROTEST?

The internet tax protests have been considered a success on many fronts. First, they delivered a blow to the public image of the Fidesz government and its legislative efforts. This was the first time—and to date, the only time—that any Orbán government was forced to respond to popular mobilization. Second, the demonstrations were successful because of both the number of people who took part in them and their heterogeneity. This success is illustrated by the fact that "by far this was the biggest political Facebook event like ever" (Adam), because thousands of people clicked the "I'm going" button on the ad hoc Facebook event page. But more importantly, success is measured by the number of people who showed up to the demonstrations: ten thousand for the first one, one hundred thousand for the second one. This surprised the activists, as Bálint said: "It was very a big surprise for us, there were a lot of people in the first protest." Daniel concurred: "Nobody . . . so we did not experience such big crowd previously. I'm sure I did not; I think most of the activists participating in the organization neither. Yeah. . . . Of course it was great." The activists communicated how rare such mass participation is in Hungary and how it is even rarer to bring together the heterogeneous crowd that showed up in these demonstrations, including individuals across ideological divides, ages, and genders. Eszter argued that "there were many young people in the streets, which usually never happens, and also the supporters of Fidesz were against the internet tax. This is why they stepped back." The activists believe that the mobilization of different constituencies, beyond the usual liberal-leftist opposition to Orbán, was a decisive factor in the government's defeat. Speaking specifically of the second demonstration, Daniel said that "there were, you know, these far-right-ish protesters next to pretty European-lover protesters, next to the previous mayor of Budapest from the liberal party, next to the American ambassador. . . . Everybody was there."[6]

Interviewees saw the popularity of the Facebook event as central to the successful mobilization of many different people. As Péter explained:

> It provided a community feeling, that I don't have to be a weirdo activist to participate in something, because it's something that normal people do, too,

now, because this is a thing that affects normal people, too. So it's not about homelessness or LGBT or those . . . but it. . . . Yeah, the Facebook event, the number of attendees on the Facebook event showed that this is not a fringe situation, but it's socially acceptable to participate.

When speaking of the reasons behind the success of the internet tax protests, some of the activists conceded that it was likely a combination of "some of the most important aspects, if you want to mobilize people" (Petra) and pointed to the heterogeneity of the motivations that might have led people to take to the streets. Nevertheless, they overwhelmingly attributed the success of the protest to its single-issue focus: the internet and the attempt to tax internet consumption. The activists chose to frame this protest as a "single-issue project" (Lászlo) in order to mobilize more people, including those who would not necessarily agree with broader left-liberal concerns or with extensive criticism of Orbán's government. In this respect, they believe that this was the main reason behind the success of the protests, as Adam explains:

> It was our main goal, and we keep it for the whole thing, that we don't want a general protest against the government, because we rather want to have a focus on the internet tax and give the people a victory over the government. Like, even an autocratic government's will can be defeated by the people. And also it was good because many people who were not necessarily in all things against the government they could connect in this one case. So . . . And this, I think this was important that the whole thing succeeded.

The single-issue focus seemed particularly successful because the internet tax was an exceptionally clear topic to talk about, as many activists suggested. Interviewees claimed that it was evident to people why the tax was bad, and that they didn't have to do any sophisticated messaging to get the point across. As one organizer remarked, "This situation was really not organized, or organized by us; it was organized by the government, we just orchestrated it somehow" (Daniel). Tamás said that it was "a very, very clear thing," for which "you don't have to talk about democracy or about such complicated thoughts" (Tamás); it was an "easy message" (Daniel), "understandable for everyone" (Petra). To explain how clear the topic of the internet tax seemed to be for the Hungarian people, the activists often compared it with other contested decisions of the government, like the wave of constitutional changes that started in 2011:

the . . . violation of the Supreme Court is a very very big thing, but how many of the youth people can really understand the importance of that? I don't want to be elitist, but I don't think than more than 10% can really understand what is the big problem, what was the big problem with that. And this was why—I don't know—600 people were taking part in the demonstration against that. So this . . . this is a comfort zone, the Internet is a comfort zone, not a very hard thing to understand why is it bad for you, if you can't use the internet. So I think this was . . . this was the big difference. (Bálint)

I argue that while the protests were visibly framed by the activists as just addressing the internet tax, their success had less to do with the specifics of the internet tax and more to do with the other policies implemented by the Orbán government: the other taxes, the cuts to public education and health care, the corruption scandals, and so on. The anger that people expressed in the demonstrations had been building up for a long time and found an outlet in these internet tax demonstrations: "Many people get really angry and actually it was not just the internet tax, I mean, not just because of the internet tax, but by 2014 we have reached a point when you know, everybody had enough, that was the kind of the last drop" (Petra). Petra also added that many people brought signs to the demonstrations that had nothing to do with the internet, which suggests that "people didn't just come because of the internet tax, they came because they had enough of the government." Lászlo explained:

> And that's what the internet tax was for the people: a very direct hit, and because they already knew that this government is very oppressive towards the people, this whole story, this whole abstract and foggy story suddenly, you know, just concentrated in one dot, and that was the internet tax and that it was. . . . So then they had, you know, we had enough.

The issue of the internet tax was particularly suitable to coalesce a series of grievances against the government into one mobilization that was formally just about the internet but opened the door for a general contestation of the government. This was possible because the protests drew upon a specific technological imaginary, which associated the internet with political concepts such as democracy, freedom, and Western modernity. The protests were never just about the internet, because technological imaginaries are not just about the technologies they refer to; they speak to the political and social role of these technologies.

THE MUNDANE MODERNITY OF THE INTERNET

The technological imaginary of the internet tax protest activists can be reconstructed through an analysis of the various reasons that led them to oppose the tax. These point to a technological imaginary that associates the internet with equality and development, the future, rationality, and mundanity. According to this imaginary, the internet is a powerful but mundane manifestation of Western modernity. This imaginary is based on classic tropes of Western modernity about the equalizing power of technology, its role in progress, and its connection to rationality, which become grounded in the everyday practices of internet use. This imaginary is particularly fruitful in a postcommunist context, because it promises a seamless coincidence between political freedom and economic freedom— a promise that was also at the core of the transition from communism to democracy and that so far has been unfulfilled. The power of this imaginary can be seen in how mundane modernity was performed during the internet tax protests, both with the iconic raising of the illuminated cell phones and with the trashing of the Fidesz headquarters.

Equality and Development

One of the main reasons the activists opposed the internet tax was, simply put, its economic impact. The opposition to the tax went beyond the fact that "people don't like taxes" (Daniel). The amount of the tax itself would have been unsustainable for many people: "This amount of money would have meant a lot to many people. . . . [L]ike many people would have been cut from the internet, because they wouldn't have been able to pay for it" (Petra). Eszter addressed the burden placed on both poorer communities and high-volume users: "Everybody could feel on his own pocket that 'I should pay money'. It was not a small amount of money, it was. . . . [S]o many people couldn't pay it, in the countryside, for example. . . . [B]ut I couldn't pay it also, because I use a lot of internet." Adam called the internet tax a flat tax because of its low threshold and its lack of progressivity, and commented: "I think flat taxes are generally not just, because everyone pays the same however income that person has . . . so like the poorest people also have to pay the amount, which is like . . . means more for them than for a rich person."

This reflection on the fact that the internet tax would exacerbate inequality was contrasted by the activists with the idea that the internet could, under certain circumstances, promote more equality in the country. Many activists spoke of the digital divide between the city and the countryside and of the necessity of reducing that gap. They suggested that the government should be concerned with increasing access and usage of the internet, rather than making it more costly. Daniel explained the connection between taxing the internet and literacy and inequality: "That's why [the internet tax] is a bad thing: because . . . so the internet leads . . . might lead, or should lead, to digital literacy which would lead to reducing the inequalities in the society, so that's why—it's a bad idea." Dávid also argued that taxing internet consumption is not the right thing to do, "because internet is a kind of. . . . [I]t practically is something like water or electricity, so why do you need an extra tax for that? I . . . uh . . . and probably for a government it is better to . . . to . . . increase the usage of internet."

Several activists argued that the internet is a public utility and that the state should have a public internet service that is free or at least subsidized. Daniel said that "the internet should be a public service" and that "it would be definitely cool to have it free"; Eszter echoed him, saying that "it's very sad that in Budapest we don't have free WiFi everywhere." Péter also argued that "the direction we should go is actually subsidize the internet and to invest into making it more and more everywhere, to people and even to companies. Because that's something that, yeah, that would really work for the country."

Others clearly connected this issue back to the need to reduce inequality. László argued that the question the government should ask is:

> How can the state take more responsibility, and working together closer with these companies, to provide internet for the people, if not for free, but for a very very low price. And how can the state, you know, provide wifi everywhere for example in the cities and especially in the villages. So that's the problem. If you are living in a village and more than 40% of the Hungarian people are living in villages, there are some villages with internet access, but you have very very little chance to have fast speed access to the internet.

Similarly, Bálint explained how inequality in access to infrastructure is connected to unequal access to information:

The good thing would be if everybody. . . . [O]kay, I don't know, it's a bit ir-
realistic, not everybody, but more and more people could use the internet for
free, because I think this informational gap between the . . . between somebody in the center of Budapest and somebody in the center of North Hungary, is very very big. So . . . I think the right thing would be the government
would work on that, to have free internet access everywhere.

It is important to note how, in talking about the divide between the
capital and the peripheral countryside, the activists reproduced a language that is common to technologically deterministic views of information technologies and development. The quotes from the interviews seem
to be in line with what Jenna Burrell (2012) described as the championing
of "universal connectivity as an imperative for the progress of developing
countries" (p. 133), although they are applied to poorer rural areas within
Hungary.[7] These discourses are not alien to the dominant technological
imaginary of Silicon Valley either, which often portrays the digital divide
as the single most pressing challenge that needs to be addressed in order
to guarantee prosperity and freedom.

Future

The Hungarian activists also believed that the internet tax went against
the future. Their notion of the future is conflated, as it often is, with the
idea of progress. Adam suggested that "it's just so backwards thinking to
tax the internet" and explained that "this was in trend with how the government generally thinks about many modern things" and that the "modern world has the internet as a tool for lots of things." Bálint reframed
this, saying that the internet tax is "a good symbol that Fidesz don't know
anything about the youth."

The criticism about the backwardness of the government extends to
implicitly criticize the ideal of illiberal democracy as a return to an authoritarian past. The backwardness is not just political, it's also economi-
cal; the interviewees conveyed the sense that the government's inability to
appreciate technologies is blocking economic development. Péter talked
about the fact that investing in the IT-related sector would help Hungary be less vulnerable to global economic changes, but argued that "the
main problem is that for some reason our government doesn't have any

day-dreaming about technology" and that "if you have that kind of attitude for something that will define the next decades, yeah, pretty much you've already lost." Dávid compared the internet tax to other controversial decisions of the government, like the mandatory closing of retail stores on Sundays (Pállinger, 2019, p. 71), and argued that "the internet story and closing the shops are very very similar . . . both stories are against more or less the economy. Making the life of the people harder." For the interviewees, the internet tax was thus another step away from the future. Péter's words clearly communicated the sense of frustration with the direction of the country:

> Right now, we are working our way back to, I don't know, the middle of the 20th century. I don't know if you've been to the countryside. It actually looks like it's the 1950s and people live like it's the 1950s. And we had a dictatorship in the 1950s under socialism! . . . Is that the future?

No, the activists would argue, the future is the internet.

Rationality

Another theme that emerged from the interviews is the apparent stupidity of the internet tax. Indeed, the tax proposal had some serious issues of feasibility that the government was never able to address. But the activists communicated this by calling the tax "stupid, absurd" (Adam) or "not really sane" (Daniel). They regarded the internet tax as something that would go against rationality. László implied that the tax would never have been proposed by anyone who had "some experience with reality."

The activists conveyed the sense that it would be nonsensical to even think about taxing the internet. Adam said it was "so visibly a stupid thing"; Tamás argued that it was "totally crazy"; Daniel called it "nonsense" (several times); and Bálint recalled that it "was so silly and so unrealistic, that I can't really imagine to be honest, how could it work." Péter explained more in detail: "So it was evident that it won't happen. In that way, because it just can't. . . . [I]t wasn't a policy issue, it wasn't something coming from an ideological standpoint of the government, it was just a bullshit screw-up."

The interviewees suggested that the internet tax was not "a very thoughtful idea" (Bálint), a mistake, "a stupidity of the government"

(László). After all, how could someone rational even consider taxing the internet? The recurrence of terms that indicate the nonsensical and stupid nature of the tax proposal reinforces the notion that taxing the internet would mean going against rationality. This discourse is in line with teleological views of technology that emphasize that technological progress is the manifestation of rationality.

Mundanity

The fourth theme that emerged from the interviews is the mundanity of the internet, which the activists saw as a key component of the success of the protests. Eszter contrasted the issue of the internet tax with other controversial decisions of the Hungarian government, like the Media Laws or the amendment of the Constitution, which she found not only less easily understood but also less universal: "It was for everyone, I mean, because they made many many things that are much worse than the internet tax, but the other things are not affecting everyone in the country, but this one was affecting everyone." The demonstrations were successful because people could weigh the tax against the importance of the internet for their daily lives. In the interviews, the internet emerged as something very personal, a space of personal freedom: a private sphere in which the government should not be allowed to intervene. The internet, said Dávid, "is so involved in our everyday life, that everything which relates . . . touches it. . . . [W]e act really sensitive on that." Bálint also remarked that people "got furious because they felt they can really lose their personal stuff."

Eszter and Petra both associated the internet with people's homes in order to express the deeply personal and everyday nature of the internet:

> Every part of the society, everybody understood what does it mean when they put a tax on the internet, and well . . . at least they understood that they need to pay more and they understood that it's something which would really . . . like . . . how to say? which would really affect their personal life, and their, you know . . . so something which would get into their bedroom, let's say it this way. (Petra)
> I think on one hand it was a big amount of money, but on the other hand, it was like that they are. . . . [T]he government goes into your house. It's your private thing that you use everyday. Of course, you use it for work, but

it's your private life, and I think in Hungary many people is addicted to Facebook, but really. . . . They live their lives there, communicating with each other there, organizing events, everything on Facebook. And it was about that, that they want to take away one thing from your life. (Eszter)

Notice here how "bedroom" and "house" signal a connection between the internet and a sphere of life that should be considered private and protected from government intervention.

Another aspect that emerged from this mundane and personal vision of the internet is that it is conceived as a space in which everyone is free to access and consume content. It is a freedom that is constructed around consumption, not necessarily expression: the freedom to access information, to watch movies, to share copyrighted material. Dávid even remarked how one torrenting site decided to take a position on the internet tax by alerting its users about how much each download would be taxed. Bálint further explained people's concerns about the impact of the tax on their downloading habits: "It's funny because we saw calculations about how [much] one episode of *Game of Thrones* would cost. . . . There were some speculations about going to Slovakia and Austria and torrent things, and then come back."[8] In his analysis of discourse opposed to the Anti-Counterfeiting Trade Agreement (ACTA), Jakub Nowak (2016) also showed that piracy has become an everyday online practice overlaid with an ethos of freedom. Being free to choose what to read or watch— including pirating copyrighted material—is embedded in these visions of the internet as a private and personal space in which people can do what they please. As Adam summarized, "This is your space, you decide what you, what you read and don't need to. . . . [Y]eah, so like, you decide what you read. It's personal."

The Mundanity of Modernity

Three of the four themes identified in the interviews—future, equality and development, and rationality—are key concepts associated with Western modernity (Giddens & Pierson, 1998). Here they are equated with the internet, which is seen as representing the future, the achievement of equality and development, and rationality. Taxing the internet is wrong because it goes against modernity. As Adam summed up nicely, "It's against modernity, it's against common sense. Yeah, it's against common sense. And it's socially unjust, and also even hard for jobs. You have lots of reasons, I think I used this anti-modern comment, against common-sense, it's like a collection of arguments." Although Adam was not talking about academic definitions of modernity, his argument clearly illustrated how the internet is associated with rationality, with the future, and with equality and development; the internet tax represented a threat to these three important aspects of modernity. Yet this modernity is experienced through mundane, everyday practices: checking Facebook, downloading pirated content, reading the news. Experienced through the mundanity of smartphones and torrenting websites, modernity becomes a domesticated, everyday practice (see Appadurai, 1996). When the internet is equated with it, modernity becomes something that we can hold in our hands.

Taylor argued that "the sanctification of ordinary life" (2004, p. 102) was part of the experience of modernity. Here the mundane and ordinary aspects of the internet reinforce the power of the idea of modernity. It is through this dual association of the internet with both modernity and mundanity that the technological imaginary of the internet tax protests can symbolically counter Orbán's illiberal democracy: by using the internet as a symbol of the modernity that the government is rejecting, but that is mundane for the protesters.

The Freedoms of Mundane Modernity

In talking about the internet tax protests, international media often explained this mobilization as one about internet freedom. The interviewees overwhelmingly rejected this frame and suggested that foreign media probably used it to make the Hungarian protests legible in relation to the American and European debates on net neutrality that were happening at that time. Tamás rejected the idea that internet freedom was at the center of the protests: "I think in Hungary it's, you know, the 20th priority. Sorry, you know, when you have so many problems in a country, you cannot say. . . . [I]t's also, of course, it's an important part, but." And yet, freedom comes up again and again, both in the interviews and in the slogans of the protests; "Free country, free internet" ("*szabad ország, szabad internet*") was one of the most popular.

So what is the freedom that was envisioned in the internet tax protests? I argue that through the lens of mundane modernity, we can highlight the dual meaning of freedom in the protests: on the one hand, the liberal political freedom of modernity, on the other, the private consumer freedom of mundanity. Far from contradicting each other, these two meanings of freedom reinforce the power of the imaginary of mundane modernity, especially in the context of a postsocialist society, because of the specific conditions of the transition, which promised the simultaneous achievement of liberal democracy and market-driven prosperity (Offe & Adler, 1991); such promises have been frustrated in many ways (Bohle & Greskovits, 2012), yet their legacy helps explain the particular power of mundane modernity in the Hungarian case.

The way in which modernity is associated with the internet carries with it a notion of freedom that is predicated on Western liberal democracy. In Hungary, this should be interpreted in the context of the communist regime and its legacy, but also of the more recent turn to illiberal democracy proclaimed by Orbán. Petra explained both aspects. First, she said that by the time the government announced the internet tax,

> Fidesz made it quite clear that they wanted to have an illiberal democracy. They, you know, made strong friendship . . . with dictatorships and so . . . they became an ally with Russia, and stuff. And you know, it is kind of hard for the Hungarian people, since we had the Russian occupation, you know, the Soviet occupation and stuff. And it was for many people also kind of symbolic, that the internet meant freedom, and you know, somehow a connection to the West.

What emerges from Petra's words is a powerful mainstream discourse that connects the internet, democracy and Western liberalism. The internet tax protests drew on this discourse by turning the internet into a symbol of Western modernity and freedom, which could stand in opposition to Orbán's illiberal democracy.

Furthermore, the association between mundanity and the internet carries a set of additional meanings about the notion of freedom, which is understood in terms of the freedom of individuals to consume content. Notice how Bálint defined it in relation to media consumption:

> [People] didn't want to lose the freedom of the internet. I think we don't, we don't have to have theories more complex than that. This was the only really

important thing for them, to watch their series free, to watch their football games for free, and . . . and this was threatened by the government.

Péter echoed this notion of freedom: "People wanted their real actual existing practical internet freedom to be able to use the internet in the next month and the month after that, and the month after that." The internet, in their words, appears as a vast market of content that consumers should be free to choose from.

If this tech-oriented overlaying of market freedom and political freedom sounds familiar, it is because it features prominently in the dominant technological imaginary of Silicon Valley, too. In line with neoliberal principles, Silicon Valley's imaginary does not distinguish between political and economic freedom: political freedom is imagined to be achieved through the use of digital technologies available on the "free" market. In talking about the myths of cyberspace, Mosco (2004) argued that the discourses that celebrated digital technologies in the 1990s also promoted market-driven notions of citizenship and called for the deregulation of technological markets.

In the postcommunist context, the conflation between political and market freedom carries additional political relevance. A parallel to be drawn here is with the circulation of samizdat under communism (e.g. Kind-Kovács & Labov, 2015), which took on the character of a political practice even when it involved "commercial" entertainment content. In line with Petra's quotes, we might speculate that the legacy of the communist past is present in the concern for a freedom that is based on personal and quotidian choices of consumption, not just in more abstract notions of democracy and political equality (see also Deák, 2011). The political relevance of consumption is also reinforced in Hungarian postcommunist society by the cultural consequences of the neoliberal "shock therapy" that the country had to endure after the transition. According to Wilkin (2018), the legacy of these neoliberal policies can be found in the emergence of "a form of consumerism in which consumers are encouraged to define what is good through personal gratification" (p. 21).

As I have shown, the technological imaginary of mundane modernity is influenced by the political contradictions of the Hungarian sociopolitical context; it is a response not only to the emergence of an illiberal state, but also to long-term political phenomena that have their origins in communist times and in the transition to democracy.

Performing Mundane Modernity

The technological imaginary of mundane modernity was performed by the internet tax protesters through two different prominent actions that took place during the demonstrations: the recurrent use of illuminated smartphones and the trashing of the headquarters of Fidesz. As can be seen in figure 1, protesters lifted their phones up high, in what became one of the most recognizable actions of these protests; as previously mentioned, this action was borrowed from the Umbrella movement in Hong Kong (see Lee & Chan, 2018).

The Hungarian protesters did this several times, even though only two of the interviewees mentioned it in the interviews. When asked about the origin of the action, Eszter explained:

> Actually, we saw a demonstration in China, I think it was in China, where they used this—but not regarding the Internet. I don't remember on what issue. And we thought that we should use this, because it shows that . . . shows something, the people do something in the demonstration, and it . . . I think this thing can present the future, the internet . . . that it's connected, and so on . . . and also that we are together.

What Eszter was trying to convey with her explanation of this protest action is that it helped illustrate the meaning of the internet for the protesters and its connection to the future. The Hungarian protesters did not borrow the action from Hong Kong to stage an elaborate comparison between the Hungarian and Chinese states. As Eszter's quote shows, the organizers did not even remember the grievances of the protesters in Hong Kong. That action resonated, for the Hungarian activists, not so much because it was borrowed from a prodemocracy demonstration, but because it channeled a complex set of aspirations about modernity into something as easily accessible and mundane as a smartphone. The gesture embodied the symbolic power exerted by the association between the internet, political freedom, and Western modernity: it allowed the Hungarian activists to visually perform the technological imaginary of mundane modernity.

Figure 1. Protesters lifting illuminated smartphones during first internet tax protest in Budapest, October 26, 2014. *Source*: Photo by Dr. Stefan Roch (used with permission).

The second performance of the imaginary of mundane modernity took place in a much more unplanned way, during one of the main incidents of the protests. After the end of the first demonstration, a small crowd of protesters headed for the headquarters of Fidesz, Orbán's party. Upon arrival, they started throwing old pieces of IT equipment—modems, routers, keyboards, and even monitors—against the building. The protesters also attempted to tear down the protective fence and break the windows. No one was injured, and only the exterior of the building was damaged. The organizers did not plan this action, but they could not stop it, either.

What the organizers had wanted was for people to have something to do during the demonstration, instead of solely listening to speeches. They asked participants to bring their old electronic goods to the protest and planned to end their demonstration outside the Fidesz headquarters. A video, prepared by the organizers of the protests and distributed via YouTube, invited protesters to bring their obsolete devices along with them. One of the organizers was portrayed in the video with different types of old electronic equipment, saying: "In order to block this unjust tax, bring along ruined electronic devices. A broken router, an overused keyboard, an old cell phone, a ruined laptop, or damaged cables. Bring as much as you can, as much as you can carry to succeed" (Százezren az internetadó ellen, 2014).[9]

While organizers encouraged people to show up with broken devices, they did not really have a good plan for how to use them; it seems that they intended for people to deposit these gadgets on the doorstep of Fidesz's headquarters. However, given the unexpectedly large size of the crowd, the organizers had to redirect the demonstration to a larger square nearby (Heroes' Square). After they proclaimed the end of the demonstration, part of the crowd went to the Fidesz building anyway, computer parts in hand.

But why did the activists decide to ask participants to bring old electronics? Some of the activists said that they wanted to visually represent the internet in a way that would look good in pictures. But others explained that the old computer parts were meant to be something more than a cool photo op: they helped convey the message that the internet tax was an obsolete way of thinking about the internet. Adam said that they "asked the people to bring you know, all the mouses [*sic*], bad computers, to place in front of the Fidesz [building] as a symbolic gesture that their idea to tax the internet is very outdated"; Dávid echoed him: "Simply show them that ... bringing the old things ... how they are thinking about the whole thing is such [*sic*] old."

This episode illustrates how the old devices came to represent not only the internet tax but the political backwardness of the government. As Péter argued:

> Somebody came up with it, and everybody just went with it, that okay, what if we say that, bring some old IT equipment with you and let's make a heap of garbage out of them, to show the government that this idea to try to restrict the internet it's way behind us, it's ... it's the mindset of the 1990s and it belongs to the same garbage dump.

The internet tax thus became a metonymy of the backward-looking attitude of illiberal democracy: this is what the activists meant to communicate by asking people to bring their obsolete electronics along. The fact that protesters started throwing the technology against the Fidesz headquarters further underscores that the demonstrators thought about the internet tax as a proxy of the government's shortcomings, as Eszter explained:

> Actually I think this protest was not only about the internet. But it was about.... [I]t was also anti-government protest. Because otherwise they wouldn't destroy the headquarters of Fidesz. And I think for some people it was only about the internet, but for many people it was also about the government.

The organizers' decision to ask protesters to bring obsolete electronics and the vandalism against the Fidesz headquarters both point to a performance of the imaginary of mundane modernity in opposition to illiberal democracy.

APPROPRIATION: SILICON VALLEY IN A POSTCOMMUNIST CONTEXT

The technological imaginary of mundane modernity constructed and deployed by the Hungarian activists is one of appropriation: the activists embraced both the key elements of the technological imaginary of Silicon Valley and the digital technologies that emerge from that imaginary. In fact, mundane modernity is aligned with the three tenets of the dominant imaginary: the equation of digital technologies with freedom and democracy, technosolutionism, and the ancillary role of Silicon Valley in neoliberal capitalism. First, mundane modernity is based on the association between the internet and Western modernity; as explained earlier, this means equating the internet with both market freedom and political freedom. But the Hungarian activists also envisioned a connection between the internet and democracy, which they deployed to protest against Orbán. Petra also explained this connection between democracy and the internet in historical perspective:

> I think the internet symbolizes, you know, openness, and like all the possibilities.... So it's ... you know, it also symbolizes that the internet is, somehow symbolizes freedom, the West, you know, belonging to the West instead of the East.... [B]ut you know what I mean, like symbolizing democracies, like versus dictatorships.... Symbolizing progress. So....

In this quote, Petra made explicit the association between the internet and freedom, the West and democracy, which underpins the imaginary of mundane modernity but is also the foundation of Silicon Valley's dominant technological imaginary. Further, the promise of direct democracy through digital technologies, one of the dreams propagated by Silicon Valley, seems particularly appealing for Hungarian activists, given the rampant corruption of the Hungarian post-transition democratic system. Second, mundane modernity sees the internet as a solution to different socioeconomical problems, such as inequality and underdevelopment, as articulated by the activists in the interviews. But mundane modernity also coalesces aspirations about democracy and prosperity into a techno-solutionist vision of technology, expected to deliver what the state and the market could not deliver in the previous thirty years. Third, the imaginary of mundane modernity does not problematize how Silicon Valley's visions of technology support and benefit from neoliberal capitalism. While the activists express their desires for some forms of public welfare correctives, such as free public Wi-Fi or public subsidies for internet consumption, there is a substantial normalization of market-driven notions of technology; this is evident in the conflation of market freedom and political freedom that characterizes mundane modernity, as well as the dominant technological imaginary of Silicon Valley. The other component of this imaginary of appropriation is the fact that the Hungarian activists adopted Silicon Valley technologies in their daily lives and in their organization of the protests. Further, they attributed at least part of the success of the internet tax protests to their use of these technologies, particularly Facebook.

As evidenced by the choice of the term *appropriation*, mundane modernity does not simply reproduce the dominant technological imaginary of Silicon Valley; mundane modernity is an imaginary that *reinterprets* Silicon Valley's ideas in a way that made sense in the Hungarian context of 2014. In particular, this appropriation is shaped by the ideology of left-liberal Hungarian activists; the characteristics of the Hungarian political system and the legacies of the transition to democracy; and the technological imaginary of Orban's illiberal democracy, which is exemplified by the internet tax itself. I first address the influence of the Hungarian political context, in order to better explain the ideological positions of the activists.

Political Context

The imaginary of mundane modernity contextualizes Silicon Valley's imaginary in the Hungarian postcommunist context. As highlighted previously, the discourse of mundane modernity casts the internet as capable of simultaneously delivering economic development and political freedom. In this imaginary, the internet then becomes a powerful solution to the unsolved contradictions of the transition, in that it is seen as offering that bundle of democracy-with-prosperity that was promised after 1989 but not quite achieved. In framing the internet as a symbol of Western modernity, this imaginary touches upon long-standing—and now contentious—dreams of "catching up with the West," that is, of resolving the contradictions of the transition through fast economic development (Ágh, 2017, p. 34).

In addition, the appropriation of Silicon Valley's imaginary through that of mundane modernity is shaped by the fundamental political cleavages of post-2010 Hungarian politics: modernity versus tradition, pro-West versus anti-West, pro-EU versus anti-EU, cosmopolitan versus ethnonationalist, urban versus rural. Although these cleavages are not new to Hungarian politics—which has seen a clash between democratic-liberal and authoritarian forces throughout its history, as highlighted by Wilkin (2018)—Viktor Orbán rearticulated these cleavages in postcommunist Hungary and used them to turn Fidesz into the central political force of Hungarian politics. He positioned himself and his party as offering "anti-modernism and anti-cosmopolitanism/Europeanism as a viable alternative to neo-liberal democracy and the market economy" (Pap, 2018, p. 2). It is to these cleavages that Orbán returns whenever his policies are contested domestically or internationally; time and time again he has defended Fidesz's decisions by pitching his government as the defender of the Hungarian nation against the outside threat of an international power (Ágh, 2017, p. 36), chiefly the EU.[10]

Mundane modernity allows the left-liberal activists to insert themselves in the cleavage articulated by Orbán, but not in a subordinate position: to offer a cool version of the modernity they aspire to, a version of modernity that cannot be readily criticized on ethnonationalist grounds and that might even be more powerful than international institutions. In this activist imaginary, the internet then becomes the hip and mundane face of Western modernity, that Hungarians can hope to "catch up with." This is not the modernity of the International Monetary Fund (IMF) and the EU technocrats but the "cool" modernity of Silicon Valley, with its gadgets and its promise of prosperity and tech development; not the bureaucratic democracy of the international institutions, but the democratic ethos of Silicon Valley. If, as Appadurai (1996, p. 9) wrote, modernity is an elsewhere, then Silicon Valley is a better modern elsewhere to hang onto, compared to Brussels.

The internet tax protests thus appropriated the dominant technological imaginary of Silicon Valley within a political context that sees a struggle over modernity and the West as its core cleavage. Drawing on the imaginary of Silicon Valley allowed the protesters to cling onto aspirations of modernity and Westernization through the mundanity and "coolness" of technology, which cannot be readily subsumed in the nationalist discourse of Orbán's government.

Ideology

It is within this peculiar political context, marked by the legacy of the communist regime and the politics of the transition, that we should understand the ideological affinity between the Hungarian left-liberal activists, including those who mobilized in the internet tax protests, and the dominant technological imaginary of Silicon Valley. While this left-liberal activist scene is somewhat diverse, they agree on a few fundamental issues beyond their opposition to Orbán: they are pro-Europe, they are concerned with environmental issues, they support civil rights, and they are critical of the political establishment. But unlike most leftist social movements in the West, Hungarian leftist activists are generally more accepting of neoliberalism. In a way they *have* to be, because of the truncated and reversed political space they inhabit. As Endre Borbáth and Theresa Gessler (2020) explain, in post-transition Hungary, as in other postcommunist CEE countries, a "left-right consensus emerged on questions regarding privatisation, property rights and free markets as they came to be conceived as a progressive break with the past" (p. 5). This means that it is very difficult for any political actor, including social movements, to question capitalism; it also means that, as explained in the previous section, the fundamental demarcation between political positions is not on the socioeconomic axis but rather on issues of authoritarianism/liberalism and of culture and identity. This neoliberal consensus is grounded in the legacy of the immediate post-transition period, in which leftist parties embraced fiscal austerity in an effort to distance themselves from the communist past; conversely, rightist parties supported increasing public spending (Tavits & Letki, 2009). This resulted in an ideological space that is truncated to the left, because what we would consider as a traditional left-wing position on socioeconomic issues, that is, a critique and/or rejection of capitalism, is not tenable in Hungary, due to its association with the pre-1989 regime. But it is also a reversed ideological space, in which it is right-wing forces that are more likely to oppose neoliberalism, albeit on cultural and ethnonationalist grounds, while left-wing actors are more likely to embrace it because of its connection to the West (see also Wilkin, 2018). Just consider how much Orbán has attacked the institutions that have promoted neoliberal capitalism, such as the EU and the IMF, on nationalist grounds. This means that any attempt to criticize the same institutions from a social justice, anti-capitalist perspective risks being construed either as support for Orbán himself or as a throwback to communist times.

This truncated and reversed ideological space makes it difficult even for social movements to mobilize against neoliberalism; it is no surprise then that the internet tax activists are not interested in critiquing the connection between capitalism and Silicon Valley. It is not that any of the interviewees actively *like* neoliberalism. Indeed, many of them are concerned about economic inequalities and are critical of austerity politics. It's just that, as much as they might dislike neoliberalism, they dislike Orbán more.

The technological imaginary of mundane modernity thus reflects the ideology of these activists, especially in its combination of market freedom and political freedom. The fundamental equation of technology with freedom and democracy that is one of the key aspects of the dominant technological imaginary makes sense to the Hungarian left-liberals. The fact that these ideas are coupled with an adherence to neoliberalism does not prevent the activists from embracing the ideas of Silicon Valley; rather, the vision of technologies as free, democratic, and empowering helps make neoliberalism easier to accept, in service of their opposition to Orbán.

Other Technological Imaginaries

Finally, the imaginary of mundane modernity is constructed and deployed by the Hungarian activists in opposition to Orbán's illiberal democracy. For these activists, illiberal democracy carries with it a specific technological imaginary, which is exemplified by the internet tax itself.

The activists criticize Orbán and his government for their inability to use and understand the internet and digital technologies, something that they think explains Fidesz's general attitude toward modernity. The interviewees were often amused and sometimes outraged when they told me that Orbán and other top Fidesz politicians are really not familiar with new technologies. Bálint said he did not "think that a lot of Fidesz politicians are really good with iPhones." Daniel added that it is common knowledge that Orbán does not really know how to use a computer. Adam explained that "the Prime Minister personally does not really use new technologies" and that "he doesn't really understand modern technology"; to support this claim, he said that when Orbán is photographed at his desk, such as in a famous Facebook profile photo, one can clearly see that he does not have any electronic devices around him. When I asked him if Orbán's presumed scarce knowledge of technology meant that he could not be a good politician, he replied: "Okay, I don't want to exclude the chance that he could be a good leader without knowing it, but like . . . how [do] you avoid it? Completely . . . so much in your life, to don't really use these things." Péter linked Orbán's limited digital literacy to the internet tax: "It was really obvious that Viktor Orbán had this idea. He heard about the internet. . . . [H]e doesn't even really use a computer, on a daily basis."

Dávid argued that Orbán's lack of familiarity with digital technology means that "Orbán's government is a government who are not able to really understand the new time, the new technologies." Péter added that the government is not necessarily hostile toward technology: "I don't think they hate it or they are negative about it. It's just something that meh . . . who cares?" Daniel recalled another occasion when Orbán seemed to ignore the importance of digital technologies:

> [T]here was once something Orban said: yeah, it's very good to have 'those little startups, investing in like future and modern technologies, but we are building the society based on work here.' . . . Which like, I think somehow meant, yeah, it is not work what you are doing in so-called 'high tech start-ups,' just some bullshit, but we make work.

In retelling this anecdote, Daniel used his hands to form scare quotes when paraphrasing Orbán's sentence and when saying the words "high tech startups," to further underscore how he found Orbán's position absurd. Notice how, in Orbán's position as detailed by Daniel, there is a stark contrast between the future and modernity of digital technologies and traditional "work," which we can imagine to be associated with how Orbán would describe the traditional values of the Hungarian nation. This minor episode thus serves to illustrate how illiberal democracy has its own technological imaginary, which downplays the importance of digital technologies. While this technological imaginary might not be explicitly or officially articulated by Orbán, it was picked up by the Hungarian activists, who constructed mundane modernity in response to it.

CONCLUSION

The imaginary of mundane modernity constructed and deployed during the Hungarian internet tax protests of 2014 associates digital technologies with both Western modernity and mundanity. It sees the internet as an enabler of development and equality, as the future, and as rationality—all key tropes of Western modernity; at the same time, the activists underscored the importance of the internet as something mundane, crucial for everyday life in a personal way. Further, this imaginary fuses together a vision of the internet as supporting political freedom and allowing for market freedom; this fusion takes on an oppositional symbolic meaning in the Hungarian postcommunist context but is also aligned with the dominant technological imaginary of Silicon Valley. I argue that through the technological imaginary of mundane modernity, the activists were able to connect the internet tax to larger political demands and turn the protests into a more general contestation of Orbán's illiberal Hungary.

Mundane modernity is an imaginary of appropriation, which embraces both the use of Silicon Valley's technologies and the core ideas of the dominant technological imaginary of Silicon Valley. In fact, mundane modernity associates the digital with democracy and freedom and pitches technologies as the way to solve sociopolitical issues. This imaginary of appropriation is meaningful within the post-2010 Hungarian political context, which has seen the resurgence of the political cleavage of modernity versus tradition. The appropriation of Silicon Valley's imaginary is thus influenced by the heightened political relevance of Western modernity in the contemporary Hungarian political scene. But this appropriation is also shaped by the ideology of Hungarian left-liberal activists, in the internet tax protests and beyond, who are more accepting of neoliberalism than leftist social movements in other contexts; while these activists are not enthusiastic about neoliberalism, they are nevertheless stuck with embracing it as part of their general endorsement of Western liberal ideas in opposition to Orbán. Finally, the imaginary of mundane modernity is also shaped not only by the activists' rejection of Orbán's illiberal democracy, but also by what they perceive to be the technological imaginary of illiberal democracy, of which the internet tax is an illustration.

The imaginary of mundane modernity was performed by Hungarian protesters through both the attack on the Fidesz building and the iconic lifting of illuminated phones to the sky. As mentioned, the latter action was taken up by other protesters across CEE, in demonstrations that had nothing to do with the internet. If mundane modernity has a symbolic meaning not just in Hungary but across different national contexts, it is because it draws on the dominant discourses that have been popularized by Silicon Valley over the past few decades. It is through the lens of the dominant technological imaginary that illuminated smartphones can be read as a political symbol, which can be deployed in a postcommunist political context as an attractive version of Western modernity and capitalism, a cool modernity that can be symbolized by something as mundane as a smartphone.

While Hungarian activists find it useful to embrace the technological imaginary of Silicon Valley to fight against illiberal democracy, the other movements I examine in this book approach this set of dominant discourses as fundamentally opposed to their own political ideas. I now turn to how these activists construct and deploy imaginaries of negotiation.

4 Fighting the System with the Tools of the System

LUME'S IMAGINARY OF NEGOTIATION

It was cold, damp, and dark. That's what I remember the most about the first time I attended a meeting of LUMe, the Metropolitan University Laboratory, in its newly occupied building in Milan, Italy. This open meeting, announced with a Facebook event, took place in December 2017, in the location that LUMe had just recently occupied: a large vaulted space, a depot originally built in the late 1700s as part of the system of defensive walls adjacent to Porta Venezia, and currently owned by the Municipality of Milan. The activists had tried their best, but the heating was not really working, and the lamps barely illuminated the center of the room. The occupied space betrayed long years of neglect. During the meeting, a newcomer inquired about a rumor they had heard: Was it true that LUMe maintained a list of buildings in Milan that could be potential targets for an occupation? The activists never confirmed or denied the existence of that list but made it clear to the participants at the meeting just how complicated it is to occupy a building. There's the fact that occupation is not only illegal, but also defined as a criminal act in the Italian penal code, which leaves activists open to criminal prosecution. But the activists also underscored another aspect that makes occupations risky: they require a lot of activist work. An occupation is not just breaking into a building; it requires reopening it for public fruition, repairing it, and putting in place organizational structures that allow for the occupied space to run well.

The magnitude of this labor was immediately clear to me when I reentered LUMe's occupied depot in June 2018 to conduct my first interviews. The environment had completely changed: the activists had put in a wooden floor, a bar with functioning beer taps, a sink, and a refrigerator. They upgraded the heating system with a more complex set of pipes. They added couches and a foosball table. The walls were now covered with the posters of their many events. The labor put into the occupied space is a point of pride for the activists. The cold, damp, and dark space I had encountered months before was no longer an abandoned depot. It had become a space for concerts, theater plays, movie screenings, political meetings, protest planning, and just hanging out. It had become a cultural space. A political space. It had become an "urban commons" (*bene comune urbano*), as the activists like to say.

LUMe is a radical leftist collective, composed of students and recent graduates of the universities and art academies in Milan. They describe themselves as "antisexist, antiracist and antifascist" and are widely known in the Milanese activist scene for their commitment to promoting grassroots culture. LUMe is what Italians call a *centro sociale*, a social center: a radical social movement whose defining practice is that of occupying buildings for political use. Occupations are direct confrontations with power. They are precarious, they are risky, and they are illegal. Yet they are also incredibly widespread among Italian activists. And occupation is more than a tactic: maintaining an occupied space is a source of collective identity, which entails certain types of political beliefs and political practices. This collective identity is rooted in the history of Italian occupied spaces, which activists remember and reinterpret.

The core principle guiding the praxis of the social centers is that of self-management (*autogestione*), which is based on a critique of representative democracy, a rejection of hierarchy, and an embrace of horizontal organizational practices (Montagna, 2006, p. 296). Self-managed social centers bring together an opposition to capitalism with prefigurative practices, combining "radical struggle with grassroots initiatives for alternative models" (Casaglia, 2018, p. 483). Identifying as a social center already implies specific political commitments, which are taken for granted across Italian social centers: a general leftist orientation, based on Marxist (broadly defined), anti-capitalist, and anti-imperialist ideas (Casaglia, 2018; Montagna, 2006; Mudu, 2018).[1] The politics of social centers usually includes a militant stance against the resurgence of neofascist formations and against the mainstreaming of xenophobic and racist positions by right-wing parties. At the same time, social centers have also long rejected moderate center-left parties like the Democratic Party, as well as the populist Five Star Movement (5SM).

Social centers have been part of the Italian political landscape since the 1970s, when the occupation of buildings emerged as a tactic of the extraparliamentary Left (Edwards, 2009; Mudu, 2004). Despite its risks, occupation remains a popular practice even today. LUMe belongs to a new wave of social centers, established by a generation of activists whose formative events were the financial crisis of 2008 and the Anomalous Wave student movement of 2008–2009. In Milan, where the urban development process preceding the 2015 Milan Expo (the Universal Exposition) was also a catalyst, this wave of social centers includes LUMe, Macao (Cossu, 2018; Murru & Cossu, 2015), and ZAM (Barassi, 2015); similar centers have also sprung up in other Italian cities, for instance Làbas in Bologna (born in 2012). This newer generation has critically reinterpreted the legacy of the social centers, while attempting to be more open, that is, less identitarian and more integrated with the neighborhoods in which the social centers are situated. As is evident in the cases of Macao and LUMe, a core focus of these newer social centers lies in the promotion of cultural events. For the activists of LUMe and other social centers, occupying unused buildings means liberating them from neglect, reopening them for public consumption, and filling them with politically meaningful cultural content. This newer generation of social centers has also been marked by an intense use of mainstream corporate digital media, especially Facebook, as a way to communicate with their activists and the general public.

LUMe's "antifascist, antiracist, antisexist" and anti-capitalist politics, the importance of occupations as a practice and an identity, the legacy of Italian social centers, and the emergence of populist parties in the Italian landscape are all defining elements of how the activists of LUMe think about digital technologies. Using the words of the activists, I describe their technological imaginary as "fighting the system with the tools of the system"; for the activists, digital technologies are flawed and complicit with power, but they are also indispensable for social change. This is a technological imaginary of negotiation: the Italian activists criticize the key aspects of the dominant technological imaginary of Silicon Valley, yet they rely on Silicon Valley's technologies in their activism. To show how this imaginary of negotiation unfolds in the case of LUMe, this chapter starts with a description of what LUMe activists stand for, what they have done, and what this means in the Italian political landscape. I then highlight the centrality of Facebook and WhatsApp in the life of the collective; in particular, I show that Facebook is so crucial for the movement that it powerfully shapes how the activists think about digital technologies in general. Using in-depth interviews and drawings produced in the visual focus groups, I reconstruct LUMe's technological imaginary. This imaginary rests on two criticisms that the activists make of internet technologies: an anti-capitalist critique of how corporate power operates online and a skeptical stance about the purported democratic-ness of the internet. However, despite these stark criticisms, the activists believe that digital technologies are crucial for activism and that there is no alternative to them: they are an expression of the system and a weapon against the system. LUMe's technological imaginary of negotiation thus brings together a rejection of the ethos of Silicon Valley with a reliance on corporate digital technologies. This negotiation is shaped by a specific combination of three political factors: LUMe's anti-capitalist, leftist orientation (its ideology), which guides how LUMe's activists navigate their ambivalence toward corporate social media; the legacy of the Italian social centers and the practice of occupation, which gives LUMe a lens for thinking of digital spaces in relation to offline occupied spaces (political context); and the salience of another technological imaginary in Italian politics, that of the 5SM, one of the main Italian political parties and a key government partner between 2018 and 2022. The 5SM's imaginary, which reinterprets the technological imaginary of Silicon Valley, is predicated on a discourse of digital utopianism, which has been used to justify nondemocratic practices within the party (see Natale & Ballatore, 2014; Treré, 2018). LUMe's activists distance themselves from the 5SM and from its technological imaginary of "authoritarian sublime" (Treré, 2018).

LUME: RADICAL POLITICS AND GRASSROOTS CULTURE

LUMe was born in April 2015, during the occupation of an empty, multistory building dating back to the sixteenth century and located next to the University of Milan. In the two years that the collective spent in that building in Vicolo Santa Caterina, LUMe grew rapidly, taking advantage of its proximity to the university and becoming an important hub for young artists and university students in Milan, hosting concerts, theater performances, and art exhibits. The occupied space, which the activists cleaned, painted, renovated, and opened up to the public, brought together "young activists with experience as militants of social centers, students of the University of Milan and beyond, artists, musicians" (*Tre Anni Di Viaggio*, 2018). Their focus on art and culture as a form of political activism made them unique in the Milanese scene. During this time, LUMe grew to include between eighty and one hundred activists. Most of them had never been involved in activism before joining the collective.

The police evicted LUMe from the Santa Caterina building in the summer of 2017. The eviction was a rather traumatic event for the collective. The activists were not notified of the eviction in advance; the police cleared out the occupied space in the early morning, and LUMe activists only found out because an activist of another collective happened to witness the eviction. The loss of a physical space weighed on the collective. Meeting in activists' apartments and in spaces provided by other movements, LUMe's members spent the summer of 2017 planning their comeback. They organized open assemblies and movie screenings in the square adjacent to the building they no longer occupied. They promoted a petition to the Municipality of Milan, which gathered more than twenty-eight hundred supporters on change.org (LUMe, 2017a). In September 2017 they organized the "cultural siege of Palazzo Marino" (Assedio culturale a Palazzo Marino): a one-day event, with speeches, live music, theater performances, and a march from the Santa Caterina building to the main seat of the municipal government of Milan, Palazzo Marino. With the cultural siege, LUMe aimed to highlight its contribution to the cultural life of the city and to the precarious life of the Milanese youth; to defend the practice of occupation; and to claim "the right to a legitimate sociality, to a critical, independent and self-organized culture" (LUMe, 2017b).

In October 2017 LUMe conducted a brief occupation of the foreclosed Cinema Orchidea, reopening it to the public for free movie screenings, jazz concerts, and debates. The occupation of the movie theater was brief and marked by confrontation with the Municipality of Milan, which owns the building. The movie theater had been closed to the public since 2009; the municipal government approved and financed its renovation in 2015, but at the time of LUMe's occupation (late 2017), the movie theater had yet to undergo any repair work (LUMe, 2017d; Venni, 2017). LUMe publicly pledged it would leave the building as soon as the Municipality of Milan resumed the renovation work on the movie theater (Vazzana, 2017). On October 25 the municipal government announced that the renovation of the Cinema Orchidea would start before the end of 2017. LUMe declared victory and announced it would leave the movie theater on that same day (LUMe, 2017e). As of 2024, the Cinema Orchidea is still not open to the public.

A week after leaving the Cinema Orchidea, on November 2, 2017, LUMe occupied the municipality-owned maintenance depot (*magazzino del verde*), where the group is currently carrying out its activities. The depot is a vaulted space; it includes a larger room, which activists use for concerts and performances; a long, L-shaped corridor with a side room used for storage; and a large entryway. While the new occupied space has its own challenges, such as the damp and cold climate, it has given LUMe the possibility to resume its cultural and political activities; in the Facebook post where it claimed responsibility for the occupation, the group explained that it wanted to "make this space a home for arts and culture, to push forward [its] horizontal and inclusive model, to give back to citizens a place that has survived the unstoppable transformation of the city of Milan over the past 250 years" (LUMe, 2017f).

LUMe's political commitments shine through the myriad of activities, assemblies, and events promoted by the collective: the activists are critical of neoliberal capitalism and of right-wing populism, which in the Italian context is best exemplified by the League, the xenophobic, right-wing populist party led by Matteo Salvini, but they are also decisively to the left of mainstream center-left parties, such as Partito Democratico, which they oppose at both the national and local levels.[2] The shorthand that most of the interviewees used to explain the politics of LUMe to me, and which is included in all of their online materials as well as public presentations, is that they identify as "antifascist, antiracist and antisexist." This translates into three visible threads running through their many events: promoting anti-fascist mobilizations and cultural events, organizing against "state racism," and hosting feminist and queer artists and speakers. When I conducted my fieldwork, the Italian cabinet was formed by a coalition between two populist parties: the League and the 5SM. LUMe fiercely opposed both parties, and the resulting Conte I Cabinet (2018–2019), organizing protests and direct actions with other movements in Milan. While the League has often been an explicit target of its protest actions, LUMe is clear in talking about the general anti-immigration stance adopted by Italian parties as "state racism" (razzismo di stato), that is, widespread racism across the Right and the Left. In February 2019 LUMe and other movements symbolically occupied a ministerial building to protest against the government's anti-immigration policies ("Milano, Studenti e Centri Sociali Occupano," 2019). Some of LUMe's activists also spent time volunteering with the NGOs running the "20K" project in Ventimiglia, the border town between Italy and France that has become a central node in migrants' journeys to Western Europe (Giuffrida, 2018). 20K is a grassroots effort to support people in transit and monitor their treatment by the Italian and French authorities (Progetto 20k, 2017). Anti-racism and anti-fascism are common traits for Italian social centers, but the same cannot be said for anti-sexism. LUMe, however, appears friendlier toward women and LGBTQ individuals than what has (sadly) typically been the case for social centers. This is also reflected in its participation in Pride events in Milan and organization of a festival, "Body Politics: Body Self-Determination," thought of as a collective consciousness-raising moment directed at eliminating gender disparities. Held in March 2018 around International Women's Day, the festival was organized in collaboration with a feminist collective and the local group of the feminist movement Non Una di Meno (Not One Woman Less).

What characterized LUMe from the beginning is its commitment to supporting grassroots cultural production as a form of political engagement. The activists approach art in a profoundly political way: not just to promote politically relevant artistic content, but also to provide a collective, political way of doing culture together. In other words, they see culture as a primary locus for political contention. LUMe activists describe their work as centered on promoting grassroots culture (*cultura dal basso*), self-organized cultural production that is of high quality but also accessible to all, regardless of income. In practice, this means that LUMe takes great care in selecting who performs there, prioritizing emerging and engaged young artists; all artists are compensated; and the performances are accessible with a modest suggested donation of €2–3. This aspect of economic accessibility was crucial for LUMe to engage youth and university students, who typically do not have much disposable income. It was LUMe's jazz collective that pioneered its political approach to grassroots culture. Jazz—not the kind of music one would imagine finding in an occupied social center—rapidly became one of LUMe's distinctive features; its Wednesday evening jazz performances featured established musicians, music students, and jam sessions that were open to all. LUMe's theater group also took to heart the activists' dream of not only hosting cultural events but also producing them. In fact, LUMe aspires not only to be a space that hosts concerts or plays, but also a place where collective cultural production can happen, on the basis of a common political consciousness. Because so many of LUMe's activists are artists or aspiring artists themselves, this attention to sustainable cultural programming has been crucial for the collective, which has been able to create a loyal public for its events. And in a city like Milan, which has become unaffordable for many and is known for exploiting creative workers, the fact that LUMe is offering a venue for artists to perform (and get compensated) and for a broad public to watch live performances for a small price is in itself a highly political stance. It means prioritizing the quality and sustainability of cultural production over its profitability. As LUMe declared during its cultural siege of 2017, "Culture for us is like bread: you need a lot of it, and it shouldn't cost much" (LUMe, 2017c).

FROM OCCUPIED BUILDINGS TO URBAN COMMONS

For LUMe, political activism and cultural production go hand in hand with the occupation of buildings. The activists express this by using the idea of "urban commons" to refer to LUMe, which highlights that the occupation is meant to have a social and political function for the city of Milan and its people. The idea of commons has been central for social centers over the past fifteen years. *Commons* can be defined as "social systems at different scales of action within which resources are shared and in which a community defines the terms of the sharing, often through forms of horizontal social relations founded on participatory and inclusive democracy" (De Angelis, 2014, p. 302). Although the idea of commons has been important to political philosophers for a long time, recent contributions focus on the way in which commons can be a response to capitalist enclosure that can be put in practice through a process of "commoning," i.e. through "social labor and the corresponding forms of cooperation that are located within commons" (De Angelis, 2014, p. 302). It is in this vein that LUMe defines itself as "urban commons" (*bene comune urbano*). Over and over again, in both the interviews that I conducted and in their public statements, LUMe activists explained that their occupations of buildings are really liberations, meant to open up and revitalize urban spaces, transforming them into commons that have an important social, cultural, and political function. Yet these urban commons are also challenges to power and to the increasing repression of sociality outside of the logics of capitalism. In a Facebook post in which LUMe activists celebrated the importance of urban commons, they invited other activists to join them in fighting "the rise of sovereigntist fascisms, the complicity of populists and the neoliberal centrist parties", through "the strength and transparency of the practices, the ideas, the communities, and the networks we will manage to build" (LUMe, 2018). Framing their work as directed at the creation of an urban commons, LUMe activists also see it as a response to populist, (neo)fascist, and neoliberal forces.

The occupation of buildings and their transformation into commons provide a strong collective identity to LUMe's activists. The identity work performed by the practice of occupation became even more evident to activists when they were evicted from their first occupied space in 2017. As Mario, one of the activists, explained: "Even if LUMe, even if any collective, cannot be reduced to the physical structure that hosts it in that given moment, that physical structure nevertheless contributes to giving you an identity, to giving you a certain mindset," which he likened to a rhythm to keep up with. Even though a social center, as a collective actor, can survive without a physical occupied space, the practices of self-management that sustain an occupation give activists a way of thinking about their activism and its meaning.

LUMe's activists are acutely aware of the legacy of the social centers and consciously situate their occupations within that historical trajectory. However, as both a young social center and composed by young activists, LUMe has critically reflected on which parts of that legacy it most wanted to embrace. In fact, after an extraordinary growth and increase in popularity during the anti-globalization movements of the 1990s–2000s, Italian social centers went through a period of political and organizational division (Casaglia, 2018, p. 490), which led to the perception of social centers as sectarian and self-righteous, more interested in cultivating loyalty within an inner circle of longtime activists than in incubating inclusive mobilizations. As part of a newer generation of social centers, LUMe has tried to avoid the pitfalls encountered by older activists; they chose to do things differently and were successful in attracting people. Ilaria, another LUMe activist, told me that "LUMe was a hybrid between a classic social center and a cultural center, more in line with what had always been my interests. That's why I joined and then I got super-politicized." Jessica echoed this: "You know, one might think that social centers . . . that only certain types of people go there. But what I always liked about LUMe is that you could find anyone there, really." Like other collectives of this newer generation, LUMe is reclaiming the label of social center, acknowledging the great contributions and the many shortcomings of those centers' forty-year history, while trying to forge a different path. Its reimagining of the legacy of the social centers plays a clear role in how the collective envisions the role of digital technologies.

HORIZONTAL STRUCTURES, CORPORATE DIGITAL TECHNOLOGIES

LUMe's use of technology should be understood within the horizontal organizational practices that characterize the collective. In particular, two aspects of LUMe's organizational structure have a strong impact on what they do with digital technologies: the fluidity and autonomy of LUMe's thematic working groups, which require constant coordination; and the commitment to assembly-based horizontal decision-making, which limits the extent to which decisions can be taken through digital means. Like many contemporary leftist movements, LUMe is run according to the principle of horizontality, and its structure is decentralized and multilayered. The collective is made up of various working groups (*tavoli*), which have changed during its years of activity. The working groups meet regularly and enjoy a high degree of autonomy, although they are held accountable by the collective during regular assemblies. LUMe's structure is flexible and adapts to the ebbs and flows of its activity, with new groups being formed and established groups (such as LUMe jazz or the writing collective) sometimes fading out after a while. During my fieldwork, the active working groups were politics (Collettivo Politico), cinema and video (Lumeteca), theater (Lumo Teatro), and art. A special working group is in charge of social media. In addition to the working groups, LUMe has different types of assemblies. Usually held twice a month, the operational assembly (*assemblea gestionale*) is a horizontally run, semi-open assembly, in which activists of the various working groups meet to make decisions about the day-to-day operations of the collective (and of the occupied space). In contrast, plenary assemblies are held every two or three months. They aim to be open to all the activists of LUMe. They are devoted to discussing big picture topics and make general decisions about the social center. In addition, LUMe holds monthly assemblies that are open to the public. The aim of these is to offer potentially interested people a venue to get to know what LUMe is about and also provide a space for different individuals to pitch an idea to LUMe.

LUMe's participatory horizontal structures are woven together by the group's digital communication practices, which are both inward-facing, helping keep the activists plugged into the life of the social center, and outward-facing, directed toward the public, powerholders, and potential new activists. Silicon Valley technologies are the backbone of LUMe's internal and external communication practices. On the internal front, LUMe relies heavily on both Facebook and WhatsApp. The activists run a closed Facebook group with a number of active members, around seventy when I conducted the interviews. The main purpose of the group is to update activists on what is happening at LUMe, so they can be plugged into the life of the collective even when they are not able to come to the occupied space. On WhatsApp, LUMe has an organizational group chat, which is smaller than the Facebook group but highly active. The group chat includes LUMe's most active members, roughly forty people. This is the space in which urgent information gets disseminated and questions that require a quick answer are posed. The group chat is also used to raise issues for further discussions and make decisions that require immediate attention by LUMe, especially those concerning the occupied space. The working groups have also created their own private Facebook groups and group chats on WhatsApp. Last, there is a shared Google Drive folder, which contains a messy archive of documents, leaflets, videos, and photos. Most importantly, it hosts two shared files mentioned by many interviewees: a calendar and a scheduling spreadsheet. It is through these Facebook groups, WhatsApp chats, and Google folder that LUMe activists coordinate their activities, check in with each other, announce assemblies and meetings, and generally organize to run the occupied space. However, it is very rare for these activists to entertain deep political discussions or actually make important decisions in these online spaces; those political processes are reserved for the in-person meetings and assemblies in the occupied space.

For its outward-facing communication, LUMe is entirely dependent on commercial social network sites; the collective is very active online through its Facebook page (https://www.facebook.com/pg/LUMe .occupato/), Twitter account (@LUMe_occupato), and Instagram account (@lume_occupato). In 2019 LUMe also created a short-lived Telegram channel, which had about two hundred subscribers. However, at the time of my fieldwork Facebook was by far its most used social network site. Through LUMe's Facebook page, the activists create and post Facebook events for the activities they organize, from demonstrations to concerts; they share and provide commentary on media coverage of various issues, such as immigration policy; they circulate pictures and videos of recent events; and they distribute their own press releases. The page thus functions as an information hub for all that concerns the collective. In addition to the main LUMe page, individual working groups have their own Facebook pages, through which they typically promote their events and share posts from the main LUMe Facebook page.

LUMe's social media activity is managed by an ad hoc working group, LUMe Social Media, which draws activists from different working groups and others who have graphic design and video editing skills. The social media group is in charge of the collective's accounts on Instagram and Twitter, and most importantly, its Facebook page. The social media group enjoys a high degree of autonomy in its work. The larger collective is usually not aware of what will be posted on LUMe's social media; the group's trust in the social media collective comes through in all the interviews in which the group is mentioned. When asked about problems that might have arisen in LUMe's use of social media, no activists pointed to tensions within the collective around what the social media group had posted. This is remarkable, given the documented tensions around the management of collective accounts, for instance in the Occupy movements (Gerbaudo, 2012; Kavada, 2015; Terranova & Donovan, 2013).

The intense day-to-day work of the social media group is organized around navigating the known features of Facebook Pages, while still adhering to LUMe's principles, such as the necessity to produce quality content and to incorporate horizontal decision-making. The activists are acutely aware of the existence of peaks and ebbs of attention on Facebook and speak of the need to optimize when they post, to make sure that their public has the highest chance of being exposed to their content. The marketing language that permeates the back end of Facebook Pages is clearly echoed in how the activists talk about their communication practices. Mario, who is not a member of the social media group, understood the mechanics of the process in the following way: "Posts are programmed in a rational and rationed way. They go out at time X of day Y because that's more suitable. . . . [T]hese kinds of methods allow you to maximize the efficacy of your communication." Ilaria, who is part of the social media group, confirmed Mario's impression of their work. But she was also quick to justify their actions: "I mean, we don't sell anything, we don't earn anything, so it's not about getting more clicks and more likes. It's about the broadest possible diffusion of information. For us it's important that people read what we think and know what we do." But LUMe also uses other features of Facebook Pages in a more proactive and political way. In particular, Facebook Pages offer the possibility to draft posts in advance and schedule their publication. This allows LUMe activists to time the publication of the posts, but also to collectively edit them before they are published. Activists in the social media group think of this as a small-scale newsroom, in which they edit each other's writing and learn from one another.

Although LUMe also maintains a Twitter and Instagram account (which the activists have used more and more since my fieldwork), it is on Facebook that the activists focus their efforts. This became evident in a discussion that I witnessed, and which I discuss in chapter 1, on the hot topic of creating a website for LUMe. LUMe did create a blog-based website in 2015, which is no longer updated. Overall, activists regret not having a functioning website. They also have different ideas about what the website of a social center should look like: an archive? a portfolio? or an alternative publication, in the spirit of Indymedia? But they all agree on the fact that building and maintaining a website would be too much for them, on top of the labor they put into managing their Facebook page. The activists all recognize that it would be great to have an online space that is not constrained by the predetermined functions of Facebook, but at the same time they feel that they do not have the technical skills or the free time to take care of the website, on top of their existing social media work. This is also why the original blog was abandoned; it was just too much, when there was already so much work to do to optimize their Facebook (and Instagram) presence. The website can wait. It's Facebook that really matters.

LUME'S INTERNET: BETWEEN CORPORATE POWER AND THE ILLUSION OF DEMOCRATIC-NESS

LUMe's activities are planned, coordinated, and publicized through multiple channels on social network sites. Activists talk to each other on WhatsApp, promote events on Facebook, and showcase performances on Instagram. They are intimately familiar with digital media platforms and the way they operate. So how do they think about them? What does LUMe's technological imaginary look like?

There are two fundamental and intertwined critiques that the activists of LUMe make of digital technologies: first, they criticize the corporate, capitalist, exploitative models of digital technologies and the power of internet corporations; and second, they criticize what they call "the reality" of the internet, by which they mean that the internet, as it is, does not live up to its promise of being a free and democratic space. Both of these critiques strike at the core of Silicon Valley's dominant technological imaginary. LUMe's activists end up taking issue with both the neoliberal business model of Silicon Valley and the discourses that pitch digital technologies as inherently democratic and empowering. What the activists are saying is that this internet is not what was promised. And it cannot be, because of the immense power and the business model of the Silicon Valley companies that control the internet today. These two intertwined critiques run through the visual focus groups that I conducted with the activists, in which I asked the activists to collectively draw what they thought the internet was like and gave them a space to discuss how they saw digital technologies and their role in society. Their critiques manifested in their final collective drawings, as well as in numerous sketches and doodles that the activists drew to support their discussions.

In both visual focus groups, activists spent a significant amount of time articulating their Marxist, dialectical reading of society, of the internet, and of how power operates on the internet. This first critique—of the power of corporations and of digital commodification—is central to the collective drawing developed by the activists in the second visual focus group (see figure 2). This drawing represents the internet as an iceberg.

The upper part, visible above the water, is comprised of benign, everyday activities: streaming, gaming, information seeking, the publication of multimedia content, and the consumption of porn. The invisible part contains more problematic processes, which undergird the daily experience of the internet but remain hidden. These processes are control of information, information manipulation, privacy violation, and data commodification. On the right side of the iceberg, activists depicted the state as a submarine. While the submarine sees what is happening both above and below the water, it does not intervene. On the left side of the iceberg, corporations are represented as an oil platform, which extracts value from the bottom of the iceberg (where the activists drew the symbols of the US dollar, the euro, and the British pound). The submarine and the oil platform are meant to represent how power operates on the internet.

Figure 2. Collective drawing produced in second VFG, January 7, 2019. *Source*: This
work is licensed under CC BY-SA 4.0 DEED. To view a copy of this license, visit
http://creativecommons.org/licenses/by-sa/4.0/.

In the other visual focus group, activists also wrestled with this critique,
particularly in terms of visually representing how they think about the internet in relation to power and capitalism. For instance, Emanuele drew
the internet as an "interregnum" (in his words), which he represented
graphically as the overlap of two rectangles, as can be seen in figure 3.

In his words, the internet interregnum represents:

> on the one hand, the users, who are the ones that could actually make it a
> space of freedom and democracy, and on the other, corporations and states.
> I mean, it's an interregnum in the sense that it's a field of struggle. If I had
> to imagine it, I would imagine it as something that sits in-between two other
> things. (Emanuele)

Emanuele then went on to clarify his sketch to explain the powerful and
the powerless as two parallel entities, which are both "touched" by the
internet, which then becomes the field where the contention between

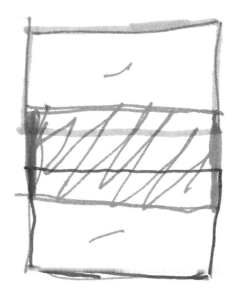

Figure 3. Emanuele's drawing, first VFG, November 8, 2018. *Source:* This work is licensed under CC BY-SA 4.0 DEED. To view a copy of this license, visit http://creative commons.org/licenses/by-sa/4.0/.

these groups is possible. Emanuele's drawing generated a long (and unresolved) discussion about whether the internet should be considered a terrain of conflict or simply a tool of conflict, which echoed some of the key questions raised by the literature on digital labor (e.g., Andrejevic, 2013; Lazzarato, 1996; Terranova, 2000). In this vein, the activists also spent time debating whether the internet operates as a factory and what would qualify as "means of production" in the internet landscape. They considered the music streaming service Spotify and its tracking of users' listening patterns to generate profit. But they weren't fully satisfied with this analysis, as Emanuele conveyed: "Considering data as the means of production, considering that the machines of the factory could become the data, with all the evident differences. But then . . . I mean . . . I have to admit that I am finding it a bit difficult." His (and everyone else's) attempts to put together a Marxist reading of the internet speak to the complexity of identifying precisely how power operates on the internet. Paolo initially proposed to draw

> a worker who is modelling some clay, in which the internet is society, so the internet is the one who is shaping the clay, but he's actually not a worker, he's

a puppet . . . while the one holding the reins . . . so those who have the tools to build the internet and have people use it are the ones who actually have the capacity to direct the puppet to create what they want. (Paolo)

Paolo's idea was never drawn, partially because of its complexity, partially because the activists found that it did not account for the multiple sources of power that operate online. Maria proposed a revised version of the drawing, which can be seen in figure 4.

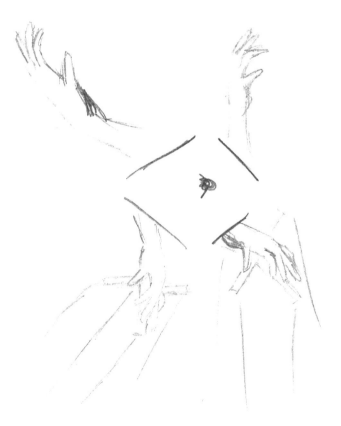

Figure 4. Maria's drawing, first VFG, November 8, 2018.
Source: This work is licensed under CC BY-SA 4.0 DEED. To view a copy of this license, visit http://creativecommons.org /licenses/by-sa/4.0/.

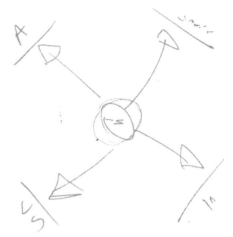

Figure 5. Paolo's drawing, first VFG, November 8, 2018. *Source*: This work is licensed under CC BY-SA 4.0 DEED. To view a copy of this license, visit http://creativecommons.org /licenses/by-sa/4.0/.

The drawing used the image of the puppeteer but allowed for the existence of multiple hands—multiple puppeteers—corresponding to multiple sources of power. These sketches were quickly abandoned because they did not fully encapsulate how the activists saw the internet. The main difficulty they found in articulating this Marxist perspective lay in the age-old question of structure versus agency. In fact, many of the objections they raised to each other had to do with the agency of internet users and the necessity to account for the possibility of creative and resistant uses of the internet. Graphically, this was rendered in the drawing shown in figure 5, which represents the interaction of different actors, shown as vectors, around a central circle, the internet. The actors represented in the drawing changed during the discussion.

Before converging on the image of the iceberg, the activists in the second visual focus group also discussed the role of users' labor, data commodification, and platform power in how they experienced the internet. These processes clearly became a key component of the final drawing: commodification is a key element in the hidden part of the iceberg, while the power of corporations and of the state are represented as an oil platform and a submarine, respectively. The image of the oil platform, used to convey the extractive processes with which corporations generate revenue from internet activities, was also brought up many times during the focus group. It emerged in conjunction with another image, one that was never quite put on paper by the activists: the "money machine" (*una macchina da soldi*). Their discussion used different images but touched upon many of the themes articulated by the first visual focus group, speaking to a common (although somewhat vague) dialectical, Marxist view of society and of the internet that permeates LUMe as a collective. Stefano's heated remarks highlight this aspect:

> Alright, yes, but I mean, for me the biggest problem of the information on the internet is not that Salvini [leader of the League] yells or spreads populism on Instagram. For me it's the fact that, I mean, over the last five years it has become the biggest money machine of the world, out of nothing. Like a money factory out of nothing, basically . . . making you work on. . . . I mean, making you create value on the internet, which you can't actually benefit from. And all of this through this "Okay, you are doing this, and I'm letting you do this, because you are using my service, so you are lucky that I am allowing you to do this." That's why I am saying that . . . the situation has gotten out of hand.

As Stefano eloquently argued, the power of corporations to control our online interactions and to generate profit from them is a key problem for LUMe's activists. As he underlined, this power is reinforced by a certain discourse used by these corporations, one that does not acknowledge the digital labor of users and seeks to justify their exploitation of users' labor through their provision of "free" services. But this reference to the legitimizing discourse of corporations also speaks to the strength of the dominant technological imaginary of Silicon Valley and its promise of empowering and democratic technologies, which LUMe activists are deeply skeptical of.

And this is where the second criticism of the internet raised by LUMe comes into play. LUMe's activists merge a critical reading of the power relations that shape digital spaces with a general discomfort about the uneasy relationship between the lived reality of society and the internet. In the first visual focus group, activists grappled with the idea of the internet being a mirror of society, that is, reflecting all that is happening in society; for the activists, this mostly meant reflecting the struggle between the powerless and the powerful. However, for these activists the internet is not a mirror that simply reflects what is going on in society; it also shapes

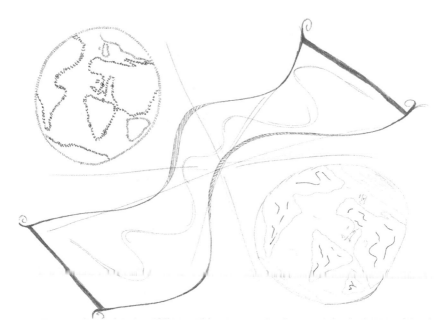

Figure 6. Collective drawing produced in first VFG, November 8, 2018. *Source*: This work is licensed under CC BY-SA 4.0 DEED. To view a copy of this license, visit http://creativecommons.org/licenses/by-sa/4.0/.

it. While they could not exactly determine, and thus draw, how this shaping occurs, they acknowledged it by representing the internet as a funhouse mirror, the distorting mirror seen at the center of their drawing that reflects and distorts society (figure 6). On the lower right activists drew a globe, to represent society as it is; on the upper left, a globe made of numbers and letters to represent code, which stands for society as it is shaped by the internet. The two globes are purposefully similar, but different, to account for the fact that the internet is shaping reality in a distorted way. Maria explained: "It's a mirror, not of society as much. . . . [I]t's an illusory mirror of society. It's a distorter of society . . . because that is never actually the society, but in some ways it works like a small world, a small society." In theoretical terms, this drawing and the discussion that generated it attempted to engage with the idea of the mutual shaping occurring between society and the internet, while acknowledging the existence of powers that alter this relationship.

LUMe's critique of the "reality" of the internet also includes a strong critique of the disconnect between what the internet is and what it is portrayed to be. This is a theme that also clearly emerged in the group drawing that depicted the internet as an iceberg to differentiate between what part of the internet is visible and what processes are hidden. Although the activists conceptualized this disconnect in different ways, they all converged on the idea that something is flawed in the way that the internet is talked about as a free and democratic space. LUMe activists are deeply skeptical of the idea that the internet can be thought of as democratic, for two main reasons: on the one hand, because they know that structures of power and inequality exist online, and on the other, because they feel that information and relationships are filtered and distorted online.

Prompted by a provocative question, activists debated at length whether the internet can be considered a democratic space.[3] One of the participants even wrote, on the margin of their questionnaire:

> It is democratic in terms of the possibility of sharing and accessing content, but its potentialities are threatened by the control over information and by the fact that a 'web democracy' presupposes a universal level of participation, something that seems utopic. (Anonymous)

This nudge toward the promise of a "web democracy" is to be taken as criticizing the core of the technological imaginary of Silicon Valley: LUMe does not see digital technologies as inherently freeing or democratic. It also shows how LUMe stands in stark contrast with the "myth of the web" (Natale & Ballatore, 2014), on which the 5SM constructed its early following, and which pitched digitally mediated participation as a form of direct democracy, intended to replace representative democratic processes. This mythical view of the web, communicated through slogans such as "one equals one" (*uno vale uno*), meant to convey that all individuals are equal online, is very much criticized by LUMe.

As highlighted in the previous section, in the visual focus groups, LUMe activists discussed at length the presence of structures of power and exploitation on the internet. It is this fundamental lack of real equality that drives their critique of the democratic-ness of the internet. Emanuele criticized the idea that the Facebook posts of a regular internet user would receive the same attention as those of a political leader, arguing that while this might be true in theory, the reality is quite different. And this is also why Maria called the internet "illusorily democratic." Alessio, in the other visual focus group, argued that whether people can experience a democratic internet depends on how good they are at using digital technologies:

> I mean, it depends on how well you can use the internet. Because you can use it democratically, in the sense that it is open to everyone, because everyone has . . . according to how well one can use the internet, a possibility to express themselves. If you don't know how to use it, and you just see what the internet shows you, it's not that democratic.

In so doing, Alessio cast digital literacy and savviness as a significant barrier to the achievement of a truly democratic internet.

It is LUMe's daily experiences with the internet, and corporate social network sites in particular, that push the activists to question its democratic-ness. For instance, the activists lament that the internet seems to distort how information is transmitted, and thus also to distort human relations. This came up often in the interviews and seems very important for the activists, because of their reliance on Facebook and WhatsApp for their internal communication. Boris, for instance, talked about "filters" that "virtual means of communication" introduce in conversations and that alter how political discussions unfold. Other interviewees contrasted online modes of communication with face-to-face meetings. They spoke of the existence of filter bubbles (Ilaria) and echo chambers (Paolo). As Ilaria argued, "You know, social network sites really distort the mode in which you relate to others." In particular she talked about WhatsApp as an "anonymous and misunderstandable medium," which ends up being "a bit violent" and "really bring[s] out the worst in people." This negativity identified by Ilaria was felt by other interviewees, too. Many of them mentioned disagreements and misunderstandings that LUMe encountered in using WhatsApp and Facebook; they typically explained them as problems created by how these services are built. If for Mario, LUMe's internal WhatsApp group chat can be "confusing and messy," this is not something that has to do with the activists themselves but is rather "inherent to the WhatsApp group chat" as a digital space. Given these concerns over the quality of information and interactions, it is easy to understand why LUMe activists would be highly critical of any attempt at depicting the internet as a democratic space. Crucially, though, LUMe's activists read these negative aspects of their experiences as consequences of the way power operates online and as evidence that speaking of a democratic internet is an illusion.

NO ALTERNATIVES

Despite its strong criticism, the collective uses Silicon Valley technologies extensively. LUMe activists attributed their reliance on social network sites, and Facebook in particular, to their power, reach, and ease of use. Activists explained that "everyone has Facebook now" (Boris) and that "they reach more people . . . simply because today it's the easiest way to reach the most people" (Valeria). Boris argued that social media offer a general audience to movements, one that is not necessarily already politicized; they "have a strong power because they can reach many people, because they already have their own public, that maybe hates what movements do." Several activists also said that it is easier for a movement to be found on Facebook than by simply searching the web with a search engine. Boris scolded me, after I raised some objections, telling me: "I wouldn't demonize social network sites in this way, though, because they nevertheless allowed us and still allow us to become known and to let people know about our events and what we think." Activists thus clearly consider social media as a great opportunity to get more people interested in what they are doing. Ilaria specifically praised corporate social media for their "propulsive" role in the Arab Spring and in the international women's mobilizations of recent years, saying that activist content is exactly the content that should be on social media. She added that for her, that should be the main aim of these platforms: "I mean, social media should be a public square, meaning a space full of content, politics, and culture. I couldn't care less about what someone ate for lunch, honestly."

However, the activists' unanimously positive accounts of the role of social media in their political activity are peppered with many individual objections, often having to do with how they use (or do not use) these platforms in their private lives. Some activists took long breaks from Facebook or created ad hoc accounts to avoid the platform's data collection.

Boris deactivated his Facebook account for four years after finding that he was spending too much of his free time using the service; he now has a Facebook account, activated prior to joining LUMe, which he reportedly uses mostly to find out about events and interact with LUMe's social media. Mario told me he has a Facebook account he shares with a friend; although this shared account was born out of necessity, when Mario did not have reliable internet access, he now seems to enjoy having an account that can confound Facebook's algorithms by being operated by different people: "I always found the idea of messing up the algorithm pretty fun" (Mario). Jessica spoke of the relief she felt when her Facebook account was temporarily suspended. Some of the activists openly talked about their fear of the power of social media; they reported that fights which broke out on social media had taken a toll on their personal lives. Maria and Ilaria relayed their impression that social network sites exacerbate loneliness. Maria experienced a moment of estrangement with her family that was due to hidden political tensions that manifested as a fight over Facebook posts and Maria's unfriending of her father on the platform. Jessica talked of her fear of surveillance, of the fact that so much data is being collected through this platform. She described herself as using social media "in a terrible way." By this she meant to convey that she felt unable to stop relying on social media, even though she was aware of their problems and their power: "And anyway, the fact that I know . . . it actually makes me feel, quote-unquote, worse because anyway this awareness does not lead me to safeguarding myself" (Jessica). Like Jessica, many LUMe activists expressed their frustration with corporate social media.

It is somewhat of a paradox to hear LUMe activists relay that they should use Facebook "because everyone is there" while they are themselves not really there, while they themselves are concerned about social media or actively trying to avoid Facebook. Most of them also reported joining LUMe because a friend introduced them to the collective or brought them to an event. So even though they themselves did not join LUMe because of Facebook, they seem convinced that this is the privileged avenue for getting to know about the social center. The belief in the importance of Facebook is also reinforced by the sense that there would be no alternative to Facebook. Although they do not state this lack of alternatives explicitly, it emerges from many of their arguments. Jessica, barely hiding her embarrassment, told me she did not know how to respond to a guy who was potentially interested in LUMe but who did not use Facebook: "I did not know what to tell him." But she also rationalized that something like this would happen rarely: "one in every 1,500 people that come through" (Jessica).

After talking about what he felt was a difficult moment for radical leftist activism, Stefano bitterly commented, "The internet is all we have." However, it is clear from the interviews and from the discussions and drawings in the visual focus groups, that "the internet" largely means Facebook for these activists. Its opaque algorithms, its exploitative business model, and its penchant for surveillance are very much at the forefront of how the activists think of digital technologies in general. Activists' thoughts about Facebook influence all of their thinking about technology and its power. Maria encapsulated this feeling in a remarkable quote: "Facebook is the new television." The metaphor is particularly telling. It highlights the mainstream appeal, power, and outsized relevance of Facebook—just how inevitable it is. But there is an added layer to this metaphor: in the Italian context, television has been particularly fraught for left-wing activists, because of the dominance of Berlusconi in the TV landscape for such a long time and the consequent difficult relationship that the Left has had with the medium. To call Facebook "the new television" is also to acknowledge how activists can be critical of that social network while still feeling dependent on it as an avenue for reaching out to the public.

FIGHTING THE SYSTEM WITH THE TOOLS OF THE SYSTEM

LUMe activists hold contradictory thoughts about digital technologies. They have strong political criticisms of social media. But they think that they are inevitable. They are critical of the technologies' power, but also think that they should take advantage of this power. They personally distance themselves from Facebook, but also believe that Facebook is the most important tool with which they can reach people. How do they make sense of these conflicting ideas?

LUMe's technological imaginary bridges the inherent contradiction of believing in the usefulness of digital technologies while rejecting many of their aspects: for LUMe, digital technologies are simultaneously flawed and indispensable for social change. These technologies are flawed for the reasons that LUMe activists articulated in the interviews and visual focus groups: because they are embedded in a capitalist system of power and because they don't live up to the expectations of democratic-ness. Yet they are also indispensable, because activists believe in their power, reach, and ease of use: there are no alternatives to these technologies, because they are held to be the most efficient way to get in touch with other people. While this imaginary might appear simple, if not simplistic, in practice it requires constant political discussion and fine tuning. In their own words, LUMe activists rationalize this technological imaginary through variations of the sentence "using the tools of the system against the system."[4] Valeria's quote fully expressed LUMe's technological imaginary:

> Our idea has always been to use the tools of the system against the system, let's say. We did not pass value judgments on the thing itself, we thought about the fact that it was available to us and how we could exploit it to our advantage. It was that. And we have mostly used Facebook, and I have to say that it works. I mean, many people come to us because they saw something on Facebook. And this shows you that it's a tool that reaches many many people. But I mean, we use it with reason and awareness. And always in line with our principles.

Valeria's words show the kind of careful internal deliberations and political consideration that support LUMe's technological practices of using corporate social media in opposition to the system that created them. Others are even more forceful in identifying the internet, and Facebook in particular, as being representative of a capitalist system that provides tools that activists can turn against the system. Paolo explicitly called internet technologies "the tools that capital gives you," which he argued "can be used to spread diametrically opposed content." Ilaria illustrated how LUMe navigates this:

> We thought about using those tools—obviously in a critical manner, meaning that we know we are. . . . [I]n the end, we are incoherent, in using these media to then go and criticize the system. I mean, it's a dog biting its tail. We had a lot of scruples at the beginning. We had a political discussion. And we agreed that our position was that of exploiting the system to fight the system. Not to be hermits that keep out of social media, that retire, that give up

on communicating, and thus give up on creating consensus, on a popular base for consensus. Because that's what social networks are today. . . . Instead, we want to use them in a critical way.

Ilaria's words capture the political work that LUMe puts into making digital technologies work for its political ideology and objectives. This is why I argue that LUMe's technological imaginary can be classified as one of negotiation. LUMe rejects the core of Silicon Valley's dominant technological imaginary: it is critical of the neoliberal underpinnings of digital technologies and refuses to see the internet as inherently freeing and democratic. Despite rejecting the system (in LUMe's terms) and the imaginary (in mine) of capitalist Silicon Valley, the activists nevertheless rely on Facebook and other corporate platforms for their activism. The process is not frictionless; it requires a constant negotiation among themselves and between them and these technologies. The frictions they encounter are generated by the clash of two technological imaginaries—LUMe's and Silicon Valley's—which come to the surface when LUMe attempts to use digital media tools in accordance with its political principles and not Silicon Valley's. Silicon Valley's imaginary is encoded in its technologies; by using these technologies, LUMe activists have to negotiate with an imaginary they do not endorse. How this negotiation unfolds in practice is influenced by three political factors: LUMe's anti-capitalist ideological positions, the political context of Italian occupied social centers, and the strength of the technological imaginary of the "authoritarian sublime" (Treré, 2018) of the 5SM, which LUMe opposes.

Ideology

LUMe's anti-capitalist politics is at the forefront of how the collective envisions digital technologies. Whether represented as an iceberg that hides processes of data extraction and commodification or encapsulated in sentences like "the tools that capital gives us," it is clear that LUMe's take on digital media is profoundly influenced by its Marxist political orientation. The activists' critiques of the internet are centered on power and on the political economy of digital technologies: the internet, and social media in particular, are flawed because of their corporate exploitative model and their inability to foster truly egalitarian and democratic spaces. LUMe's technological imaginary of negotiation is thus powerfully shaped by the clash between its anti-capitalist ideology and Silicon Valley's embrace of neoliberalism in both its discourses and its technologies.

LUMe's imaginary of negotiation is a balancing act: How can the activists maintain their political identity while using these digital platforms that they find indispensable? This is what Valeria hinted at in the quote in the previous section, when she spoke of using Facebook "in line with our principles." Negotiation is not an easy process. It is rife with contradictions and powered by extensive discussions. Activists are fully aware of how negotiation is full of imperfect solutions. Ilaria, quoted in the previous section, conveyed that the activists are aware that they can be seen as "incoherent" in their use of capitalist tools to pursue anti-capitalist politics. Boris was also conscious that LUMe could be considered "not really coherent" with its ideology:

> I mean, if you are against certain things and you fight . . . [you have] your politics, your ideals, and if the company whose services you utilize doesn't respect them, you should. . . . I mean, ethically, in your militancy, in your political activity, in your contestation, you should boycott it, or contest it. And that's fine. But this leads you to certain problems.

While fully aware that the most ideologically coherent option would be for LUMe to reject and boycott Silicon Valley technologies, Boris also said that this would, however, lead to problems: it would most likely make it very difficult for LUMe to reach out to people and operate smoothly. Once again, the use of social media seems completely unavoidable and indispensable.

Sometimes activists from other movements take issue with LUMe's use of social media and its supposed lack of ideological coherence. Ilaria mentioned that creating an Instagram page was regarded as a bad look for a social center. Mario recalled his meeting with an "old militant hacker" who vehemently objected to LUMe's use of social media, which he saw in stark contradiction to the tradition of social centers. Mario engaged with the hacker's objections, but concluded:

> Yeah, that's one way of seeing it. It is a very purist way of seeing it, I'm not sure how to say this. It has its charm. But if you want to spread an idea, you do it through whatever channel allows you to do it. You even do it through Facebook.

LUMe activists don't feel like refusing to use social media is the way to go. As Mario argued, it's a purist, doctrinaire solution to ideological incoherence, but not a very useful one.

LUMe's solution, instead, is to use internet technologies "in line with our principles," as Valeria said. This might mean using Facebook "with reason and awareness," as Valeria explained, or "in a critical manner," as Ilaria suggested. Many of the activists came back to this idea of using digital technologies purposefully and critically, foregrounding their political objectives. They envisioned a common intentionality that enables a critical use of social media, which rejects the capitalist premises of the technological imaginary of Silicon Valley. As Mario explained, by using Facebook critically, LUMe can push back against the intended uses of this platform:

> We try to fill this container, this container that is given to us, with as much content as possible. Because in the end, that's how you make a difference. While many only use this with a profit logic, only with a logic of banality and . . . I mean, despite everything we know about demagogy, and populism, and how much Facebook can be shit, you can try to fill it up with content. Because it allows you to reach a wider audience than if you didn't use it. Then at that point you have to try . . . to, quote-unquote, "trick the system." Because you are trying to transmit something of value on this platform that would otherwise become the shitter of the internet. . . . That's the mission. Trying to make as meaningful as possible what you do on that platform. I believe that's the only way to use it with awareness.

Mario's words show that LUMe believes it can use Facebook in a critical, intentional manner, to insert political content into the discussion, to promote an engagement with the news, and ultimately to criticize the system. This way of using Facebook is a way to put meaning into this otherwise terrible platform, while allowing the collective's members to still be themselves, to still maintain their political identity.

LUMe's ideology shapes its technological imaginary of negotiation. When the activists talk about "using the tools of the system to fight the system" (or "to fuck the system"), they are acknowledging that digital technologies are part of the capitalist system that they would like to take down. Yet they are also assigning a crucial role to these technologies in helping them get closer to taking down the system. Their technological imaginary of negotiation holds these contradictions together by envisioning a critical, intentional use of Silicon Valley's technologies, which is based on constant internal deliberation.

Political Context

LUMe's technological imaginary of negotiation is also powerfully influenced by the peculiar political context in which the collective is immersed: the long history of Italian social centers and the importance of occupied spaces for the Italian radical Left. Occupying a space does not just give activists a venue to host their activities; it is also part of their identity as a collective and links them to long-standing political practices of occupation that have characterized Italian activism since the 1970s. Occupied spaces and the legacy of Italian social centers then play a role in how LUMe envisions the political role of digital technologies. In fact, LUMe activists are anchoring their use of corporate social media platforms to their occupied space. Although they are very open about the crucial role that Facebook plays for them, they frequently contextualize it within their offline practices: their assemblies, their horizontal decision-making process, and their self-management of the occupied space. Activists often repeat that even if extensive conversation and exchange of information happens in their internal Facebook group and WhatsApp group chat, decisions can only be taken in an assembly. It is such a cardinal rule that almost all interviewees repeated it to me. The offline space—particularly the political space of demonstrations or the occupied space itself—is where politics happens.

Ilaria encapsulated this idea by arguing that LUMe's use of social media cannot be divorced from its presence in offline political spaces:

> I mean, to me Facebook is making an event, inviting people, and then seeing them in real life (*dal vivo*) and "doing politics" in real life. To me Facebook means posting an article on migrants dying in the Mediterranean, so that people can develop some critical thoughts and then come to demonstrate the following week. . . . For me Facebook is not the only place where politics happen, absolutely not, otherwise it would be terrible.

Ilaria's words show how LUMe rationalizes its use of Facebook as a prelude to actual political engagement, not as a locus of political engagement in itself. This is part of what the activists think of as their critical, intentional use of corporate digital technologies: being aware that they can be used to recruit and connect with people, but that they cannot take the place of offline political practices, such as open assemblies or direct action. Maria observed that LUMe's spike in popularity on social media happened in the interim period between the eviction from the Santa Caterina building and the occupation of the Cinema Orchidea, in summer 2017, when LUMe did not have a physical space. She detailed:

> LUMe's first social media boom was after the eviction. The eviction period, the new occupation, that's the moment LUMe's social media . . . because not having a space, not having a place to gather, and the spaces were usually secret . . . I mean, the spaces where we were meeting. . . . [I]t was important to meet in a plenary assembly to decide on the occupations or . . . mostly, the occupations. [Social media] were the only way to interact and to interact with the outside. Since we didn't have a space where people could come and talk to us. And that's when it boomed.

Maria thus traced a link between LUMe's peak use of social media for external communication and the absence of a physical offline space. Ilaria made a similar connection with respect to LUMe's internal communication, remarking that the current occupation, which is in a less hospitable building, needs online communication more than the Santa Caterina one did: "If we had the physical space to spend time together. . . . [S]ince we don't, we use [online communication] more." Although this link does not emerge explicitly from other interviewees' accounts, it serves to further highlight the importance of offline, occupied spaces in LUMe's technological imaginary. The occupied space grounds LUMe's negotiation of the dominant technological imaginary of Silicon Valley: it puts the activists' reliance on digital media in perspective. It allows LUMe to understand its use of digital media as subordinate to the self-management (and enjoyment) of the occupied space.

But the practice of occupying a space is not just about having a venue for meetings and activities. The occupation is part of LUMe's political identity, and it situates LUMe within a long historical trajectory of Italian occupied social centers. LUMe activists respect this history and draw upon it, even as they feel the need to innovate what can be done in and through a social center. In this sense, foregoing the centrality of occupied space in favor of virtual—and corporate-run!—spaces would seriously violate some of LUMe's political principles. Stefano clarified the stakes:

> The elimination of sociality, let's say . . . that's a plague you run the risk of spreading yourself, if you begin to only do everything in a virtual manner . . . then the space doesn't exist anymore. It's a different space, but it lacks the main component of what you initially wanted to do—to share a different model of culture. We never thought it would make sense to build our own universe on the internet. It's always been a tool for us. I mean, it would go against everything we believe in, at all levels.

According to Stefano, moving all activity online not only would be against the collective's beliefs, but could also jeopardize the occupied space. Stefano made it very clear that while LUMe has been taking advantage of corporate social media, they would never want to feel that they were contributing to the demise of occupation as a political tactic. They want to be part of the context of Italian occupied social centers, not break away from it. Offline occupied spaces thus offer LUMe a way of anchoring its negotiation of Silicon Valley's imaginary and digital technologies; both the self-management of its space and the political meaning of the occupation allow the activists to envision digital platforms as one of the avenues where political participation can be encouraged, but not the primary space where politics happens.

Other Technological Imaginaries

The third element that shapes LUMe's technological imaginary of negotiation is its contempt for the 5SM. While the collective strongly criticizes the party for its (since foregone) alliances with the League and populist positions, it also rejects the discourses about digital technology that the 5SM has popularized. These discourses, which were particularly important to the 5SM in its initial years, constitute a very specific and powerful technological imaginary. As Simone Natale and Andrea Ballatore (2014) suggested, the Five Star Movement's technological imaginary is an adaptation of the Californian Ideology (Barbrook & Cameron, 1996) to the Italian context. Beppe Grillo and the late Gianroberto Casaleggio, the founders of the party, used a powerful techn-outopian "myth of the web" (Natale

& Ballatore, 2014) to differentiate themselves from other Italian parties, seeking to cast the 5SM as a revolutionary force that would destroy old party structures, just as the internet has destroyed older technologies. However, as Treré (2018) argued, the appeal to digital utopianism has only served to strengthen authoritarian, top-down practices within the 5SM itself. Treré (2018) convincingly termed the imaginary of the 5SM as "authoritarian sublime," by which he described how "the cyber-libertarian discourse of the 5SM, based on the myths of horizontality, leaderlessness, and digital democracy, was used to conceal and legitimize political practices associated with authoritarianism, populism, and strong leadership" (p. 124). Although LUMe activists rarely connect their technological imaginary to the 5SM in an explicit way, many of their concerns about the presumed democratic-ness of the internet and its unequal power dynamics have been strengthened by what has unfolded in the 5SM. Consider, for instance, how Valeria expressed a concern about people's risk of being manipulated:

> If you approach the internet without knowing what you are getting into, you run the risk of being maneuvered, rather than being the master of your own self. Maybe you even think that your idea comes from that, but . . . I don't know, personally, I'd rather be informed, to find things out from other channels as well.

Valeria was explaining that using the internet without taking the kind of critical stance that LUMe activists find so important can be dangerous, because it may lead people to be taken advantage of. Further, in the Italian popular imagination, supporters of the 5SM are associated with a lack of digital literacy (and sometimes of literacy as well), like the spreading of disinformation or the intense use of Facebook in a cringeworthy way, including bad grammar errors and the extensive use of all caps and exclamation marks (Boni & Ricci, 2015).[5] Sometimes LUMe activists grapple with this issue in terms of digital literacy. They see the younger generation to which they belong as being more aware in their use of digital media. They often talk to me about their parents, or other older people, to explain how they see their own self-aware use of Facebook as different: savvier, more detached, more strategic. However, this contrast between savvy and unsavvy uses of social media does not just have a generational connotation for LUMe's activists: it is profoundly political.

Some of these themes emerged in the visual focus groups, in which activists talked at length about how "awareness" and "savviness" changed one's relationship to the internet, especially in terms of experiencing a more democratic internet. Activists are skeptical about the idea of the internet being democratic also because they perceive that many people lack the literacy and savviness—the awareness—that would (maybe) allow the use of digital tools in a more democratic way. In the second visual focus group, Alessio even proposed to represent the internet as a ship leaving port, "where someone got stranded, because someone always misses the ship." LUMe's activists find this lack of awareness, this acritical use of digital technologies, particularly problematic, and they tie it directly to the 5SM and its use of social media. Stefano made this point, connecting a lack of awareness to the belief in the democratic-ness of the internet, to highlight how it can make people vulnerable to political exploitation:

> There are generations who don't have the same way of disentangling online things that we have, who think that something they read on the internet is way more authoritative. And then there's the fact that the internet has opened to. . . . I mean, it's cause and consequence of the enormous opening towards populism that we have seen in recent years. I mean, it's true that it is not the primary engine of the phenomenon—the fact that we have fake news online—but it comes full circle, with the model that the internet chose, in terms of information.

Here Stefano made a connection between social media and populism, linking together the business model of corporate platforms, the lack of digital literacy that characterizes ample swaths of the Italian population, and the emergence of populist forces that can exploit the situation. LUMe activists see a lack of awareness and digital savvy, far from simply being a generational grievance, as politically problematic, because it leaves people more exposed to populist forces. This is one of the reasons they are skeptical about the presumed democratic nature of digital technologies, why they criticize the immense power of digital platforms, and ultimately, why they reject techno-utopian discourses about technology, whether coming from Silicon Valley or from the 5SM.

LUMe's technological imaginary of negotiation is thus a response to the technological imaginaries of both Silicon Valley and the 5SM. By relying on the idea of using corporate social media in a critical, intentional way, LUMe activists understand their social media practices as producing meaningful political content, which allows them to "use the tools of the system to fight the system." At the same time, they also distance themselves from discourses that picture the internet as a democratic space— ideas they see as instrumental to contemporary forms of populism.

CONCLUSION

The activist technological imaginary developed by LUMe fully expresses its ambiguous relationship to digital technologies, particularly commercial social media platforms. For these activists, these technologies are unavoidable; there is no credible alternative to them. Yet these technologies are also deeply problematic for LUMe. As this chapter shows, the activists in the collective express a strong critique of web technologies: they identify a strong connection between capitalist structures and online processes, they reject the idea of a democratic internet reality, and they question how internet technologies mediate and distort human interaction. Their criticism hits at the core of Silicon Valley's technological imaginary: it uncovers its connection with neoliberal capitalism, rejects its belief in an inherently liberating and democratic nature of internet technologies, and refuses its technological solutionism. And yet by relying on the same technologies that were created within the dominant imaginary, LUMe activists end up having to navigate how Silicon Valley's imaginary manifests in the affordances of those technologies. LUMe's technological imaginary is thus one of negotiation: activists are actively engaged in tweaking and justifying their use of Silicon Valley's technologies so that it can best match their beliefs and praxis. In the activists' words, as highlighted previously, this process is described as "fighting the system with the tools of the system."

The framework I propose in this book theorizes that activist technological imaginaries respond to the dominant technological imaginary of Silicon Valley in ways that are shaped by their political ideology, the political context in which they are situated, and the presence of other prominent technological imaginaries. In the case of LUMe, negotiation is shaped by LUMe's Marxist orientation, its existence within a long historical trajectory of political occupied spaces (the social centers), and the strength of the technological imaginary of the 5SM. First, this chapter examined in detail how LUMe activists apply a Marxist reading to the internet, which drives their criticism. Interviewees identified data commodification and the power of online corporations as the main problems of the internet. They did not, for instance, talk about internet companies violating users' privacy as a violation of civil liberties; they understand surveillance within capitalist processes of exploitation. Their negotiation attempts to square their anti-capitalist critique of digital technologies with their belief in the unavoidability of corporate social media and requires constant discussion to make sure that it is compatible with their political beliefs. Second, the political context in which LUMe is embedded—the Italian occupied social centers—also guides how the activists relate to technology. LUMe activists are conscious of being part of a long tradition of political occupations, and they are committed to this practice. Their use of corporate social media is functional to the goal of sustaining their occupation, not supplanting it. Moreover, LUMe activists draw an important distinction between on-line and offline spaces, arguing that it is in the latter that meaningful political participation actually happens, whether in the occupied spaces or in the streets. This political context thus plays an important role in how LUMe situates itself in relation to the dominant technological imaginary of Silicon Valley and its technologies. Third, LUMe's technological imaginary stands in opposition to Silicon Valley's imaginary, but also to the imaginary of the 5SM, the populist party that was so influential in the 2010s in Italy. In its critique of democratic-ness and reliance on a critical, intentional stance as a key for navigating its use of social media, LUMe implicitly, and at times explicitly, rejects the 5SM's authoritarian sublime (Treré, 2018). Indeed, it even seems that LUMe activists interpret Silicon Valley's imaginary through the lens of their experience with the 5SM, thus reinforcing their rejection of both imaginaries. Silicon Valley's dominant imaginary is untenable, for LUMe, also because it enables and justifies the kinds of authoritarian and populist practices that the 5SM has been enacting. The influence of LUMe's Marxist orientation, the legacy of occu-pied social centers, and the prominence of the technological imaginary of the 5SM thus shape how LUMe's negotiation of the imaginary of Silicon Valley unfolds.

5 Organizing Where People Are

PHILLY SOCIALISTS' IMAGINARY OF NEGOTIATION

The facilitators asked all of us to state our names and our pronouns and to talk about the worst job we had ever had. I was sitting in a packed room in a building in Northern Liberties, a historically working-class and now gentrified of Northeast Philadelphia, rented for the day by Philly Socialists (PS) to host the group's monthly "mass meeting," announced on Facebook and open to anyone interested in learning about the organization. It was July 2018 and Philadelphia, like many other cities in the United States, had just seen an unexpected surge of mobilization against the repressive immigration policies of the Trump administration, under the name Occupy ICE. Members of neighborhood PS were among the organizers of Occupy ICE in Philadelphia, which included a four-day occupation of the area outside the local ICE office, demonstrations, working groups, and another occupation near City Hall, which lasted twenty-two days. Their role in organizing the protests was recognized by the media, from the local *Philadelphia Inquirer* to *Jezebel*. On a Sunday afternoon weighed down by the sweltering Philadelphia heat, more than thirty people had shown up to get to know PS.

A table right by the entrance held the colorful copies of the *Philadelphia Partisan*, PS' self-produced magazine; a pamphlet with a lot of information about PS and its activities; and a sign-up sheet, whose importance became clearer to me in subsequent months, and which asked participants for their name, contact details, and what "projects" they would be interested in being connected to.

After going around the room and bonding over crappy wages and horrible bosses, we listened as PS organizers stood up and introduced the many different projects developed and run by the organization:

The Philadelphia Tenants Union (PTU), started by PS but now fully independent, fighting slumlords and advocating for tenant rights through direct action.

English as a second language (ESL) classes, run by volunteers in two different areas of the city—a vehicle of solidarity between immigrants and nonimmigrants.

The *Philadelphia Partisan*, the group's quarterly alternative magazine, managed by an editorial collective and open to written contributions by members and sympathizers.

The Cesar Iglesias Community Garden, PS's own land redistribution project: an empty lot in North Philadelphia turned into communal garden and run by activists and neighbors.

Student socialist organizing at Temple University, Drexel University, and the University of Pennsylvania, the three largest campuses in the city.

A design collective, responsible for all things PS and design, including posters and T-shirts.

I tried to follow along in the pamphlet I had picked up at the entrance, but organizers kept mentioning other projects they wanted to test out or that they were looking to solidify, new projects that were not even included in the long list that populated the pamphlet:

Dignity, PS's worker organizing project, which was just starting at the time of that assembly and has since become a full-fledged organization with its own membership.

An inkling of coalition-building around immigrant rights, emerging from the strength and success of Occupy ICE Philadelphia.

A domestic violence rapid response team, an idea developed by the Dolphin Caucus, the PS working group for members who are not cisgender heterosexual men.

What came through when PS members talked about their activities was a sense that the hands-on work happening in the projects deeply motivated them; it was exciting and meaningful and a great way to get involved. As one of the speakers summed up: "Come for the values, stay for the work."

In the weeks and months that followed, PS organizers called my phone, left me voicemails, and sent me emails inviting me to their events and to the work sessions of the projects I had selected when filling out the sign-in sheet at the assembly. As I learned by interviewing organizers, attention to the projects and to following up with potentially interested people are at the core of how PS members operate.

PS is a socialist organization committed to revolutionary politics. Active since 2011 in Philadelphia, its dues-paying membership is diverse in terms of age, gender, and race, although the core organizers serving in leadership positions have mostly been white and/or male. The PS idea of socialism is based in the concept of "base-building": building working-class power outside of the electoral arena. Within base-building, projects such as a tenant union or a community garden are crucial, because they serve the needs of the working class, while also recruiting people to socialist organizing. Borrowing a slogan from the Black Panther Party, PS organizers explain their work as "serving the people, fighting the power." For base-building to work, organizers need a well-functioning system that helps them recruit people who might be coming in for the values and get them to keep coming back for the work. This is what they simply call "organizing."

I studied PS during what looked like a "socialist moment" in contemporary American politics, a period of heightened attention to socialist politics during the Trump presidency (2016–2020), likely spurred by Senator Bernie Sanders's participation in the Democratic presidential primaries in 2016 and the election of Alexandria Ocasio-Cortez to the US House of Representatives in 2018. Although this socialist moment had brought interest to PS, the group was not necessarily thrilled with how the mainstream conversation about socialism has been co-opted by the electoral politics of the Democratic Party. Within this context, the group has become even more forceful in articulating how base-building distinguishes it from other socialist organizations, like the popular Democratic Socialists of America (DSA): PS is committed to organizing the working class, not running candidates in elections.

It is this vision of organizing that shapes how PS members think about, and use, digital technologies. Their complex and overlapping technological practices—Facebook pages and groups, emails, listservs, newsletters, a Twitter account, a website, phone calls, texts, CRM software—are in service of an idea of organizing within the perspective of base-building. Their technological imaginary, which I condense in the phrase "organizing where people are," recognizes that the digital technologies of Silicon Valley are not ideal for the Philly Socialists, but they are good enough for recruiting people, and recruiting people needs to happen where people "already are," even if that means corporate digital platforms. This is an imaginary of negotiation, because the organization rejects the dominant technological imaginary of Silicon Valley while relying on its technologies. This negotiation is based on a strategic use of the notion of "organizing," which allows the group to frame its technological practices as one piece of a more complex online and offline strategy. With the emphasis on organizing, this imaginary of negotiation is clearly influenced by the ideological commitment to base-building that characterizes this movement. It is also shaped by the lessons members draw from the history of socialist organizing; they explicitly reference the idea of using any available mainstream technology, whether a typewriter or Facebook, to disseminate socialist ideas to the people. Finally, I argue that this imaginary is based on a rejection of another technological imaginary, "activist networking"—that is, performative lifestyle activism, which the Philly Socialists members see as prevalent in the US Left and which they strongly criticize.

THE PHILLY SOCIALISTS: FROM OCCUPY TO THE SOCIALIST MOMENT

PS was founded in summer 2011, right before the beginning of the Occupy Wall Street movement in the United States, by a handful of white male activists who had recently relocated to Philadelphia and had prior experiences in radical social movements, student organizing, and antiwar demonstrations. It can thus be considered as originating in a wave of mobilization that brought young Americans to the streets after the financial crisis of 2008 and the subsequent loss of trust in the Obama administration's capacity to steer the country in a more progressive direction. But while many of the movements of the postrecession period have long been gone, more than ten years after its founding PS is still gaining new members and implementing new projects. In January 2019 its dues-paying membership amounted to 170 individuals; in addition, dozens more people participate in its projects in the city, even if they do not hold formal membership.

A number of the group's current members got to know the organization during Occupy Philadelphia and its two-month-long encampment near City Hall in fall 2011. Besides participating in Occupy Philadelphia, the founders created the first projects of the organization, volunteer-run general educational development (GED) and ESL classes. They also started organizing in North Philadelphia, particularly hit by the recession and with empty lots scattered throughout, discovering that residents were interested in having a community garden; they identified a piece of land that had been abandoned due to tax delinquency and turned that into a garden. Since then, PS organizers have established several community gardens in Philadelphia, which they maintain with the involvement of the neighborhoods. After what one of the founders described as a "lull period" between 2012 and 2013, PS directed its efforts toward tenant organizing in 2014–2015. Inspired by the Seattle Solidarity Network, PS started to organize tenant fights against landlords in West Philadelphia.[1] What began as support for one resident's struggle against a negligent landlord (Thompson, 2019) later became a full-fledged organization, the PTU, founded in 2016. The PTU is now an independent organization, but its membership, and at times its leadership, overlap significantly with PS.

In the long campaign leading up to the presidential election of 2016, the candidacy of Senator Bernie Sanders in the Democratic primaries stoked people's interest in "democratic socialism" and socialist organizations. Although PS does not support Sanders or other candidates for office, it benefited from the national media attention to Sanders and his reclaiming of the label "socialist," albeit within the confines of the Democratic Party. After the election of Donald Trump in 2016, the Philly Socialists experienced another spike in the number of people who showed an interest in its activities and participated in its public events, including several mass meetings with hundreds of people, which took place right after the election. The group tried to channel the frustration (and excitement) of the early anti-Trump protests into its various projects. PS also took part in the rallies of late January 2017, when thousands of people took to the streets to protest against Trump, who was in Philadelphia for a Republican Party retreat (Hesse, 2017). Since this post-Trump growth, PS has expanded in different directions and experimented with new projects, such as its worker-organizing initiative, Dignity. The organization also had a change in leadership in 2018, which signaled the "retirement" of its founders from leadership roles and the emergence of a more diverse cohort of leaders in the elected positions of the organization.

In summer 2018 PS was among the organizers of the Occupy ICE protests in Philadelphia. These protests were part of a nationwide surge in activism against the repressive immigration policies of the Trump administration and the targeting of immigrants by ICE (Levin, 2018). Portland, Oregon, was one of the main centers of the protests. In Philadelphia, organizers such as PS, the Philadelphia branch of DSA, and Reclaim Philadelphia started occupying the area in front of the ICE offices. Despite the summer heat and the rain, the protesters continuously occupied the site for four days, building an encampment and collecting donations (Gammage & Irizarry-Aponte, 2018a; Orso & Feliciano Reyes, 2018). The protesters were forcefully evicted on July 5. A second encampment was created next to City Hall on July 6 (Sasko, 2018); the new encampment spurred a mass meeting on July 10, at which activists attempted to create a more stable structure of working groups. The occupation lasted for twenty-two days. In Philadelphia, the Occupy ICE protests supplemented the nationwide demand to "abolish ICE" with two more local claims: (1) a request to (then) governor Tom Wolf to "shut down" the federal detention center in Berks County, which holds parents and children who are awaiting immigration or asylum decisions; and (2) a request to (then) mayor Jim Kenney to end PARS, a data-sharing agreement that allowed ICE to access information about arrests in the city of Philadelphia (Gammage & Irizarry-Aponte, 2018b). The protests were successful on the local level, in that Kenney announced on July 27 that the city would not renew its contract with PARS, which terminated on August 31, 2019 (Gammage &

Irizarry-Aponte, 2018b). The announcement put an end to the encampment outside City Hall (*"Occupy ICE" Activists Vacate City Hall*, 2018). The local success of Occupy ICE Philadelphia brought an increase of media attention to PS, which was recognized as one of the main actors behind these protests (Brey, 2018; Orso & Feliciano Reyes, 2018).

The mass meeting described at the beginning of this chapter brought together many people who were seeking to get involved in PS after Occupy ICE. Besides the many projects introduced in that open meeting, organizers have since also expanded their political education work and created a "prison-organizing project," which organized drop-in letter-writing sessions, providing materials, postage, and advice on how to write to incarcerated people (Philly Socialists, 2019). Each project is coordinated by a working group, typically composed of dues-paying members but open to nonmembers; the General Assembly and the Central Committee oversee all of the activities and allocate a budget for them.

Veterans of the organization often remarked on how much PS has grown and changed over the years, in terms of membership, leadership, and organizational structures. But in all of this change, the organization has held onto its ability to bring together protest, direct action and project-based work. This emphasis on organizing and base-building is key to how PS defines its political orientation.

BASE-BUILDING

PS is a broadly inclusive socialist organization. It welcomes people who are interested in radical leftist politics regardless of their ideological beliefs. In its own words, the group is a "multi-tendency" organization, with an "eclectic" approach to socialism. Amy clarified what this means:

> How it works is that we don't require people to subscribe to kind of a specific and more abstract set of political beliefs to be involved. . . . Right now really we try to let our projects speak for themselves. If you believe in the things that they are fighting for, then we can work together, kind of. And so, if you believe in tenant power and worker power and you believe in immigrant rights and right to land for like collective use then we're on the same page because that's what our projects are about.

It is really the work going on in the different projects that anchors the politics of PS and steers it away from the electoral process and toward a revolutionary perspective. As Tyler explained:

> We are . . . we accept people who identify as anarchists, people who identify as Trotskyists or Stalinists or what have you. We don't have like a specific strongly held ideological core belief, but generally, the organization moves in a revolutionary direction, the long-term stated goal is a revolution and the tactics tend to downplay the importance of elections and to focus more on direct action, mass action, right? Mass struggles, protests and community organizing. Our approach to elected officials tends to be more oppositional and antagonistic.

While being broadly inclusive of different leftist orientations, the fundamental line of demarcation that PS draws is about electoral politics. The organization is not interested in taking part in the electoral process at any level; instead, its activities are geared toward protests, direct action, and "serve the people" work—what members call base-building. As we can see in Tyler's words, they think of this organizing work as leading toward a socialist revolution in the United States.

In a small pamphlet issued in 2018, PS explained what it means to be socialist in relatively simple terms: "Socialists believe in democracy and the right to a decent human life. The 'right' to profit and private property should never impinge upon our basic rights to human dignity" (Philly Socialists, 2018a). The text explained in more detail by juxtaposing three "We are" phrases—"socialists," "building a political base," and "serving the people, fighting the power"—with three "We are not" phrases: "a political theory club," "funded by grants," and "supporters of the two capitalist parties" (Philly Socialists, 2018a). In line with Tyler's words, the three instances of "We are not" articulated in the pamphlet are a direct way for PS to distinguish itself from orthodox, sectarian, socialist groups ("political theory club"), from nonprofit organizations ("funded by grants"), and from the DSA ("supporters of the two capitalist parties"), which have recently become more directly involved in the politics of the Democratic Party, particularly after the 2016 election cycle. It is as important for PS members to describe who they are as it is to describe who they are not; this necessity to differentiate PS from other groups is a recurrent theme in the interviews, too.

This need to demarcate itself from other socialist organizations, especially the DSA, might be especially important for PS given the unexpected media and public attention to socialist politics in the United States since 2015–2016. In the years immediately preceding my fieldwork, mainstream media had been preoccupied by the emergence of a "socialist moment" in the United States. *PBS Newshour* asked: "Is socialism having its moment in U.S. elections?" (Greenfield, 2019); a segment on NPR's program *Fresh Air* declared, "Socialism isn't the scare word it once was" (Nunberg, 2019). The pages of the *New York Times* hosted discussions on the rise of socialism in the US political landscape: in August 2018, an opinion column was titled "The New Socialists: Why the Pitch from Alexandria Ocasio-Cortez and Bernie Sanders Resonates in 2018" (Robin, 2018); in May 2019, the *NYT*'s website hosted a conversation with Bhaskar Sunkara, the founder of the socialist magazine *Jacobin*, under the title "The United States of Socialism?" (Douthat et al., 2019). But the predominant frame that news media used to cover the "resurgence" of socialism was undoubtedly that of defining it in generational terms: the emergence of "millennial socialism" in the United States was announced, for instance, by the *Economist* ("Millennial Socialism," 2019); the *Chicago Tribune* (Chapman, 2018); the *Guardian*, which declared that US millennials "fell in love with socialism" (McGreal, 2017); and the *Nation* (Mead, 2017).

This media attention to socialist politics was sparked by Senator Bernie Sanders's run in the Democratic primaries in 2016 and reinforced by the election of Congresswoman Alexandria Ocasio-Cortez, a member of the DSA, in 2018. In no small part due to the media frenzy surrounding Ocasio-Cortez's election, Trump even talked about the threat posed by the rising popularity of socialist ideas in his 2019 State of the Union address. His remarks undoubtedly contributed to the continued media coverage of socialist organizations. In particular, given its connection to Sanders and Ocasio-Cortez, the DSA has benefited from this intense media attention. Founded in 1982, the DSA is now the largest socialist organization in the United States: its membership grew from six thousand in 2015 to more than fifty thousand in 2019 (Henwood, 2019; Stein, 2017), and reached ninety-two thousand in 2022 (Democratic Socialists of America, n.d.).

This national attention to socialism trickled down to the local level, too. During the same period, PS experienced a surge in membership, public participation, and media coverage. Its dues-paying members went from 32 in 2014, to 72 in August 2016 (Philly Socialists, 2018c), to 170 in January 2019. After the Occupy ICE protests in Philadelphia, in summer 2018, PS received a lot more media attention and several members were quoted—and even photographed—in the *Philadelphia Inquirer*'s coverage of the protests (Gammage & Irizarry-Aponte, 2018a, 2018b; Orso & Feliciano Reyes, 2018); the *Philadelphia Weekly* put PS on the cover of the magazine, with the headline "A Full-Fledged Socialist Party in American Politics: Just a Dream? These Folks Beg to Differ" (Brey, 2018). While welcoming the increased media coverage and the growth in membership and participation, PS is skeptical of how the national conversation about socialism has been skewed toward socialists' participation in the electoral process via the Democratic Party. Michael reacted as follows to my questions about this "socialist moment":

> I think it's yet to be seen, because I think you can say socialism as a word has gained resurgence, but if that just means [it was] whipped into the Democratic party, that's not a socialist moment. Socialism means independent working-class power, at the end of the day. . . . I'm talking about just our own independent political power that is not hung at the collar to the Democratic Party, [if we don't have that] then it's not a socialist moment.

While Michael saw this contemporary moment as one that might mark the resurgence of socialism, he was nevertheless suspicious about the way in which the national conversation on democratic socialism had largely been about Democratic socialism, that is, about co-opting socialist organizing in the electoral process.

In contrast, as Michael's words highlight, for PS socialism means "independent working-class power." Building working-class power outside of the electoral system is the core of base-building, which is the guiding principle for PS organizing. Lisa explained the main advantage of base-building, contrasting it with running candidates for elections:

> A lot of people want to do. . . . I find it the easy route. . . . Of like doing elections and stuff, which is good, people want to do elections that's okay. But I don't think that should be your only focus. Historically, and also just recently, real change comes from when you do a lot of the base-building kind of work. So that's the kind of work that I think we should be focusing on, personally. Many people want to do elections and stuff, but that's I feel is

more Democratic politics. Because there's not a party . . . like for instance I am not a citizen. None of those parties, I would be able to have any political. . . . I wouldn't be able to vote. But doing the kind of work that I'm doing, I am able to actually move the politics to where I want them to be moved.

Lisa's quote is helpful to highlight two key aspects of the PS base-building approach: first, the idea that "real change" comes from the direct, grassroots mobilization of the working class, and second, that base-building is the only approach that can actually aim to include all of the working class, given the electoral disenfranchisement of marginalized groups. While Lisa pointed out the disenfranchisement of immigrants, other groups are also largely excluded from the electoral process, including many poor voters of color and formerly or currently incarcerated people. The contrast between the inclusive grassroots work of base-building and the exclusionary nature of electoral politics in the United States was also at the core of a chapter that members of PS contributed to a published collection of essays from activists and scholars of the socialist Left (Corcione et al., 2019). In that chapter, PS organizers argued that "pursuing an exclusive electoral strategy" essentially makes it impossible to engage with working-class people who cannot vote (or do not want to); in contrast, base-building aims to create a working-class movement capable of seizing power for itself: "We build power outside the electoral system by creating our own institutions and programs. And it is through these, not primarily through electoral efforts, that we build a mass for socialist politics. Our projects directly meet people's material needs by 'serving the people and fighting the power'" (Corcione et al., 2019). While "serving the people" is accomplished through the numerous projects put in place by PS, "fighting the power" happens through direct action and advocacy. PS credits the Black Panther Party for inspiring its dual power approach of "serving the people/fighting the power" (Corcione et al., 2019). To this day, the PTU remains the best example of PS's success in bridging direct action and political campaigning: while the PTU promotes direct actions against landlords, such as eviction protections, it also puts pressure on elected officials to pass legislation that can help everyone in the city, such as the 2019 "Good Cause" bill, which protects tenants in short-term leases against arbitrary eviction (see Corcione et al., 2019). The success of PS also inspired other local socialist organizations, which came together in 2017 to create a US-wide socialist organization focused on base-building, called Marxist Center, which is now defunct (Horras, 2022).

But what does base-building look like in practice? In articles penned by a member of PS, it is described as "door-knocking, one-on-one conversations, serving the immediate needs of the masses, fighting the power of local oppressors alongside them" (Horras, 2017b) and as "organizing the unorganized" (Horras, 2017a). All the projects promoted by Philly Socialists operate under the umbrella of base-building. To make these projects work, PS members have created an elaborate organizational structure that brings together the centralization that is typical of socialist organizations with an attention to horizontal practices that resonates with neo-anarchist movements. They also built a complex multiplatform communication system that helps them communicate with each other and with the public.

A MULTIMEDIA STRATEGY FOR ORGANIZING

PS has created a complex organizational structure to manage its many activities; its members operate with a relatively high degree of decentralization while still maintaining the typical leadership structure of a socialist group. Figure 7 provides an explanation of the different elected positions within PS (at the time of my research): the Central Committee (CC), which during my fieldwork included two cochairs instead of one chair, and the arbiters.

A 2018 restructuring turned the CC into a task-based leadership body in which each elected member has an assigned set of responsibilities, as can be seen in figure 7; it also added three rotating at-large members to the CC, who are randomly selected from the dues-paying membership to serve for a period of three months. The membership also elects two arbiters, who serve independently from the CC; according to the PS Constitution, they are "responsible for accepting formal complaints (grievances) and handling appeals" and can be approached by any member "to help resolve an interpersonal conflict" among members (Philly Socialists, 2017, art. II (F)).

However, this codified structure of elected positions coexists with more horizontal processes, influenced by neo-anarchist practices. Per the

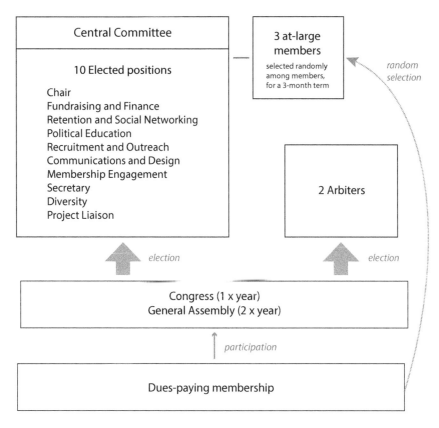

Figure 7. Leadership positions and selection procedure, PS. *Source*: 2017 Constitution (Philly Socialists, 2017) and interviews conducted with members of the organization.

Constitution, members can create autonomous groups and affinity groups (Philly Socialists, 2017, art. 3(B)). The General Assembly is run by facilitators, not by CC members or the cochairs. Working groups and caucuses— such as the Dolphin Caucus, which welcomes members who are not cisgender heterosexual men, and the Ability Caucus, open to members with disabilities—also operate in a less hierarchical way (e.g., they meet whenever they choose to meet and do not have elected leaders). While PS retains a centralized leadership structure, each project is managed by a working group, which can choose how to operate; this work is largely carried out in a decentralized way. In addition, the different student branches (at Penn, Temple, and Drexel), as well as the PTU, operate as separate entities from Philly Socialists proper. Michael joked that PS was "the most anarchist socialist organization" he had ever encountered. Jokes aside, even if they do not acknowledge it explicitly, it is clear that PS members blend traditional socialist structures (such as the Central Committee) with elements of neo-anarchist horizontality (Taylor, 2013), which are more familiar to younger generations of activists who have been involved with the Occupy movement or other recent movements.

The intricate organizational structure of PS is mirrored in an equally complex set of technological practices across multiple types of media. Its external communication relies on corporate social media (Facebook, Twitter, and Instagram); a website (www.phillysocialists.org); and the *Philadelphia Partisan*, its self-produced magazine and blog. It also uses mailing lists, housed on Nationbuilder, and phone banking. Three actors coordinate the external communication across these different channels: a director of communications, an elected member of the Central Committee who coordinates a media team tasked specifically with managing media relations; a social media team; and the editorial collective of the *Partisan*.

The PS website hosts information about who PS members are, how to join the organization, and how to get involved in the projects; it includes links to various social media pages and discussion groups of PS, as well as links that allow users to pay membership dues or make a donation to the organization. The main purpose of the website, according to the interviewees, is to come up in Google searches: "So our website is mainly for people who Google us. It's like, 'Oh I want to know socialists in Philly'. . . . If anybody is interested in socialists in Philadelphia, this is what they're going to find" (Lisa). PS's approach to the website is very pragmatic and in stark contrast with how LUMe activists talked about creating and maintaining a website as a political practice.

The bulk of the external communication of PS happens through corporate social media: Facebook, Instagram, and Twitter. At the time of my fieldwork, the Facebook page of PS was by far the most active of the profiles: it was used to post memes, invite people to meetings and events, and share and comment news items. The Instagram profile is mainly used to visually document the activities of the organization, including with the "Stories" function, through which PS provides short videos of its events and organizing work. The Twitter account is less active; Michael commented on the fact that he would like to see it used more: "I think we should be focusing more on Twitter, if we could, but we don't have anybody who's like a Twitter monster." Although Twitter and Instagram are also considered important, it is Facebook that provides the most useful tools to PS, including the Event feature and the discussion groups, which I examine when describing PS's internal communication practices.

Despite the high volume of content posted by PS pages and its intensive use of Facebook Events, interviewees report that there is no specific social media strategy: "Basically, it's like we just post so much that eventually it ends up building our social media following" (Michael). The different social media accounts are managed by the social media team; the interviewees explained that different members tend to "specialize" in one of the platforms, but there is overlap between the people who manage the different accounts. Lisa reported that the Facebook account, in particular, has almost twenty administrators, given the amount of work that tending to that platform requires. Similarly to LUMe, members of the social media team are not bound by any particular rules when posting.

PS started publishing its quarterly alternative magazine, the *Philadelphia Partisan*, in 2017. Its print version is a visually appealing, colorful, sixteen-page stitched booklet, which PS distributes for free at its events and at coffeeshops in Philadelphia; a digital version, supplemented by blog posts, is available on the *Partisan*'s website and shared via the dedicated Facebook and Twitter accounts. Publishing in print has been historically important for socialists, but PS tries to make the *Partisan* appealing to people who would not otherwise be interested in a social movement publication or in radical politics, to cover issues related to Philadelphia, and to do so without the jargon that so often characterizes socialist publications. It is not a theory journal, but a well-designed and accessibly written magazine.

Finally, PS also communicates with potentially interested people (those who gave their contact information) via a mailing list and phone calls. After volunteering my contact information at an open meeting, I received regular newsletters with updates about the organization and its projects, usually every week. The newsletters were written in an informal tone and included reminders of upcoming assemblies and events, accompanied by social media links (usually to the Facebook Events of the gathering being promoted). I also received phone calls (and voicemail messages), which invited me to or reminded me of events. Phone calls are made by PS organizers during ad hoc "cadre" meetings. PS manages people's contact information and sends newsletters through Nationbuilder, which is a customer relationship management (CRM) tool developed for election campaigns; it is nonpartisan and has been used by different parties and a variety of causes (McKelvey & Piebiak, 2016, p. 902). While its appeal lies in its all-encompassing nature (McKelvey & Piebiak, 2016), PS has found that it does not live up to expectations: "It's basically just like a giant contact database with tags and that's all it does for us, so it feels like a lot of money to pay for just that" (Amy).

What I just described as the discrete use of different communication technologies should actually be understood as part of a multimedium, multistep strategy for recruitment and retention that Philly Socialists has perfected over the years. Lisa explained this in detail during the interview:

> On a regular month, we have what will be like a recruitment kind of like event. We will go table to a festival or do something. And then we would do what's called a "Cadre Meeting," where we call those new people that we get information from and then we invite them to an event that is either on Facebook or something. And then after that we invited to that event, then we have retention kind of thing which would be a social. So that's how we usually do it. And then the social and those events will be usually on Facebook and things because it's easy. You have the map, they can easily find the map, they have all the information on there. So, it's part of a whole plan thing. It works pretty good, I think.

As can be seen in the quote, the recruitment process blends online and offline components. PS organizers collect contact information at events where they set up a table with information about the organization; they then follow up through phone calls with the people who left their contact details, inviting them to an upcoming event, which they can typically also find advertised on Facebook. Besides the event—which would usually be either connected to the different projects or an open assembly—people are also invited to a social gathering, such as a picnic, a potluck at an organizer's house, or a concert in a bar. In a document that contains organizing tips compiled by PS, the organization outlined its recruitment and retention strategies (Philly Socialists, 2018b). The tips include a detailed explanation of best practices for tabling; among those is the advice to focus on collecting phone numbers rather than email addresses, because "phone calls to invite new recruits to meetings and events [have] proven to be the most successful way to get people in the door once they sign up/express interest" (Philly Socialists, 2018b, p. 6). Retention is obviously not just about calling interested individuals, but rather entails creating a steady stream of activities of different kinds that people can join to get involved with the organization: (1) "regular meetings, events, projects to keep people involved"; (2) "political education events to build a shared culture and understand the diversity of opinions and approaches on the Left"; and (3) "socials to create strong ties within the organization" (Philly Socialists, 2018b, p. 6).

The extensive web of external communication practices of PS should thus be framed in the context of this recruitment-retention process. Seen through this lens, the intense social media production of PS is less about expressing how the group feels about different political issues and more about drawing in as many potentially interested people as possible. Michael articulated this with a metaphor:

> I always think of social media as the dragnet, it's the big net that you cast to bring in as many people to your circle as possible, and then the job of an organizer is to be like a good fisherman of people, I guess like Jesus. . . . And it's like, go through that dragnet and pick out . . . throw away the bad fish and some fish will slip through, but make sure you catch the right fish.

Tabling at events and posting on social media serve the same aim, according to Michael: helping PS drag in as many people as possible. However, the organizing work only begins once people have been caught in the its net and can then be involved in the work of the organization. The highly structured nature of the recruitment-retainment process comes into play in PS's technological imaginary; in fact, it is the idea of "organizing," predicated on this recruitment-retainment process, that allows the group to imagine its use of internet technologies as only one aspect of its political work.

Once interested individuals become members of PS, they find that the organization uses an equally complex multiplatform approach to communicate internally. In particular, PS employs Facebook groups (some secret, some public but closed), internal listservs hosted on Google groups, Signal, Slack, and informal messaging through texting and Facebook Messenger.[2] PS has seventeen Facebook groups; the most important is a secret one, called the "Discussion group." In the interview, Donna reported that this internal group includes seven hundred members and feels "more personal" than the Facebook page of PS; Lisa also explained that it is used to debate all sorts of topics. Michael detailed the kinds of posts that get shared in the discussion group: memes, reminders about events, articles, updates from ongoing actions (such as the Occupy ICE protests), and "general calls for last minute help." On the PS website, the "secret" nature of the group is explained thus: "Unfortunately, the group is 'secret' to avoid a massive influx of requests and to make sure that the group is mostly people who are interested in supporting our work" (Philly Socialists, n.d.). The other Facebook groups have a more specific target, either a specific project (e.g., the community garden or the Design collective) or a specific group of organizers (e.g., the nonwhite caucus).

Crucial to the internal communication of PS is also the "strategy" listserv, which all members (and only members) should subscribe to. This listserv is seen as a key avenue to spread information within PS, discuss what the organization should do (hence the "strategy" label), pitch ideas, and remind people of upcoming events. The other platforms that PS utilizes in its internal communication are Slack, a cloud-based collaboration tool, and Signal, a privacy-oriented encrypted messaging app. Members also often talk about "messaging" each other, but they don't clarify whether this means using a specific app or just text messages.

A GOOD ENOUGH SPACE FOR NOW . . .

Given this complex multimedia strategy, how does PS make sense of its relationship to digital technologies? In the interviews, members argued that the internet can be a relatively good space for socialist politics, in particular because it makes it easier to spread information and to organize events, since people already use digital technologies for other reasons. They are not enthusiastic about using corporate social media for politics or in their personal lives, but they highlight the useful features of these platforms. While the interviewees also consider "the internet" more broadly, they tend to focus on Facebook, as already highlighted in the case of LUMe. For instance, Michael argued that "most socialist groups don't have independent, fleshed out, comprehensive communication structures. And Facebook just offers that to us. So, we're just trying to . . . in the absence of having something built, this is like what we're gonna use." Facebook thus functions as a universal platform that supports organizing. Donna echoed Michael's words and claimed: "I think that part of organizing is making connections and getting information and spreading information. I think Facebook is one of the best tools we have for it right now." As in the case of LUMe, Facebook looms large in the PS technological imaginary.

Several interviewees praised the internet for its usefulness in making information more accessible and organizing more efficient. Tyler compared the internet to earlier technologies:

> Technology, overall, is much more helpful. I was very fortunate to have mentors who came up in the movement in the '80s and '90s. At that time, if you wanted somebody to come to a rally, you had to call them. If they weren't around, they didn't have answering machines, so you had to actually physically meet them. It was more difficult to move people.

Although Tyler had no direct experience of pre-internet organizing, his sense was that coordinating people was much harder without digital technologies. Lisa argued that the internet is particularly good for information sharing. Donna echoed Lisa's remarks:

> I definitely feel like I have had more access to information and more involvement in radical politics through the internet, especially like . . . like I'll literally just add random people who have good mutual friends on Facebook. You know, people who I would've never met before and I think it's also really helpful for those of us who have like chronic medical conditions and yeah, confronting ableist ideas of organizing where you have to be like out all the time, while not all of us can. So, I think it's been really helpful with that.

In relaying experiences with digital technologies and radical politics, Donna underlined the importance of the internet for people who have disabilities and chronic conditions that limit their possibility of being physically present. According to Donna, digital technologies thus help challenge the ableist assumptions about participation that still shape politics. Donna further underscored this point by adding: "As someone who's episodically both mentally and physically disabled, like, I think technology is honestly one of the saving parts of community for me." Alexander, who has been part of several leftist organizations besides PS, also contended that the internet has been empowering for radical politics:

> There are people who are far away from anyone else that shares their same concerns, far away geographically, so meeting face to face is hard, or they have children, or they have physical disabilities, or they're kind of like me, fairly introverted, so I'm not gonna go to social meetings so much.

For Alexander, the internet can thus allow radical groups to be more inclusive for those who, for different types of reasons, cannot always commit to physically participating.

According to the interviewees, the reason digital technologies—and Facebook in particular—are so effective for information dissemination and organizing is that people already use them, whether they are interested in activism or not. That "people are already there," that is, on social media, is a mantra repeated by PS interviewees (as well as by LUMe activists, as seen in chapter 4). Michael spelled it out in these terms: "People are on Facebook, people are on Twitter, they don't wanna switch." Alexander concurred:

> You should just be using Facebook. It's where everyone is. You go to the people; you don't try and build your own platform. So, for me it's always that, I use Facebook because it's what everybody else uses, and you wanna get a message out, Facebook's really good for getting a message out.

Because Facebook is where people are, socialists should be using Facebook to recruit and spread information. PS members seem to have taken this idea to heart, given how much of their internal and external communication is channeled through Facebook.

In sum, the PS interviewees felt that, although digital technologies, and especially Facebook, have very clear problems, they are so useful and efficient that organizers cannot afford not to use them: "Right now, those social media platforms seem like the easiest, best tools that we have." (Michael)

BUT NOT AN IDEAL SPACE

Although PS members endorse the use of digital technologies by social-ist groups, interviewees point out the limitations of these platforms. Lisa fully expressed how PS regards digital technologies as good enough, but not ideal:

> I think it's a great space for radical politics. I think it gives people a lot of ac-cess to different ideas that they didn't hear before, but it also can be a little toxic. People can get a little . . . can try to debate online. I personally don't think it's the best space for debates.

PS members raised three main criticisms of digital technologies: as seen in Lisa's quote, that they can be toxic and are not good spaces for debate, unlike the offline world, and also that they can be used for surveillance. The first criticism raised by the PS interviewees was the perceived toxicity of digital spaces and the meanness they experienced in these spaces. Lisa explained:

> Most of our followers . . . a lot of them are very far left and if you post the most. . . . We had people who just don't like the memes, or they will just com-plain. Sometimes we have a lot of right-wing people leave really mean . . . people who have the opposite of the politics, or who are too far into the poli-tics and it's like, "Oh that's like not Marxist enough," or something like that. But that's just silly, that's harmless. But then there is people who are going through our stuff and they would try to haze our members or people who comment on our things because they have the opposite politics.

As Lisa explained, PS members have to navigate both "purist" attacks from people who perceive them as not Marxist enough and harassment from right-wing users. Donna, who is part of the social media team, also recounted how often they see "reactionary content" as well as actual hate speech when managing the PS Facebook page: "I think you always get the trolls, and you always get like Nazis coming in and like trying to say whatever bullshit or a lot of transphobic people." Michael also said that social media are "very toxic" and that "sometimes people are just mean. I don't know. And social media creates social distance that allows you to be meaner." Lisa also spoke of how mean people can be online: "It's just like the worst of people comes out. They're just really mean." Alexander concurred: "If you start debating people you don't know, it goes downhill really quick".

But it is not just individuals who disagree with the politics of PS who can be "mean" online. Digital media facilitate meanness even among PS members. As Alexander argued:

> If you start debating over something, Trotsky, Marx, Lenin, you know, should we work with the unions or focus on something else? Then it becomes a lot harder. So, having a discussion on proposals like what do the Philly Socialists do can become pretty messy. Yeah. So, the other thing, and I. . . . So, it reinforces the gender dynamics in the organization, and the dominance. Like men, I think us men have an even easier time dominating online discussions than they do in person discussions, and they dominate both, so. . . . And also, people of color.

Alexander's words suggest that online spaces, especially when used to debate strategy or political positions, can become unruly and end up replicating existing inequalities; in particular, he found that white men are very comfortable in online spaces and that this results in women and people of color having an even harder time in online discussions.

The second limitation of the internet identified by interviewees is its inability to generate the same kind of connections that can be fostered offline. The organizers mostly talked about this in terms of the impossibility of truly debating ideas online. For instance, Lisa, who talked about how mean and toxic people can be, concluded: "I can have the same debates with people in real life and I feel that it's more interesting, it's more engaging." Similarly, Alexander argued that in social movements "most of the decisions are made face to face. And that's when you can really get the debate and the discussion. People actually listen to each other face to face, I think, a lot more." He concluded: "you don't want to build a base online. It's just a waste of time."

Echoing Alexander, other interviewees remarked on how the internet cannot be the only space where organizing happens, because the offline world is still crucial. Michael explained:

> The reality is that our lives are not lived on social media, our lives are lived. . . . [A]n eviction occurs in real life, it doesn't occur on social media. Like losing your job occurs in real life, sexual assault and sexual abuse, that

occurs in real life not in social media. And so, we need to be able to. . . . [I]f all your organizing is online, then I do think that you will inherently run into this issue of "how do I know that you'll show up in the real life where my real problems are?"

The distinction drawn by Michael between online activities and "real life" offline is also shared by others. In his explanation, organizing cannot be an entirely online activity because the challenges that people face—evictions, joblessness, sexual harassment—have a strong bodily and material component; because these problems happen offline, organizing also needs to happen offline, so that people will know that PS will be physically there for them. This quote reveals how PS members think of the internet as an inferior space compared to the offline spaces of meetings and protest actions; it also highlights the assumptions about embodiment and materiality that support the kind of ableist conceptions of political activism that Donna, for instance, criticized.

The third major criticism of digital technologies brings to the fore their potential for surveillance. The interviewees mostly thought of surveillance in terms of law enforcement, not corporate, surveillance; they worried that using social media might expose them to US law enforcement agencies. Tyler talked about how people involved in social movements worry about being surveilled: "There's a lot of security concerns, right? Concerns about being able to track people. Being able to . . . the government being able to spy on them, which are legitimate." Lisa reported how she and other prominent Philly Socialists organizers receive "a lot of fake friend requests from fake people" on Facebook; she believes these fake profiles are managed by cops in order to gain access to closed Facebook groups and to keep an eye on activists whose profiles are not publicly accessible. However, Lisa also said that she is not personally worried, although "people generally worry about surveillance." She added:

> Look, if they wanted to know what we're doing, they already know what we're doing. We are like all over social media. So, if we going to be using social media, which is a very public space, we just have to be upfront with the things that we're doing.

In Lisa's view, social media are so public that no one should have any expectation that their information will not be seen and/or recorded; for an organization like PS, this means being "upfront"—that is, assuming that whatever is said online is fully public and thus also visible to law enforcement. Donna agreed with Lisa's remarks: "Ultimately you should just, like, assume we are being surveilled and like, it's just about not saying illegal shit or that when you're going to do illegal things but using it to make connections." Amy concurred: "Yeah, I have concerns about surveillance, but to me, spending time worrying about them over spending time organizing, it's not a good trade off."

Donna was the only interviewee to weave together Facebook's data collection and law enforcement surveillance. However, as can be seen in the following quote, Donna showed resignation to Facebook's policies:

> I mean of course, like, you give your information to Zuck, the Zuckerberg gods, but it's just like this looming figure that controls all our data but I personally feel pretty able to say whatever the hell I want via Facebook even though I'm sure my FBI agent isn't happy about it, . . . [B]ut yeah, I think technology is overall a good thing as long as you know boundaries, like don't talk about illegal shit. I've had people who've had like FBI agents show up at their work just saying some like, what I would consider like a petty, not a real threat. He said he wanted to punch Donald Trump in the face and the FBI showed up, which sounds like something else was . . . yeah. I think as long as you know boundaries and also know in cases like that what to do, it's ultimately a good thing.

In that long quote, Donna showed how they think of Mark Zuckerberg as an entity in control of all the data of Facebook users, but that they still feel like their freedom of speech is somewhat guaranteed on the platform, as long as they accept specific boundaries, for example, what they can and cannot say. This is striking, particularly because during the interview Donna also explained how they had been unjustly banned by Facebook for a few days. However, the most salient element that emerges in the quote is how Donna has internalized both the need to adhere to Facebook's content policies and the presence of law enforcement monitoring and surveillance on the platform, which leads them to feel free to speak their mind, while actually self-censoring. The joke about making their assigned FBI agent unhappy, coupled with the story about their friend allegedly being investigated for a Facebook message about Trump, points toward the crucial role that surveillance plays in how Donna—and PS members in general—think about digital technologies.

It is important to note that in contrast to LUMe activists, the PS inter-viewees rarely explicitly connected their critique of internet technologies to the corporate, capitalist nature of these platforms. When some of these concerns about the connection between digital platforms and capitalism emerged, they were usually subsumed by the preoccupation with surveil-lance. See, for instance, how Tyler approached the topic:

> The other part of how the internet works is it's channeled through and con-trolled by big corporations, which doesn't usually have the effect of the gov-ernment directly stepping in and censoring us. Although, maybe someday, but more that maybe they hold the keys and can. They have that ability. There's the ability to trace back everything that's happening and identify people, which could be problematic down the road. They have the, more im-portantly, the ability to kind of direct or redirect traffic.

Here Tyler was interested in how big tech corporations control and chan-nel content on the internet, and how that ability can be used for monitor-ing and surveillance of political activities. That internet technologies are powered by processes of data extraction and commodification is not part of the criticism that Tyler waged. In another moment in the interview, Tyler went back to explain how the internet has become very centralized:

> As time has gone on, as anything under capitalism, things become more consolidated. Now you have issues where the vast majority of traffic gets funneled through a couple of websites and that gives enormous power to these, the owners of those websites, whereas before maybe traffic had been more spread out.

Once again, Tyler was concerned with the power of tech corporations insofar as it allows for a concentration of traffic and attention, but he did not question the connection between digital media and capitalism per se.

The scarce presence of a Marxist, political-economic critique of digital technologies does not necessarily mean that PS ignores this aspect. How-ever, when I asked Michael directly about whether there had been any ideological opposition to social media within the organization, along an anti-capitalist line, he replied that these are not the kinds of discussions about digital technologies that the members have. He then explained:

> I don't think we think about it at the level of. . . . [W]e're not thinking,
> I don't think most . . . any of us are thinking about it at the level of, these are
> the tools of capital and therefore we shouldn't use them. It's kind of like . . .
> I mean, is it a little . . . is it wrong? I feel like a little bit, there are a lot of tools
> of capital that we need to use, because the tools of capital are really effective.
> The tools of capital are used really effectively to oppress us and to control us,
> and it goes back to the thing of you don't have. . . . [I]t's not about whether
> or not you like it or not, it's what does it take to compete and beat the capi-
> talists? And I'm in this game to win, and I'm willing to use whatever tools
> I need to win.

According to Michael, PS is not really interested in discussing how digital media are part of a capitalist system and thus how utilizing them might be inconsistent with its ideological beliefs. For Michael, the fact that digital media are "tools of capital" means that they are effective and that they must be used to compete with the capitalists. In contrast to LUMe activists, whose imaginary of negotiation is at the center of prolonged discussions in the collective, PS members appear unconflicted about the necessity to use "the tools of capital." Tyler even dismissed this conundrum by saying that it is not a concern for socialists:

> There is like a . . . more on the anarchist left, there is more of a Luddite ele-
> ment that some people, but not all of them certainly, share. That's not really
> been a big part of the socialist movement more broadly or communists don't
> really share that.

By calling these concerns "Luddite," a label that holds a traditionally negative connotation among socialists, Tyler downplayed the relevance of refusing to use technology for anti-capitalist reasons, rather than seriously considering it as a possibility. Thus, while PS is aware that digital technologies have negative sides, it does not even entertain the idea that using these tools might be rife with contradictions.

NEGOTIATION: ORGANIZING WHERE PEOPLE ARE

> I mean, yeah, I'm more than well aware that social media is
> not designed for social relationships and not designed at all
> for socialists. But until the day comes. . . . I mean I always say

the Communist party in China, they have their own little
app. Until the day comes where like Philly Socialists can do
something like that, where we can build our own apps and
we can build our own social media platforms. . . . And until
we have that kind of organizing capacity, and those kind of
resources, I have to work with what I have. Like I'm not
gonna give up email because Google runs email. I'm not
gonna give up my cell service because the capitalists run cell
service. That's just how I feel, you gotta use the tools you got.
(Michael)

This quote from Michael expresses the core of the activist technological
imaginary of PS: the idea that socialists should organize where people
are, even if this means organizing on social media. As discussed, digital
technologies are far from being an ideal space for radical politics because
of law enforcement surveillance, the toxic nature of some of these online
environments, and digital technologies do not offer the same possibility
for interaction as offline spaces. And yet, as Michael eloquently argued,
in the absence of other technological capabilities, socialists *have* to use
digital technologies, and social media in particular. They are not ideal,
but they might just be good enough—for now—to recruit people into the
socialist camp.

I label this activist technological imaginary "organizing where people
are" to encapsulate how PS conceptualizes its technological practices as
directed at reaching people where they already are, even if that means less
than ideal spaces like mainstream social media. But "organizing where
people are" also captures how the organization strategically draws on the
notion of organizing to frame its technological practices—and its reliance
on corporate technologies—as just one aspect of a much more complicated online-offline strategy for organizing.

"Organizing where people are" is an imaginary of negotiation. PS does
not subscribe to the principles that underpin the dominant technological
imaginary of Silicon Valley. It is clear that for PS, digital technologies are
not a space of freedom or liberation, as evidenced by their toxicity and the
threat of surveillance; these technologies are also not the solution to any
social or political problems, as the interviewees repeated in the interviews.

And while, as shown earlier, PS does not articulate a particularly strong critique of the relationship between capitalism and Silicon Valley, it nevertheless identifies digital technologies as tools of capital and the ruling classes. Despite disagreeing with the dominant technological imaginary of Silicon Valley in its three key aspects, PS employs the digital technologies of Silicon Valley in its organizing work—not just corporate social media, but also Google Groups, Slack, and NationBuilder, which, as McKelvey and Piebiak (2016) argued, emerged out of the culture and venture capital of Silicon Valley (p. 903). In the interviews, members tended to downplay the importance of these technologies for their organizing work, but my analysis of their technological practices clearly shows that they rely on these tools extensively.

A longer quote from Michael illuminates how this imaginary of negotiation unfolds:

> It's kind of like we're in competition with the ruling class, and if the ruling class is using this tool and that tool is productive then we have to be at the same level as them in terms of being able to compete with them. So, somebody can come up to me and say, "Oh, yeah but it was so much easier or better to organize before there was all this chatter from social media," and I'd be like, "Yeah, sure. Tough." Well guess what, whether or not it was better or worse or things are easier or harder, if we wanna compete, we have to be on the internet. That's just it. The idea that you wouldn't be organizing on Facebook or you wouldn't be. . . . [L]ike some people wouldn't be on Twitter or stuff like that, it's silly. It's ultra-left, or it's not even ultra-left, it's just nonsensical. So, I don't think things are. . . . I don't know if I would think of the internet as a good tool, I would just think of it as a necessary tool.

Michael's quote detailed how PS members negotiate their technological practices, based on Facebook, Twitter, and other corporate technologies, and their dislike of these platforms. He dismissed the idea of not using corporate social media as "ultra-left" and/or simply nonsensical. He contextualized the use of these platforms in the political competition between socialist organizers and the ruling class: if the ruling class relies on Silicon Valley's technologies, why shouldn't socialists do the same?

To make sense of this negotiation, PS draws strategically on the notion of organizing. The imaginary of "organizing where people are" allows the group to explain its use of corporate technologies as in service of organizing and to contextualize its reliance on corporate technologies within more complex organizing practices directed at recruiting, retaining, and mobilizing people. PS strongly rejects the technologically deterministic idea that social problems can be solved through the development of (new) technologies, one of the core ideas of Silicon Valley's technological imaginary. For PS, it is only slow and consistent organizing on the ground that can bring about the kind of social change the group is interested in: a socialist moment and (eventually) a socialist society. Approaching digital technologies through the lens of organizing allows Philly Socialists to negotiate its relationship with capitalist technologies and incorporate them within its political practice.

PS' strategic use of the notion of organizing anchors its technological practices to its ideological commitment to base-building (ideology); it places the group's negotiation of corporate technologies within a long trajectory of socialist politics (political context); and it creates a clear demarcation between PS and what it perceives to be the dominant technological imaginary of the American Left, what it calls "activist networking."

Ideology

The PS imaginary of "organizing where people are" casts its technological practices in service of its political commitment to base-building: organizing to build working-class power outside of the electoral system. As explained in this chapter, base-building is the crucial strategy embraced by PS, which guides its organizational practices and brings together its many projects. Base-building is what the group believes distinguishes it from other socialist organizations (chiefly the DSA). Within the perspective of base-building, organizing relies on fostering people's involvement, getting people to show up and to keep showing up. PS primarily channels its commitment to base-building through its projects, as explained earlier in the chapter. But this ideological orientation also comes through in how PS members explain their use of technology: as one aspect of their complex organizing practices, which are in service of base-building. Throughout the interviews, it was evident that the members rationalized "using social media despite the fact that we don't like them," to use Michael's words, by downplaying their importance in the life of the organization and contextualizing their use within their multiplatform organizing strategy for base-building. Notice, for instance, how Lisa explained that Facebook is only a small part of the PS organizing process:

> Yeah [Facebook is] definitely very useful, but it doesn't yield the same kind of results in real life. Because you could have 10,000 followers, but those 10,000 people are not going to show up to your event. So, you still have to do the social media kind of thing to kind of bring attention to the things that you're doing, but also . . . Because people come through social media, but we also do a lot of tabling, we do a lot of phone calls, we do a lot of emails, and we're always encouraging people to follow us or by sharing stuff. We use the social media together with the recruitment kind of like strategies. It's not on itself, otherwise we'd just be like a meme page because we wouldn't. . . . So, if we didn't have an event to invite people on the Facebook, those 10,000 followers would be kind of useless.

In Lisa's words we can trace a way of thinking about Facebook and other digital media as a component in a recruitment and organizing process that takes place online, but most importantly offline. Lisa also underlined how only relying on Facebook for their political activity would be like being a "meme page"; while PS members generally like leftist memes and share quite a few on their own Facebook page, Lisa made it clear that there is a difference between posting political content on Facebook and *actually* organizing. Michael supported her point of view, saying:

> People have this tendency to just post on our Facebook group for help, and it's like that's not how organizing works. Organizing works when you . . . you have to reach out to those people who are on the fringe and pull them in, and that's a lot of the work that you're doing, and that requires meeting people in person. Going past the social media wall and building an organic connection with them.

In line with the quote from Lisa, Michael explained how, however tempting it might be to consider posting on Facebook as a form of organizing, the work of building connections is what really matters, and that work needs to happen outside of social media. Thinking of digital media as one piece of more elaborate strategies of organizing for base-building allows PS to negotiate its relationship to the digital technologies of Silicon Valley: members use their commitment to the notion of organizing to make sense of how they rely on corporate technologies, despite not liking them.

Political Context

Drawing on the notion of organizing also allows PS members to understand themselves and their technological practices within a longer history of socialist politics. The appeal to the legacy of socialist organizing is evident in many aspects of their work; from the Central Committee to cadre meetings, it is clear that the group explicitly references key socialist practices, even as it adopts more flexible organizational structures. PS also nods to the socialist tradition in its visual iconography and in the keywords it adopts. The slogan "serve the people, fight the power," which Philly Socialists employs to talk about base-building, was used by different New Left groups, and especially the Black Panther Party, which are an inspiration for PS in general; the first part of the slogan, "serve the people," comes from a 1948 speech by Mao Zedong (1967).

This acknowledgment of the international history of socialist organizing also guides how PS negotiates its relationship to digital technologies. In the previous section I showed how Michael explained that the group has turned to corporate technologies in the absence of resources that would allow it to build its own apps or comprehensive communication strategy; to clarify his line of thought, he contrasted PS with the Communist Party in China, who "have their own little app," because they have the "organizing capacity" and the "kind of resources" that allow them to build such technology. I doubt that Michael would truly want to compare PS with the Chinese Communist Party, but his example is interesting because it shows that other socialist actors are points of reference for how PS members conceptualize their relationship to technology. This juxtaposition of PS's technological practices with other socialist organizations' practices becomes even more explicit in Tyler's words:

> Every revolutionary movement takes advantage of the technologies they have. If you read about the Bolsheviks and the Mensheviks back in the day they would smuggle in printing presses and they would set them up. Then being able to get their political . . . to articulate their politics was a really important component of what they did. They used the technology that was

most accessible to them and most efficient. However, obviously, 100 years technology has changed so the groups . . . some still, they try to sell their newspapers and that's not really, we think, the most effective approach.

Tyler compared PS's technological practices to those of the revolutionary socialist movements of the early twentieth century; in this comparison, social media are for PS what the printing press was to the Communist revolutionaries in 1917. Tyler directly placed PS's use of corporate technology in a long historical trajectory of socialist organizing. The lesson that he drew from that history is a specific one: the need for socialists to use the "most accessible" and "most efficient" technology available, whatever it may look like. This appeal to the socialist heritage thus further contributes to the PS imaginary of negotiation, by contextualizing its relationship to technology within a socialist history that is imagined as entailing the use of (capitalist) technologies in the service of organizing for revolution.

Other Technological Imaginaries

The third factor that shapes PS's imaginary of negotiation is its strong critique of what it perceives to be the prevalent technological imaginary in contemporary American leftist circles. The group calls it "activist networking."[3] By that, PS means something akin to "lifestyle activism" (Johnson et al., 2012; Portwood-Stacer, 2013a); the group understands this as an attitude toward activism that is very individualized and focused on self-expression, as opposed to organizing. See, for instance, how a member of PS explained this idea in an article that makes the case for base-building: "Activist networking is what might be called lifestyle activism, in the sense of individuals who form their identity around being an activist and derive the majority of their social life from activism. These are the type of people who do not engage with, are not comfortable around and are not friends with non-activists or non-theory types, and whose weekly and monthly schedules are a busybody itinerary of meetings, discussion groups, protests, and conferences" (Horras, 2017a, para. 9). Activist networking, as defined by Horras, is more concerned with giving a social identity to individual activists than it is with organizing for social change (or revolution). This is one of the reasons PS advocates for base-building and does not describe its members as activists, but rather as organizers.[4]

While digital technologies are not the focus of Horras's explanation, I argue that "activist networking" carries a specific technological imaginary that PS recognizes as opposed to its own. For instance, in July 2018 the PS Facebook page posted an infographic that circulated widely in leftist online spaces, including leftist Reddit (e.g., r/stupidpol), and contrasted two idealtypes: "cool kids" and "organizers" (with the implicit endorsement of the category of organizers, of course) (Philly Socialists, 2018d). The image generally conveyed the point that "cool kids" are activists interested in cultivating their own individual identity and popularity, while "organizers" do the tough work of building grassroots power. For instance, while "cool kids" "talk about working class people" and "present in a ways [*sic*] that signify they are 'political,'" organizers "talk to working class people" and "present as approachable to the people they want to organize" (Philly Socialists, 2018d). Crucially, one of the dimensions on which the two categories are compared is use of technologies: while "cool kids" "get people to follow them on social media," organizers "get people to show up IRL [in real life]" (Philly Socialists, 2018d). This infographic, as posted by PS, received more than six hundred Facebook reactions and fifteen hundred shares.

The infographic succinctly reproduced a distinction between offline "real" organizing and online activism, echoing the mainstream debate on slacktivism of the early 2010s (e.g., Gladwell, 2010; Shirky, 2011). This term was often used to question the efficacy of digital activism, depicting it as requiring the lowest possible effort and therefore as ineffective in bringing about change. As Dennis (2019) showed, these popular criticisms of slacktivism rest on flawed assumptions about the relationship between social media, political participation, and political outcomes; one of these assumptions is the "substitution thesis," the idea that slacktivism replaces other forms of activism (Christensen, 2011). However disqualified by subsequent academic research, this idea is clearly echoed in the infographic, which presents a dichotomy between online and offline engagement. It is also echoed in how PS members talk about activist networking, as this quote from Tyler illustrates:

> [The internet] helps to contribute to a culture where people aren't necessarily politically active, or they're out on the street or they're out in their communities but instead they're tweeting from home, or they build a personal

brand or reputation as an individual. Like, "I'm an individual activist"...
but they're not really representing a community. They don't have any real
loyalties or accountability to any community.

In line with the infographic, Tyler characterized this type of activism as
uninterested in community work, replacing meaningful on-the-ground
organizing with individualized online participation. He also, somewhat
harshly, directly linked the use of digital technologies to a narcissistic approach to political activism. In another part of the interview, he added
that "there is kind of a culture of media celebrity that bleeds over into
activism somewhat and that can be a problem." Some of the issues that PS
members point to in their judgment of and opposition to activist networking are indeed meaningful and have been explored in academic work in
nuanced ways. The label "activism" is indeed ambiguous and unsatisfac-
tory (Taylor, 2010, Yang, 2016), and some contemporary forms of activism
have been predicated on a very individualized vision of engagement (Bennett & Segerberg, 2013). The introduction of celebrity dynamics in social
movement spaces has been criticized at least since the 1970s (Freeman,
1972). However, it is evident that for PS, evoking "activist networking" is a
convenient way to make sense of its own technological practices: by criticizing activist networking, the group can better articulate its own technological imaginary of negotiation.

This opposition to activist networking, which is presumed to regard
the use of social media as its crucial political practice, allows PS to make
sense of its adoption of corporate platforms as just one of the tools it uses
to organize more effectively, build a base for socialist politics, and compete
with the ruling class. Tyler made this distinction between PS's practices
and activist networking very explicit:

> We're definitely in favor of using technology, but also there's a tendency
> sometimes among activists to see it as a cure all, especially during the Oc-
> cupy period. Well, if we just get everybody on these forums then we can do
> whatever. Probably somewhat similar to how Five Star became a big thing.
> Occupy was like, there were a lot of people who were techno-utopians. It
> was like if we can have direct democracy online ... and then every.... It's
> not really.... [I]t sort of misses a key component of sociality or social inter-
> action, which is that people need to have bodily presence and face-to-face
> communication is still really important. Yeah, we've kind of avoided that.

Tyler contrasted PS's approach to the "techno-utopian" impulses of other contemporary social movements, including the Occupy Wall Street movement and the Italian Five Star Movement (which Tyler and I talked about during the interview). In Tyler's view, these movements have focused exclusively on online activism, assuming that digital technologies could supplant more tiresome offline processes of organizing. PS, as Tyler concluded, has avoided this overreliance on the digital. The reference to Occupy Wall Street is meaningful, because PS was born around the same time as Occupy and because Occupy has been so influential on contemporary social movements in the United States. Here Tyler chose to remember Occupy as a movement largely skewed toward online-only action and the quest for digital democracy, minimizing the importance of embodied forms of actions, such as the encampments. In this indictment of activist networking, Tyler also clarified that, in the way PS characterizes it, this imaginary is not at all opposed to Silicon Valley's technological imaginary: while oriented toward social justice, it sees digital technologies as the primary vehicle for political engagement, as conducive to democracy, and as offering solutions to social issues. The PS imaginary of negotiation thus rejects both activist networking and Silicon Valley's imaginary; it does so by relying on the notion of organizing to simultaneously justify and downplay the use of digital technologies in service of socialist organizing.

CONCLUSION

The technological imaginary developed by the organizers of PS captures their conceptualization of digital technologies as tools that, although imperfect, can be used to recruit people into socialist politics. They use multiple digital technologies for both internal and external communication, including corporate social network sites and organizational platforms such as Slack and Nationbuilder. For PS organizers, the technologies of Silicon Valley are less than ideal spaces for radical politics. They find them to be toxic spaces, which not only allow political disagreements to turn into abuse, but also sometimes introduce unnecessary meanness into group dynamics; less conducive to debate and solidarity-building compared to offline spaces; and prone to law enforcement surveillance.

However, digital technologies also offer socialists the opportunity to communicate efficiently and to find people where they already are. They are good enough as part of a more complex organizing strategy, one that aims to get people involved in the different projects of the organization and to get them to keep showing up.

Through its technological imaginary, which I have labeled "organizing where people are," Philly Socialists downplays its reliance on corporate digital platforms by framing it as just a small piece of the group's elaborate recruitment and organizing strategy; it justifies the use of these digital technologies by identifying all of its technological practices as "organizing" and insisting on the importance of offline political practices. "Organizing where people are" is an imaginary of negotiation. PS rejects the core of the dominant technological imaginary of Silicon Valley: when members criticize the toxicity and surveillance they find on digital technologies, it is clear that they do not see these as inherently free and democratic; when they downplay their use of digital technologies and emphasize their complex online-offline organizing practices, they clarify that they don't find digital technologies to be the solution to sociopolitical problems; and when they identify digital technologies as tools "of the ruling class," "run by capitalists," they zero in on the normalized neoliberal underpinnings of Silicon Valley. As they reject the imaginary of Silicon Valley, they make sense of their technological practices by seeing them as "organizing"— casting these practices in service of base-building and portraying them as one component of their overall organizing strategy, which spans both the online and the offline.

In the case of PS, the political factors that shape its technological imaginary are its commitment to base-building (ideology); appeal to the heritage of socialist organizing (political context); and strong critique of the technological imaginary of activist networking, which the group sees as prevalent in the US Left (other imaginaries). Base-building, the idea of building working-class power outside of the electoral systems, guides the politics of PS; it is in service of base-building that the group developed its different projects and the elaborate strategies for recruitment and retainment in which its technological practices are embedded. Its reliance on less than ideal, corporate digital technologies is thus justified in light of the need to have a reliable communication infrastructure that can help the group work toward base-building. Through its strategic use of the notion of organizing, the group also shows how its technological imaginary is shaped by the lessons it draws from the long history of socialist organizing—that is, the need to use any available mainstream media technology to disseminate socialist ideas. Members even explicitly compare what corporate social media are for them to what the printing press was for the Russian revolutionaries in 1917. In this way, they make sense of their use of digital technologies by positioning themselves and their technological practices in a long-term trajectory of socialist politics. Within this historical trajectory, relying on mainstream technologies allows PS to more effectively compete with the ruling class. Finally, in drawing on the key word *organizing*, PS also seeks to distinguish its technological imaginary from that connected to activist networking, which is its way of defining some strands of American leftist activism. When members talk about activist networking, they mean something close to "lifestyle activism" (Johnson et al., 2012; Portwood-Stacer, 2013a), but also akin to the strawman of slacktivism (Gladwell, 2010); they characterize activist networking as individualistic, even narcissistic, and entirely focused on digital-only, intangible actions. PS's notion of organizing allows it to reject the idea of activist networking and justify its use of corporate digital media not as a narcissistic practice, but as one grounded in effective organizing work. Base-building, the heritage of socialist organizing, and the rejection of activist networking thus shape how PS constructs its technological imaginary and negotiates its use of Silicon Valley's technologies.

6 Conclusion

This book looks at the contested politics of digital technologies through the eyes of leftist social movement activists. It shows that activists approach technology in a political way: they think and talk about technology in relation to their political ideas and their political goals. They also understand that mainstream digital technologies have a politics of their own—that these technologies originating from Silicon Valley are the expression of a specific way of looking at the world, which may or may not be compatible with how activists think about the world. Activist technological imaginaries are how these activists respond to the politics of Silicon Valley and how they envision digital technologies in their struggles for social justice. By centering the discursive, imaginative work of social movements, this book offers a window into how activists experience the politics of digital technologies in their day-to-day lives, their power and their limits.

Activists have long been exposed to the dominant imaginary of Silicon Valley, and they respond to it, in different ways, by constructing their own activist imaginaries. I categorize activist technological imaginaries based on whether activists accept or reject the dominant technological imaginary of Silicon Valley and whether they use or refuse the digital technologies of Silicon Valley, distinguishing between imaginaries of appropriation, negotiation, and challenge. Before providing an explanation of the category of challenge, I now consider what appropriation and negotiation can tell us about the political relationship between social movements and digital technologies.

APPROPRIATION

In chapter 3 I reconstructed the technological imaginary of the Hungarian internet tax protests of 2014. I showed that the ways in which the interviewees talked about the internet reproduced classic tropes of Western modernity, which connect technology to equality and development, rationality, and the future, and I explained how these ideas about modernity were strengthened by the mundanity of the internet. I thus theorized the imaginary developed and deployed by the Hungarian activists as *"mundane modernity"*. I suggested that mundane modernity is an imaginary of appropriation, because it embraces the key aspects of the dominant technological imaginary of Silicon Valley and envisions the use of Silicon Valley technologies. I argue that this imaginary of appropriation reinterprets Silicon Valley's imaginary for a postcommunist context, such as that of Hungary, in which the modernity versus tradition cleavage has recently been rediscovered. Further, the fusion of political freedom and market freedom that characterizes Silicon Valley is appealing in a country where the transition promised to simultaneously deliver democracy and prosperity (and ended up not fully achieving either). In this context, the left-liberal Hungarian activists used the technological imaginary of mundane modernity to legitimize their opposition not only to the internet tax but also to the Orbán government in general.

I then argued that this imaginary of appropriation is constructed to respond to the peculiarities of the current Hungarian political context: the return of political cleavages such as modernity versus tradition, pro-West versus anti-West, and cosmopolitanism versus ethnonationalism. I also showed how the ideological commitments of the left-liberal opposition activists can accommodate the tenets of Silicon Valley's dominant imaginary; for instance, while not celebrating neoliberalism, these activists can tolerate neoliberalism as part of a package of Western "liberal" ideas, as a way of opposing Orbán. Finally, I explained how mundane modernity was constructed in opposition to the technological imaginary of illiberal democracy, which is represented by the internet tax itself.

The imaginary of mundane modernity, distilled in the iconic action of raising illuminated phones to the sky, became a recognizable political message not just for the Hungarian opposition, but also for other protests in the CEE region. That action was legible as a political demand exactly because it performed a technological imaginary that appropriates, in a postcommunist context, the visions of technology that form the core of Silicon Valley's imaginary. The fact that lit-up smartphones could become such a clear symbol of a complex bundle of ideas about Western modernity, liberal democracy, and political and market freedom is a testament to the power of technological imaginaries and a sign of the widespread political relevance of Silicon Valley's dominant technological imaginary.

And yet, however politically legible and symbolically strong, this imaginary of mundane modernity did not support the Hungarian activists in creating a full-fledged social movement. Although useful for the short-lived internet tax protests, this imaginary was not enough to sustain the creation of a more stable and sustainable activist infrastructure in opposition to Orbán's government. While there are also specific political conditions that made it difficult for the Hungarian activists to sustain a long-term mass movement, we can nevertheless speculate that the discourses surrounding the internet that were used in the protests were not sufficient to build a broader platform, for instance one centered on social justice. While it is difficult to pinpoint why the creation of a broader movement was not possible, it seems plausible that an imaginary that pitches technology as the solution to the lack of economic development and equality and as a manifestation of rationality might fall short as a catalyzer for a broad political movement. In both Silicon Valley's imaginary and that of mundane modernity, it is the internet, not social mobilization, that is thought to bring about social change. And if that is the case, the imaginary of mundane modernity is in itself unlikely to inspire the kind of imagination that would be necessary to bring together a sustained, large-scale mobilization in the Hungarian political context.

NEGOTIATION

In chapters 4 and 5 I explored how activists construct technological imaginaries of negotiation. Both LUMe and Philly Socialists (PS) reject the core tenets of the dominant technological imaginary of Silicon Valley; at the same time, the technologies of Silicon Valley power their daily activist work. Both groups are thus engaged in a negotiation: they try to make their technological practices fit with their politics, not the politics of Silicon Valley. How this negotiation happens, however, differs between the two movements.

In LUMe's technological imaginary, digital technologies are seen as both flawed and indispensable for social change: these technologies are tools of the system, but they can and should be used to take down the system itself. The Italian activists fiercely criticize digital technologies: they associate them with capitalist power structures, they refuse to see them as democratic spaces, and they question their impact on human interaction. In so doing, they reject Silicon Valley's ideas about the democratic nature of technology, its technosolutionism, and its seamless integration with neoliberalism. However, they employ these technologies for their perceived efficiency and reach, believing them to be unavoidable.

In contrast, the technological imaginary of PS can be summarized as organizing where people are: the PS organizers find digital technologies to be less than ideal, but good enough for recruiting people to the socialist cause. PS offers three major criticisms of digital technologies: they enable law enforcement surveillance, they are toxic, and they are not as supportive of interaction as offline spaces. PS thus also rejects the tenets of the dominant technological imaginary of Silicon Valley; in particular, its members eschew technosolutionist approaches and, as their three aforementioned critiques suggest, they refuse to think of digital media as spaces of democracy and freedom. At the same time, they use a wide range of corporate digital technologies, from Facebook to Slack. Their technological imaginary of negotiation is predicated on a discursive downplaying of the role of corporate digital media in the life of the organization: while organizers use these tools a lot, they prefer to think of them as just a small component of their multiplatform, offline-online organizing process. It is thus the notion of "organizing" that PS organizers rely on to negotiate the meaning of their use of Silicon Valley technologies.

LUMe's imaginary of negotiation is influenced by its Marxist, anti-capitalist orientation, which leads its activists to question how corporate power operates online (ideology); by their position within the long history of Italian occupied social centers, which emphasize the importance of physically occupied political spaces (political context); and by their strong opposition to the technological imaginary of authoritarian sublime (Treré, 2018) of the Five Star Movement (other prominent technological imaginaries). The PS imaginary of negotiation is influenced by the group's commitment to a specific idea of socialism, base-building (ideology); by their understanding of the long history of socialist organizing as reliant on any available mass medium to spread socialist ideas (political context); and by their critique of the technological imaginary of activist networking, which they see as prevalent in the American Left and which they characterize as individualistic and narcissistic (other prominent technological imaginaries).

Although both LUMe and PS end up developing imaginaries of negotiation, which bring together a rejection of Silicon Valley's imaginary with a reliance on Silicon Valley's technologies, these imaginaries are substantially different. Juxtaposing these two different imaginaries of negotiation makes even more evident how the politics of a specific movement shape its technological imaginary; this shows us that activists might respond to Silicon Valley's imaginary in different ways, for instance criticizing or tolerating different aspects of it, and for different reasons. These imaginaries of negotiation highlight both the power of Silicon Valley over how activists approach technology and how Silicon Valley and its technologies can be experienced and perceived differently by activists, based on their specific political conditions.

CHALLENGE

The third type of response to Silicon Valley's dominant technological imaginary that I have theorized in this book is that of *challenge*: the simultaneous rejection of the imaginary and the technologies of Silicon Valley.

This type of technological imaginary seems more difficult to find among contemporary social movements, given how much activists have come to rely on corporate digital media. When I discussed the contradictions of negotiation with the activists of both LUMe and PS, some of them mentioned the possibility of challenge. In the case of LUMe, challenge was represented by older activists of other social centers, who refused to use Facebook in their activism. In the case of PS, the imaginary was evoked in one of the first projects that the organization tried to set up (and did not manage to finalize): the creation of a "free socialist internet," a non-commercial mesh network, to be built and maintained by PS, that would provide internet access to people outside of corporate internet service providers (ISPs). Yet these inklings of challenge seemed unfeasible, for different reasons, to both LUMe and PS: LUMe activists dismissed the anti-Facebook stances of older activists as inward-looking, and PS recognized the technical difficulty of creating its own mesh network and abandoned the project.

If we look at the literature, however, we can begin to identify attempts to reject Silicon Valley technologies that might qualify as challenge, in that—we can speculate—they are motivated by a rejection of the technological imaginary of Silicon Valley. Imaginaries of challenge can further be divided into two subgroups: in the first one, challenge entails abstaining from the use of Silicon Valley's technologies; in the second, challenge takes the form of the imagination and creation of technologies that are alternative to Silicon Valley's.

The first subcategory, challenge as refusal, has recently become the object of academic interest (Fish, 2017; Hesselberth, 2018; Kaun & Treré, 2018). While the topic of technology nonuse has been more widely considered as an individual action (Hesselberth, 2018; Portwood-Stacer, 2013b), Kaun and Treré (2018) sought to investigate what they call "disconnection—for example, the choice not to use certain platforms or technologies—and how it can be adopted by social movements as a political practice. While they develop a typology of both individual and collective types of disconnection, only one of their categories—"digital disconnection as resistance" (Kaun & Treré, 2018, p. 11)—captures the spirit of what I theorize as challenge: complete or partial disconnection from specific "platforms or digital media formats" (Kaun & Treré, 2018, p. 12).

The collective and intentional dimensions of challenge as refusal are crucial. While there has been a proliferation of discourses of disconnection,
individualized practices of refusal often eschew a political dimension (see
Portwood-Stacer, 2013b) or reinforce neoliberal notions of connectivity
(see Hesselberth, 2018). Challenge as refusal is not concerned with individuals choosing to deactivate their Facebook accounts (Portwood-Stacer,
2013b), but with social movements deciding to collectively refuse to use,
either totally or partially, corporate social media because they do not
fit with their political stances. In addition to being collective, this practice of refusal also needs to be intentional; as Portwood-Stacer (2013b)
highlighted, not using a technology because it is not available or too ex-
pensive does not count as refusal. So what does challenge as refusal look
like? Kaun and Treré (2018) offered the example of radical Swedish leftist
groups (Andersson, 2016). Other movements similarly engaged in challenge as refusal must exist, but it is difficult to point out other examples;
as Hesselberth (2018) highlighted, this is certainly a bias of academic research due to the difficulty of locating these groups. A historical example
of a movement leveraging refusal, although clearly not concerned with
Silicon Valley, is the Luddites; contrary to how Luddites are popularly re-
membered (see Portwood-Stacer, 2013b), their opposition to technology
was not to the machines per se, but to the "change in the social relations of
production" (Hobsbawm, 1952) that were engendered by those machines.

The second subcategory, challenge as alternative, includes social movements' attempts to imagine and build alternative technologies. Robert W.
Gehl (2015) positioned social movements' development of alternative social media platforms in the tradition of activist alternative media (see
Atton, 2002; Downing, 2008), such as Indymedia (Juris, 2005; Pickard,
2006; Wolfson, 2014).[1] He presented different cases of activist alternative social media, such as Diaspora and rstat.us, which, he argued, "not
only [allow] for users to share content and connect with one another but
also [deny] the commercialization of speech, [allow] users more access to
shape the underlying technical infrastructure, and radically [experiment]
with surveillance regimes" (Gehl, 2015, p. 2). Presenting activist alternative technologies such as Ushahidi, Crabgrass, and Hub, Tad Hirsch (2011)
suggested that these projects "allow organizations to create communication channels that function independently of commercial offerings"

(p. 147) and that they "embody a distinct set of values, meaning that they are shaped by a different set of concerns (or at least, a different weighting among competing concerns) than their commercial counterparts" (p. 136). Milan (2013) wrote about the "emancipatory communication practices" of activists involved in creating alternatives to existing communication infrastructures, whether in the form of community radio or alternative web hosting, mailing lists, or encryption tools. Activist alternative ISPs, such as Autistici/Inventati in Italy, have also been examined in the literature (Barassi & Treré, 2012). Other movements have also created alternative platforms. According to Aristea Fotopoulou (2016), for example, feminist activists in London (UK) developed an "online social networking platform called The Café" (p. 994). The Occupy movement (Captain, 2011; Roos, 2011; Valentine, 2012), the French Nuit Debout (Russell, 2018), and most notably, the Spanish Indignados (Postill, 2014; Treré, 2018) all worked to develop alternative platforms, despite strongly relying on corporate social media. And many small projects are experimenting with the creation of technological alternatives, with different degrees of success. Black Socialists in America (BSA), a network of Black American anti-capitalist activists, worked on developing Dual Power and Stack, two apps that aim to support grassroots organizing: Dual Power wants to be "an app for democratic digital organizing and secure social networking" (Dual Power App, n.d.), built on the principles of direct democracy, while Stack's purpose is to help activists manage meetings and democratic decision-making both online and offline (Stack App, n.d.). Even more work is happening across the United States under the umbrella of "abolitionist technology" (Emmer et al., 2020).

Challenge, as both refusal and alternative, should thus be understood as the third type of response to the dominant technological imaginary of Silicon Valley. It presents evident difficulties: building alternative activist technologies requires resources, such as expertise, funding, and time, that are not always available to activists, and choosing to disconnect from corporate social media might also risk alienating some potential members or supporters. These difficulties might account for the seemingly low popularity of imaginaries of challenge among contemporary social movements. However, I suggest that the difficulties of challenge might also stem from the great power that the dominant technological imaginary exerts on all of us, including activists, which makes imagining alternative relations to mainstream technology extremely complicated.

IMAGINARIES REFLECT AND SHAPE THE POLITICS OF SOCIAL MOVEMENTS

The main argument of this book is that activist technological imaginaries both reflect and shape the politics of the social movements that construct them. Considering appropriation, negotiation, and challenge together, we can see how activist technological imaginaries are influenced by activists' ideologies, by the political contexts in which they operate, and by how they react to how other political actors construct their own technological imaginaries. Imaginaries reflect the politics of these movements, which might come to see the same digital technologies in different, political ways. At the same time, activist technological imaginaries can also shape how activists think about their political work and how they imagine their political possibilities; this can be seen, for instance, in how the reliance on Silicon Valley's technologies can limit the ability of activists to imagine technological and political alternatives.

As I have shown throughout the book, activists are keenly aware of the politics of the digital technologies they employ and that their decisions about which technologies to employ are, in fact, more political than they appear. Activists think (and talk) about technology politically. The activist groups examined in this book think about digital technologies in relation to Western modernity, like the Hungarian internet tax activists, or in terms of a capitalist system they want to dismantle, like LUMe. How they envision technology discursively is not only highly political in general, it is also very specific: technological imaginaries are tied to the specific configurations of ideologies, political contexts, and the salience of other technological imaginaries, which vary from movement to movement.

This means that different social movements experience digital technologies in very different ways. Looking at the technological imaginaries of social movements in different countries allows us to see how the same technologies of Silicon Valley, despite the universalist ambitions of the dominant technological imaginary, are far from being universal in their meaning and in their application. Instead, activist technological imaginaries reveal the existence of multiple, situated, political internets. They are multiple in the sense that the same digital technologies of Silicon Valley—the same internet protocols, the same social networking sites— are seen in different ways by different social movements. They are situated internets because they are embedded in a specific context: not just in terms of a nation-state, of an internet that might be seen differently in the United States than in the rest of the world, but also in terms of the specific situated experience of a given social movement. And they are political internets, because they are understood politically by activists, in how they represent specific sociopolitical-economic arrangements (like neoliberalism or white supremacy) and in how they might support or hinder political activism.

These multiple, situated, political internets show us the limits of Silicon Valley's universalist tendencies. Even in the Hungarian case, in which activists appropriated the dominant technological imaginary of Silicon Valley, the imaginary of mundane modernity reinterpreted digital technologies in a political way, which made sense in the streets of Budapest but not necessarily in the coworking spaces of the San Francisco Bay Area. By looking at the political ways in which these social movements imagine technology and the role it plays in their social justice work, we can push back against Silicon Valley's presumed universality. Thinking about the multiplicity, the situatedness, and the politics of these internets can help us further question and resist the political claims that are at the core of the dominant technological imaginary.

At the same time, activist technological imaginaries also shape the politics of the movements that construct them. They are certainly not the only element that comes into play in how movements perceive their political possibilities and adjust their actions, but they have an impact.[2] This is particularly visible in terms of activists' complex relationships to Silicon Valley and its technologies. Despite the existence of multiple, situated, political internets, it is clear that the imaginaries of appropriation and negotiation examined in this book show us the power and reach of Silicon Valley. Even LUMe and PS, both of which reject the visions of Silicon Valley, end up facing the dominant technological imaginary as it manifests through the digital technologies that they employ; they are still confronted with the dominance of Silicon Valley's ideas because of the way in which these ideas are encoded in digital media. As LUMe activists argued, they are in a complicated, ambiguous position: they use the tools of a system they would ultimately want to dismantle. Similarly, the PS organizers acknowledged that they use the same technologies that the ruling class also employs. It is difficult to escape from the power of Silicon Valley's imaginary, even when we reject it. On the one hand, this means that while they are opposing the imaginary of Silicon Valley, the activists are nevertheless accepting that they are part of the online economy of clicks, targeted advertising, and data commodification that sustains the business model of Silicon Valley. As some of the activists conceded, while their clicks might be directed at attacking the system, the system is nevertheless benefiting from them. On the other hand, in their negotiation the activists also end up having to rely on platforms that were not designed to support social justice efforts, but rather to further the technological imaginary (and the business model) of Silicon Valley. For instance, both PS and LUMe have to put labor into monitoring or moderating the comments that their posts receive on Facebook. The fact that the activists need to perform this kind of labor is due to the affordances of Facebook, which in turn reflect (among other things) one of the core tenets of Silicon Valley's imaginary: that digital spaces are inherently free and democratic. Yet they are not free and democratic in the way that LUMe and PS think of free and democratic spaces. To make them suitable for their politics, the activists of LUMe and PS engage in substantial imaginative work, as well as actual labor. What could these activists accomplish with the time and energy that is now being spent to try to make corporate social networks work for these movements?

But the influence of activist technological imaginaries on the politics of social movements is not just about their labor and their priorities. For instance, appropriating Silicon Valley's imaginary into mundane modernity allowed the Hungarian activists to find a way to coalesce many grievances against the Orbán government in a powerful set of ideas and symbols. But it did not help them to consolidate or expand their movement. There are likely many other reasons why these Hungarian activists did not end up creating a full-fledged social movement, but it is fair to speculate that it is at least partly tied to their appropriation of the vision of society put forth by Silicon Valley, in which it is technological innovation, supported by an unregulated global market, that accomplishes social change, not the slow work of organizing and contentious collective action. Mundane modernity did not chart a way out of illiberal democracy through collective organizing supported by digital technologies; it pitched digital technologies as the way out, or rather a way into Western modernity. It is of course unwise to deal in counterfactuals, but the limits of mundane modernity as an activist imaginary should make us question how specific activist imaginaries might end up constraining the political choices of the movements that develop them.

The argument I'm making is not a way for me to sneak some technological determinism into a book that spends so much time opposing deterministic takes on technology. I am not suggesting that it is the materiality or the affordances of specific technologies that influence how a movement thinks of its political decisions, nor am I suggesting that the politics of a movement can be derived solely from its reliance on digital technologies. This is still about how activists construct their practice-based beliefs about technology and society—their technological imaginaries—and how these are connected to the dominant technological imaginary of Silicon Valley. This is about how activists envision their relationship to technologies and how those visions might shape their political action.

Consider, for instance, how Facebook—and the other platforms owned by Meta, such as Instagram and WhatsApp—are crucial to contemporary activism. While the groups I examine in this book all use a multiplicity of digital media in addition to other offline media practices, Facebook is (at the time of writing) central to the way they communicate and organize. But it is also key to how they think about the internet. It is not accidental that so many of the quotes that I presented in the chapters discuss interviewees' experiences with Facebook. Thus, even though the internet goes beyond Facebook, this platform almost monopolizes activists' attention not only when it comes to posting and interacting with others, but also when it comes to thinking about what the internet means for them and what digital technology could do for social movements and social justice. And this will continue to have an impact even as Facebook declines in popularity with younger activists. What does it mean when one platform so powerfully shapes how activists think about technology? It is time we start thinking of Facebook as holding a monopoly not only on our online communication, but also on our imagination.

This monopoly over the imagination held by Facebook can be seen, for instance, in how LUMe and PS think about this social network site as where everybody (else) is: a vast, potentially endless aggregation of individuals, as close as anyone can get to the idea of the "general public," a public that can only be readily accessed through Facebook. This is also the dream that Facebook sells to advertisers. And for movements it is even more problematic, because it holds them captive and keeps them coming back to the platform. But we can also think about how much pressure there is on alternative, activist technological projects to be able to fully supplant Facebook and do all the things that Facebook supposedly does. This expectation that for any alternative technological project to be considered viable, it should aim to and be able to replace Facebook in its entirety, from the get-go, is not only damaging for activist tech development, it is also inhibiting our thinking about how we want technology to be different from Facebook.[3] And on an even more profound and disconcerting level, this monopoly over the imagination held by Facebook might also end up gamifying, datafying, and commodifying how we think about movements' growth and success. Metrics are embedded in all aspects of Facebook. Applied to activism, these metrics can give activists a skewed sense of how organizing works. Activists know that the number of people who click the buttons "Interested" or "Going" on a Facebook Event for a meeting or a protest will not necessarily turn up at said meeting or protest. But there are other aspects that are more subtle: what counts as high numbers of "impressions" or a high volume of "engagement" for the Facebook platform does not necessarily correspond to what activists would normally consider interest or engagement. Clicks and likes are now so often taken as measures of participation and consensus, even in how the media talk about social media content, but that idea of consensus is radically opposed to how social movements think about their participatory mechanisms and how they can arrive at consensus. The point is that this constant exposure to Facebook and its way of structuring human interaction might end up changing how activists, and regular people, think of fundamental political dynamics. This is what Bucher (2021) described as the "ontological politics" of Facebook:

its ability to "shape realities in different ways, making some things matter more than others" (p. 166)

Therefore, even if the power of Facebook is being challenged and undermined in the wake of the Cambridge Analytica scandal, its monopolistic position can have long-lasting repercussions for how we think about the role of technology in social change, even as activists gradually move away from the platform. And this holds for the dominance of Silicon Valley's imaginary writ large: even if we are gradually moving toward stronger and more explicit public critiques of tech companies, which might chip away at the dominance of the technological imaginary of Silicon Valley, we will still need to contend with how this imaginary has oriented our thinking about the relationship between technology, society, and social change for many years.

IMPLICATIONS

By emphasizing the discursive and imaginative dimensions of technology, with this book I offer a framework for the analysis of the political relationship between social movements and digital technologies. In doing so, this work makes theoretical and methodological contributions that can help us better understand the politics of digital technologies and the role they play in contemporary activism.

First, this book contributes to the literature on (digital) media and social movements by centering how activists envision the politics of digital technologies and the role of technology in their activism. With the concept of technological imaginary and the theoretical framework that I developed around it, we can better account for how digital technologies are already being imagined and experienced as political by social movements around the world. In fact, even if activists do not think about their "technological imaginaries" under this label, the empirical analysis I provided shows that they do critically reflect, either individually or collectively, about the politics of the technologies they use and how they might fit with their political identities and goals. My framework thus moves beyond the analysis of how social movements use digital technologies. Instead, it focuses on how activists imagine and reimagine digital technologies and what they might do for them and their activism. It gives us a way to account for the political and imaginative work that activists need to perform in order to navigate the politics of mainstream digital technologies.

I hope that the framework proposed in this book will help us makes sense of some issues that scholars of activism and technology have long been interested in. It can contribute to our understanding of the political meaning of specific activist technological practices, such as those at the core of media activism (e.g., Dunbar-Hester, 2014). It can help us understand how technologies come to be symbols of specific political values that can become salient in the course of mobilization. And it can support comparative approaches to the study of activism, which foreground the specific political configurations that shape how social movements relate to technology.

Second, this book also contributes to the long-standing debates on the politics of technology and the more recent body of work that has highlighted the social and political impact of Silicon Valley and of corporate technology, particularly in terms of reinforcing structures of oppression (e.g., Benjamin, 2019; Broussard, 2018; Costanza-Chock, 2020; Noble, 2018). This book brings together a strong critique of Silicon Valley with an attention to how technology is experienced and reimagined in the daily life of social movements. The framework allows us to account for the symbolic power of technology and the dominant technological imaginary, but also for how activists experience the political underpinnings of technology in their day-to-day activities. To this scholarship, the book contributes an understanding of how the politics of mainstream digital technologies interact with the politics of contentious collective actors, underscoring the importance of focusing on those who attempt to resist, reinterpret, and reimagine digital technology in service of social justice.

Last, this book also makes a methodological contribution by charting a qualitative empirical trajectory for the study of technological imaginaries. This project shows that the work of reconstructing the political meaning of technology for social movements cannot be undertaken without engaging activists directly: none of the insights provided by this book could have been reached by simply collecting the content that the activists of the Hungarian internet tax protests, LUMe, or PS post on social media. While looking at social media data can help answer some questions about social movements' use of digital technologies, it cannot account for the nuances that emerge through the qualitative investigation of movements' technological imaginaries. Further, this book shows that while textual analysis has long been the prevalent method for the study of imaginaries and other sociocultural dimensions of technology, we can gain a lot by using qualitative methods such as semistructured interviews and creative methods such as the visual focus group.

FAILURES OF THE IMAGINATION

"Maybe today no one amongst us really has a revolutionary approach to social media" (Ilaria, LUMe). Ilaria's statement came toward the end of a long interview, during which the then twenty-four-year-old talked at length about the ways in which LUMe activists discuss what the digital technologies "of the system" mean to them. Unbeknownst to Ilaria, her sentence captured some of the thoughts that kept coming to me as I worked on this research. What does it mean when social movements do not have a revolutionary approach to technology? What would a revolutionary approach to social media look like? And do movements need a revolutionary approach to technology to have a politically revolutionary approach?

Ilaria could not really tell me what a revolutionary approach to technology would look like. And I could not tell her that either. But it is high time for academics and activists to ask themselves what technologies can do for social justice. It seems that the idea that technologies are not neutral has finally become more mainstream, among academics and even the general public. But now we need to take a step further. We need to ask if the technologies we use are supporting or hindering our visions of social change. We need to ask how we can imagine technologies that can support social movements in fighting for social justice. If corporate digital technologies are reinforcing the power of the capitalist system, of white supremacy, of the patriarchy, we need to start unambiguously envisioning technologies that can support those who are already working to dismantle those powers. This might also mean envisioning technologies that obfuscate or sabotage the technologies of power.

Yet imagining different technologies in service of different futures has been very difficult. Searching for the technological imaginaries of contemporary leftist social movements has left me with the sense that the imagination of these movements has been encountering severe limitations, both when it comes to imagining the role of technologies and when it comes to imagining different futures, beyond neoliberal capitalism. Imagining different technological and social futures seems difficult, or perhaps pointless, for the movements that have emerged in the last decade, in the long tail of the global financial crisis of 2008. With all its political limitations, the global justice movement of the early 2000s unambiguously claimed that another world was possible and that a global mobilization could chart the way toward a more globally just future. The movements of the post–financial crisis wave, the Arab Spring, the Indignados, Occupy Wall Street, the European anti-austerity movements, Black Lives Matter, the women's mobilization . . . they have all, for now, refrained from or failed to imagine an alternative future. This is not to say that they haven't been important; they have been and still are very important. But they haven't truly imagined alternatives. It is no coincidence that most of their slogans and keywords have been about asserting their existence and announcing their resistance. They have carved out spaces of critique, resistance, and self-organization that fight against neoliberalism from the margins, but without necessarily imagining an alternative.

As the COVID-19 pandemic halted the world and more and more of our lives became mediated by digital technologies, I thought a lot about what this would mean for the activists I have met during this research and for social movements in general. In the midst of the horror, the loss, and the intensification of inequality of the pandemic, there was also, for a time, a sense that this could be a moment of rupture: a traumatic break from what came before and an invitation to rethink how our societies and our lives are structured. With so many people across the world talking about and engaging in collective care and mutual aid, it seemed that the pandemic had made even clearer the necessity to organize against neoliberalism and imagine different ways of living and engaging with each other. The extraordinary wave of Black Lives Matter protests in the United States following the murder of George Floyd in 2020 and the increased attention to abolitionist perspectives also opened extraordinary and previously unthinkable avenues for the dismantling of the prison-industrial complex. The pandemic has shown us, once again and on an unimaginable scale, how the system is harming us and how urgently we need to come together to imagine alternatives.

This is especially pressing now that our societies are adjusting to a new postpandemic normal, which despite the traumatic experiences of the past few years still looks like a neoliberal and white supremacist reality, with authoritarian reactionary voices growing in strength day by day across much of world. We need social movements to begin envisioning a way out of neoliberalism that is not a global dystopian authoritarian regime. We need social movements to draw on spaces of critique, resistance, and self-organization to start explicitly imagining different technologies, different societies, and different futures. Because imagining them will be the first step in the long journey toward making them a reality.

Methodological Appendix

This research grew out of my delight and puzzlement at the Hungarian internet tax protests. When I lived in Hungary between 2011 and 2014, I saw the building blocks of what Viktor Orbán would later call illiberalism: the enactment of the Media Laws, the changes in the Constitution, and the rejection of the European Union. I went to a few demonstrations. The internet tax protests of 2014 seemed entirely different in magnitude from anything I'd ever seen before (or read about). I devoured the coverage, scoured the internet for pictures and videos, and talked to my friends in Budapest. Mostly I just looked, speechless, at the images from the other side of the Atlantic.

Just a couple of years before that, in 2012, a demonstration against the Anti-Counterfeiting Trade Agreement (ACTA) was held in Budapest. There were V for Vendetta masks, pro-Anonymous banners, queer feminist drummers, handmade signs with nerdy jokes—and pirate flags, flown to the theme song from Disney's *Pirates of the Caribbean*, played on a cranky sound system. The freezing temperature that day did not help, but I thought it was great that 150 people came out to protest in the snow against an international trade agreement on copyright that was difficult to understand even if, like me, you were interested in media policy. And indeed, many people demonstrated against ACTA, including, perhaps surprisingly, many across CEE (Nowak, 2016).

But those anti-ACTA protests were honestly nothing compared to the ten thousand and then one hundred thousand Hungarians who demonstrated against the internet tax two years later. Quantitatively and qualitatively, those were very different protests, although ostensibly both were about "internet free-dom." My notes and conversations from those early days in October 2014 show all my conflicted feelings. What was going on? How was it possible that all of this would happen over a few hundred Hungarian forints? Where did this idea of internet freedom come from, and why was it so powerful?

The Hungarian protests forced me to think about digital technology in a way that I hadn't previously, to reckon with the power of narratives and dis-courses that come to be attached to technology, their political importance, and their role in social movements. How did we get to seeing illuminated mobile phones as a political symbol? What kinds of discourses about technology are the internet tax protests tapping into?

In this appendix I explain the choices I made during the course of the multi-year empirical research that informs this book, discussing my general theoreti-cal orientation to the study of social movements, research design, and research methods.

MOVEMENTS AS PROCESSES AND THE INVISIBILITY OF ACTIVIST TECHNOLOGICAL IMAGINARIES

My approach to the study of social movements is influenced, on a theoretical and methodological level, by Alberto Melucci's work (1989, 1996). I share Melucci's orientation toward studying "movements as processes" and exploring the discur-sive constructions that enable the action of social movements. His framework for the study of social movements is fundamental to my research in two ways: for its focus on the discourses that define social movements and for its insistence on discovering the invisible aspects of social movements. Both of these takeaways inform how I conceptualize activist technological imaginaries and, more gener-ally, how I think about questions of research design and methodology.

First, following Melucci (1989), I think about social movements as a process. This means that I consider the ways in which activists construct their systems of beliefs, negotiate meanings, and make decisions to be the core elements of any analysis of social movements. For Melucci (1989), in fact, discursive practices are the foundations of collective action. Such discursive practices are directed at constructing the collective identity of a movement, understood as a "sense of we" (Melucci, 1989, p. 65) that enables action. I find Melucci's emphasis on discourses very productive, and I think about activist technological imaginaries as part of these discursive process through which activists construct the environment around them—what Melucci calls an "action system" (1989, p. 27)

Second, one of Melucci's remarkable contributions to the study of social move-ments lies in his denunciation of a certain "myopia of the visible" (1989, p. 44), which leads scholars to only consider highly visible moments of mobilization and ignore the invisible foundational processes that sustain social movements during periods of "latency." Inspired by this criticism, I also focus my study of activists on invisible and taken-for-granted beliefs and practices concerning technology, which are at the core of how I theorize (and analyze) activist technological imaginaries.

I believe that embracing Melucci's perspective has specific implications for research design and methodology: how to select what to study and how to study what we select. In terms of research design, the most evident implication relates to how we can best position ourselves to investigate these more invisible activist processes. Committing to investigating these less visible aspects is not always the obvious choice, but it is an important one. In her book on the digital activism of progressive and conservative groups in North Carolina, Jen Schradie (2019) observed that much scholarship on activism treats technology as the independent variable and social movements as the dependent variable. What she meant is that researchers often end up looking at how the internet influences movements, rather than how different societal factors might influence how a movement uses the internet. This brought her to choose a research design that first centers specific movements and then looks at their digital practices. As I explain in this appendix, this was my choice, too. Schradie's critique of the scholarship on digital activism is well grounded, and I agree with it. But I think that there is another issue that runs parallel to the one that she described. Even when the scholarship on social movements and digital technologies chooses to put the study of activist processes at the forefront, it often lands on focusing on activists for whom technology is a crucial focus, a core motivation for their activism. Studies of media activism and hacktivism (e.g., Dunbar-Hester, 2014; Milan, 2013; Pickard, 2006) are incredibly valuable, and they have moved our field forward in many ways. Research on activist uses of Facebook and Twitter, protest hashtags, and digital activist campaigns (e.g., Bennett & Segerberg, 2013; Jackson et al., 2020) similarly contribute many insights to our understanding of the relationship between activists and digital technologies. However, they effectively show us how activists that are already interested in technology relate to technology. They focus on activists whose main focus is already tech, whether in terms of creating it, hacking it, or using it in specific ways. While these cases are important to consider, what would happen if we looked elsewhere? What would we be able to see if we looked at movements that might use digital technologies in their activism, but for which technology is not a core motivating concern? How do movements that don't particularly "care" about technology envision technology? This is one of the aspects I considered when thinking about the research design for this project. I had many conversations with both activists and academics, who suggested I should look at a certain movement because of its particularly interesting/sophisticated/innovative/alternative way of approaching technology. And while that would have undoubtedly been a valuable option, I preferred to select cases of social movements that did not specifically revolve around technology. I believe that this approach helps us both to nuance our findings on activism and digital technologies and to assess the actual role—and power!—of technology in contemporary social movements.

Beyond research design, adopting this Meluccian outlook on social movements also means adopting research methods that allow us to investigate the internal processes of social movements, specifically those that are harder to see. Studying activist technological imaginaries is challenging exactly because they are largely implicit and invisible and thus difficult to reconstruct directly. Digital technologies have become so embedded in our lives that trying to talk about their meaning in an interview can be challenging, even frustrating. And yet it is crucial to find methodological approaches that can help us investigate the taken-for-granted character of technology and have reflexive conversations about its power. This is why I employ a multimethod qualitative approach, which draws on the depth of semistructured interviews and the reflexivity of creative methods.

RESEARCH DESIGN

This book adopts a comparative research design that charts how activist technological imaginaries are developed by social movements in different countries. The three empirical cases that I investigate are the Hungarian internet tax protests of 2014, the Italian student collective LUMe (Laboratorio Universitario Metropolitano, i.e., Metropolitan University Laboratory), and the US Philly Socialists. This comparative approach allows me to assess how the specific political contexts in which activists are embedded might influence their relationship to digital technologies. Looking at how activists in different contexts approach the same mainstream technologies imagined and developed by Silicon Valley enables us to go beyond US-centric explanations of the relationship between activism and technology; it also contributes to decentering technology by considering how it is approached from different cultural, social, and political perspectives.

The three case studies examined in the book present similarities and differences. First, these three activist groups can be considered part of the same wave of social movements that mobilized in opposition to the growth of right-wing populist forces in Europe and North America in the mid- to late 2010s. All these groups confronted right-wing populist governments: Viktor Orbán's Fidesz in Hungary, Donald Trump in the United States, and the government alliance between Matteo Salvini's League (Lega) and the Five Star Movement (Movimento Cinque Stelle) in Italy. If these right-wing leaders can be broadly understood as part of the same right-wing populist moment, then it is important that we also consider the movements that oppose them as part of the same category, even if these movements are obviously different from one another. My selection of these cases thus encourages a conceptualization of these movement actors as part of the same cohort of movements opposing right-wing populism.

Second, the Hungarian internet tax protests, LUMe, and PS are also similarly situated to the left of the mainstream center-left in each of their respective countries. They all eschew parliamentary representation and are critical of parliamentary politics. The organizers of the Hungarian internet tax protests are part of a left-liberal activist area that represents the culturally progressive extreme Left in the truncated Hungarian political spectrum, in opposition to Orbán. LUMe is part of what is considered the Italian "radical Left", situated to the left of the institutional (center-)left in Italy. LUMe is committed to fighting against neoliberalism, racism, sexism, and fascism (which includes right-wing populism). PS is a socialist organization that embraces revolutionary politics and is also positioned to the far left of the mainstream left in the United States; it combines opposition to capitalism with a rejection of the US two-party system and of racism and sexism. Finally, these activist groups are also broadly similar in the "repertoires of contention" (Tarrow, 2011) that they draw upon: their actions include nonviolent demonstrations, rallies, and protests. Their organizational practices rely on participatory mechanisms, such as open assemblies and informal working groups.

In my case selection, I placed particular emphasis on identifying cases that were sufficiently similar on a political level. I prioritized, as much as I could, cases that presented similarities that would allow me to consider them as broadly similar movements in a political sense. I asked myself: If these activists met at an international demonstration, would they recognize themselves as being engaged in similar struggles? Based on my empirical research, I think they would.

At the same time, these cases are also sufficiently different to allow me to examine how the peculiarities of each group contribute to shaping their activist technological imaginary. The Hungarian postcommunist political space is marked by its socialist past and by the consequences of the democratic transition of the 1990s; it is also characterized by a fraught relationship with Western modernity, which affects both left-wing and right-wing politics. Although when thinking of Italy many would point to its perennial political instability as its defining trait, for my analysis what is most salient is the existence of a vibrant radical social movement scene, with a long history in which contemporary activists can ground their work. The US political context has, of course, many unique characteristics. One that becomes immediately apparent when juxtaposed with Italy and Hungary is the historical marginalization and repression of radical left-wing forces, which has greatly influenced these movements. Another striking aspect of the US landscape is its long-standing enthusiasm for technology. In addition to these macro-differences in the political contexts of Hungary, Italy, and the United States, the political orientations of these individual groups also vary, even if they can all be placed in a general radical leftist camp, to the left of the mainstream Left in their respective countries.

Some readers might feel that the three selected cases are too different to allow for a meaningful comparison. As I mentioned in chapter 1, this project does not offer a strict comparative design that identifies a few variables that neatly vary between cases and determine an outcome. It could be argued that this type of design would not work with activist groups anyway (see Barassi, 2015, p. 12). But for this specific research, which proceeded inductively, it would have been impossible to produce such a design, given that the focus of the comparison is on the processes through which activists construct their technological imaginaries and how they draw on different political factors that are salient to them in this discursive construction. It would not have been possible to identify these factors before conducting the research: while I could—and did—hypothesize that political factors would have an influence on activists' development of their technological imaginaries, I had no way of anticipating which factors would matter and how. It should also be noted that while national characteristics are undoubtedly important in my analysis, this book does not compare Hungary, Italy, and the United States as countries. The aim of this research is not to generalize from my cases to the level of the nation, identifying some "national" activist technological imaginaries to be compared. What I compare is the imaginative thinking that goes into the construction of the imaginary of each activist group and what the political elements are that come to be relevant in this process.

It is also important to say that the three cases were selected among movements in countries with which I have a great degree of familiarity; this familiarity lies not simply in having lived in Hungary, Italy, and the United States, but also in having engaged with activists in all of these countries before conducting this research (and indeed, in the case of Italy and Hungary, long before even considering becoming a researcher). This familiarity is crucial in order to undertake a comparative qualitative research project of this scope, which necessitates a deep understanding of the nuances of the different political contexts and of social movements in each country.

It is worth underlining that I did not select the three cases based on what I thought their technological imaginaries would be. While conducting preliminary research on these groups, I did encounter their social media pages or the media coverage of their actions, but I didn't pick these cases based on a specific imaginary I could see—or try to infer—from these initial encounters. Before conducting the research, I hypothesized that there might be some variation in the technological imaginaries developed by the activist groups; as explained previously, I also supposed that such variation could depend on political factors. But I did not identify the three cases analyzed in the book because I thought they would present a specific imaginary; the different imaginaries emerged in the analysis of the cases, not in the design stage.

My approach to this research was inductive. The book introduces my theoretical framework in chapter 2, before my empirical examination of the three activist technological imaginaries, but this order of presentation does not reflect how the research was conducted. When I entered fieldwork, I had developed a definition and a list of characteristics of technological imaginaries, but I had no preconceived expectations of how the activist imaginaries I wanted to examine would relate to each other and to the dominant technological imaginary of Silicon Valley. I conceptualized the categories of appropriation, negotiation, challenge after completing the empirical research and sketching out the contours of the individual activist technological imaginaries of the three cases considered. Similarly, what I show as crucial political elements that shape these activist technological imaginaries—the ideology of the activists, political context, and the presence of other salient technological imaginaries—all emerged from my comparison between the cases. In writing the book, I chose to present the framework of appropriation, negotiation, challenge before introducing the empirical chapters because I believe it enhances the clarity of the text and supports readers in understanding, and comparing, these activist technological imaginaries. But the framework itself arose from the empirical analysis of the cases.

This also means that the category "challenge" is not derived from an empirical case examined in the book, but rather from the juxtaposition of the cases of appropriation and negotiation that I analyze with the existing literature on social movements. While not looking at this issue through the lens of technological imaginaries, this literature has nevertheless begun to show a few cases of movements that might refuse and/or challenge the digital technologies of Silicon Valley. I therefore conceptualized activist imaginaries of challenge as a third possible category. In an ideal world, I would have found and analyzed three cases that each corresponded to one of the categories of technological imaginaries that I identified, but this is not what emerged from the data. I could have started searching for another case to analyze, one that would, from the outside look like a case of challenge. But this would have contradicted my approach, as described previously: I did not want to select cases for analysis based on their displaying a specific activist technological imaginary or some other specific approach to digital technology. Consequently, I decided not to search for a case of challenge.

Further, the framework of appropriation, negotiation, challenge is not meant to be prescriptive. It should not make us think that we can predict what an activist technological imaginary might look like based on the political characteristics of the movement that constructs it. The framework is more of a road map for analysis than a formula. In other words, while we might find that another socialist organization in Philadelphia is committed to the idea of base-building and identifies and rejects the imaginary of "activist networking", we cannot expect it to construct an imaginary of negotiation that is the same as that of PS. It makes sense to envision that it could also develop an imaginary of negotiation, but we might also find that its imaginary is one of challenge, or even of appropriation. This is because activist technological imaginaries are constructed through inter- action, in line with what Melucci (1989) tells us about movements; technological imaginaries are the result of collective imaginative and discursive processes and are grounded in practices. The typology of appropriation, negotiation, challenge is meant to be an analytical road map to uncover the specificities of each move- ments' relationship to technology. It is intended to support our empirical analy- ses of movements' technological imaginaries, not to offer predictions about what these imaginaries will be.

Finally, a caveat on the applicability of this research. This work only includes cases of social movements located in Europe and North America and is predi- cated on the dominance of a distinctly American, Western, technological imag- inary. The theoretical framework deployed in this book could also be used as a starting point to analyze the technological imaginaries of movements located in other parts of the world, but in order to use this framework in other contexts, we should pay particular attention to identifying what the dominant technological imaginary in a given location is. As I discussed in chapter 2, the dominance of the technological imaginary of Silicon Valley is increasingly global. However, it might not be equally dominant across the world, and its dominance might look different in different areas of the world. For instance, we could hypothesize that the technological imaginary of the Chinese government might be the dominant one to consider when analyzing how Chinese activists construct their own tech- nological imaginaries. This would then likely require a reconceptualization of the typology of activist technological imaginaries developed in this book—but one that could still be guided by the theoretical framework laid out in this proj- ect. The geographical limitations of the dominant technological imaginary, and of the cases examined here, do not minimize the findings of my research, but rather serve to underline how social movements' relations to technology must be studied in the specific political context in which movements are embedded.

METHODS

I explored the three cases—the internet tax protests in Hungary, LUMe in Italy, and PS in Philadelphia—through a multimethod qualitative approach, which combined in-depth interviews, the observation of events and online inter- actions, and visual focus groups (Ferrari, 2022). This three-pronged approach was directed at making explicit how activists thought, individually and collec- tively, about digital technology and its political connotations. The bulk of this empirical research was conducted over a period of three years, between 2017 and 2020.

Interviews

I conducted semistructured interviews with activists from the Hungarian internet tax protests, LUMe, and PS. As I mentioned in chapter 1, I used the interviews to ask participants about their experiences as activists, how they personally relate to digital technology, and how the groups they are part of relate to digital technology.

Because the interviews with the Hungarian activists were conducted earlier than the interviews for LUMe and PS, they followed a different interview guide, which was directed at understanding how "the internet" was conceptualized during the internet tax protests. By focusing on the meaning of the internet tax, activists' responses very clearly converged on what I then termed the imaginary of mundane modernity. The issue of the tax gave activists a helpful entry point to critically reflect on their relationship to the internet. When preparing the interview guides for the fieldwork with LUMe and PS, I considered how I could guide activists' reflections in a similar way. This resulted in, on the one hand, the development of the visual focus groups (as I explain later), and on the other, interview questions that were directed at discussing tensions arising in activists' relationships with digital technology, on either the individual or collective level. As explained in chapter 1, this was inspired by Susan Leigh Star's (1999) ethnographic approach to infrastructure and infrastructural breakdown and by Taina Bucher's (2016) invitation to study algorithmic imaginaries.

I conducted interviews with the core organizers of the Hungarian internet tax protests in January–February 2017, either in person in Budapest or via Skype. I interviewed seven men and two women, whose pseudonyms and ages are listed in table 1. The interviews were conducted in English. On average, each interview lasted fifty-eight minutes. These nine interviewees were the core organizers of a group that reached twenty people at most; each interviewee confirmed that my sample represented the most relevant individuals who were involved in the organization of the protests.

I conducted interviews with eight activists from LUMe, four men and four women, between June 2018 and February 2019. Their ages and occupations are listed in table 2. The interviews were conducted either in person in Milan or via video chat services (Skype and Facebook Messenger). The interviews were conducted in Italian, and their average length was seventy-eight minutes. Unless otherwise noted, all translations from Italian to English are mine. The eight interviewees who took part in my research represent different working groups in the collective; they also vary in how long they have been with LUMe: while some of the interviewees were involved in founding the collective, others joined at different times, and one interviewee had just recently become involved with LUMe when I interviewed him. This sample of activists thus captures a range of experiences

Table 1   Pseudonyms, Age at Time of
Interview, and Gender of Hungarian
Internet Tax Activist Interviewees

Pseudonym	Age	Gender
Adam	32	Male
Bálint	32	Male
Daniel	35	Male
David	45[§]	Male
Eszter	33	Female
Lászlo	33	Male
Péter	37	Male
Petra	—	Female
Tamás	45[§]	Male

[§] indicates estimate based on publicly available
information.

Table 2   Pseudonyms, Age at Time of Interview, and Gender of LUMe Interviewees

Pseudonym	Age	Gender	Occupation
Boris	21	Male	Assistant director of photography
Ilaria	24	Female	Social media manager
Jessica	27	Female	Museum staff
Maria	26	Female	Actor
Mario	25	Male	Student
Paolo	24	Male	Student
Stefano	25	Male	Student
Valeria	22	Female	Student

in LUMe; the interviewees themselves discussed my sample with me and found it representative of the group.

I conducted six interviews with members of PS; their ages, occupations, and preferred pronouns are listed in table 3. The interviews took place between August 2018 and November 2019. The interviews took place in person, in Philadelphia; they were conducted in English. Their average length was seventy minutes. As I detail later when describing the limitations of my project, the organizers of Philly Socialists were more reluctant to participate in my research than the Italian and Hungarian activists; this accounts for the smaller number of interviews. The six

Table 3 Pseudonyms, Age at Time of Interview, and Preferred Pronouns
of PS Interviewees

Pseudonym	Age	Pronouns	Occupation
Alexander	43	He/him	Web developer
Amy	30	She/her	City planner
Donna	26	They/them	Nonprofit worker
Lisa	29	She/her	Medical interpreter
Michael	24	He/him	Research assistant
Tyler	36	He/him	Librarian

interviews nevertheless offer the perspectives of organizers who had varying previous experiences of activism, work on different projects within PS, and have been members of the organization for different amounts of time.

All interviews were audio recorded with the consent of the interviewees and were transcribed either by me (Hungarian internet tax protests, LUMe) or by a professional and confidential transcription service (PS).

Observation

I observed meetings and public events organized by LUMe and PS during the three-year period in which I investigated these movements. I observed two open assemblies held by LUMe (in December 2017 and December 2018), one organizational assembly (in June 2018), and a working group meeting (June 2018). I also observed four public or semipublic meetings or events of PS: one open assembly (in July 2018), a public assembly of the Philadelphia Tenants Union (in August 2018), a general assembly (January 2019), and a book presentation held at a local bookstore (September 2018). I also visited the Occupy ICE Philadelphia encampments, which PS co-promoted, and observed a general assembly of this movement (July 2018). I took notes and collected any written materials that were available at these meetings and events. My observation of the movements complemented the data collected through the interviews and the visual focus groups; it was especially useful in providing insights into the discussions and organizational dynamics that characterize PS and LUMe. I was not able to directly observe any meeting or protest action of the Hungarian internet tax activists, because they occurred before I began the fieldwork for this project.

I also examined the content produced by these movements on their websites, social media pages/accounts, and any available documents. In particular, I analyzed social media posts and the website produced by LUMe; this content supplements the interviews and was used to reconstruct the history of LUMe, its different working groups, and its political stances. I also analyzed the social media posts and the content of the PS website; this content also included the Constitution of PS, their anti-harassment policy (available on the website), and internal documents shared on social media. I used these materials to integrate interviewees' accounts of the history of the group and of their many projects, as well as to provide an explanation of their political positions and their organizational structures. I also collected and analyzed written materials published by members of PS, which aimed to present the organization and/or explain its political stances, for instance the notion of base-building. I also collected and examined five issues of the magazine published by PS, the *Philadelphia Partisan*. Finally, I also collected and read any available coverage on these groups, across both mainstream and activist media.

Visual Focus Groups

In searching for a methodological approach that could help me uncover the unspoken assumptions about the relationship between technology, politics, and social change, I developed a new research method: the visual focus group (VFG). VFGs incorporate a collective drawing task within the traditional structure of a focus group.

As I explained in the methodological article in which I presented this method (Ferrari, 2022), the purpose of this group creative task is to stimulate participants to critically reflect on their unspoken assumptions about technology, thus supporting engaged conversations between participants and researchers. In my VFGs, I asked participants to collectively draw what they thought the internet was like. This task generated deep and critical discussions about how participants viewed the internet and how to best represent it in graphical form. They produced intermediate sketches and built on each other's ideas. Both their drawings and the transcripts of their discussions formed the basis of my analysis.

Creative methods have been quite popular across disciplines, particularly to support reflexivity in the context of individual interviews (see Gieseking, 2013; Bagnoli, 2009). To my knowledge, mine was the first attempt to employ a reflexive collective creative task, in which participants do not simply draw alongside each other but rather draw together from scratch. The advantage of embedding the creative task within a group setting is that it elicits a collective conversation among participants on how to tackle the task itself, as well as inviting participants to compare their own individual approaches and reflect on their practices within their activist community.

The VFG followed a structure in three stages (Ferrari, 2022). First, after the consent process, I asked participants to fill out a questionnaire; it included a series of questions about their technological habits, a few demographic questions, and five Likert-scale items that were designed to stimulate the participants to reflect on more political aspects of digital technologies, as can be seen in table 4.

Table 4   Close-Ended Questions Posed in Anonymous Questionnaire Distributed
in VFGs

I am concerned about how much control corporations and other private actors have
over my personal information/what I say online.

I am concerned about how much control the government has over my personal
information/what I say online.

The internet was better a few years ago.

The internet works in a democratic way.

The internet is a space of freedom.

SOURCE: Reproduced from Ferrari (2022) under Creative Commons Attribution 4.0 License
(https://creativecommons.org/licenses/by/4.0/).

Respondents were asked to choose a response on a 5-item Likert scale, ranging from "strongly
disagree" to "strongly agree."

These questions were deliberately written as "bad" survey questions that would
be very difficult to answer on a scale from "strongly disagree" to "strongly agree":
they were meant as prompts for collective discussion and they did result in such
a collective discussion, thus achieving their aim. In the second stage of the VFG,
I asked participants to reflect on the questionnaire, encouraging them to discuss its limitations. This stage was a prelude to the collective creative task, in
that participants often raised issues that would later be addressed in the course
of the drawing. In the third stage of the VFG, I asked participants to produce
one collective drawing that represented what they thought the internet was like.
I provided them with drawing supplies and paper, including a larger piece of
cardboard for their final group drawing. I explained that they could decide what
to draw and how to do it; I informed them that my only requirement was for them
to create a single drawing they could all agree with. Across the VFGs I conducted,
the collective drawing stages included deep and detailed discussion about what
the internet meant for activists; participants prepared individual sketches to
support their points of view or to validate what others were saying. The final
drawings were complex renderings of their visions of the internet, over which
activists debated in order to find common ground. After completing their final
drawings, participants were debriefed.

   Although I planned to conduct focus groups with both LUMe and PS, only
those with LUMe were held.[1] I conducted two VFGs with LUMe activists: the
first, which took place on November 8, 2018, lasted one hour and thirty-six minutes and included five activists (four male, one female); the second, on January 7,
2019, was one hour and fifty-two minutes long and included four activists (three
male, one female). Their pseudonyms and ages are listed in table 5. The VFGs
with LUMe took place in person in a space occupied by the collective and were

Table 5   Pseudonyms, Age at Time of Interview, and Gender of LUMe
Participants in VFGs

Pseudonym	Age	Gender	Focus Group
Emanuele*	29	Male	1
Maria	26	Female	1
Mario	25	Male	1
Paolo	24	Male	1
Vittorio*	21	Male	1
Alessio*	26	Male	2
Giulio*	24	Male	2
Stefano	25	Male	2
Viola*	20	Female	2

* Participant did not take part in individual interview.

conducted in Italian. Each VFG produced a collective drawing. They interviewees also created several individual preliminary sketches; I was not able to collect all of those sketches because some were thrown away by activists before I could claim them, but I was able to retain eight of them. I took pictures of the VFGs, with the consent of interviewees, focusing on the drawing process and the actual drawings and trying to minimize the presence of activists' faces or other recognizable features. The VFGs were also audio recorded and then transcribed by me.

Data Analysis

The data created through interviews and visual focus groups were coded through thematic (Braun & Clarke, 2006) and open (Corbin & Strauss, 2008) coding. In particular, a first round of descriptive thematic coding of the transcripts was conducted through the qualitative analysis software MaxQDA. Subsequently, a second round of open coding, directed at extrapolating more theoretically relevant codes from the existing descriptive thematic coding, was conducted on paper. Because the analysis was concerned with the specific technological imaginary constructed by each activist group, I analyzed the transcripts pertaining to each case separately.

The drawings produced in the VFGs—both the final collective drawings and the sketches produced by different individuals—were analyzed in conjunction with the transcript of the group discussion that produced them. The themes raised in the drawings and in the group discussions were constantly compared to those emerging from the individual interviews. As I argued in Ferrari (2022), the drawings that emerge from VFGs cannot be analyzed or presented without accounting for the discussions that generated them. When I introduced the drawings in chapter 4, I embedded them in the conversations that the LUMe activists were having in the VFGs, presenting them alongside direct quotes from participants or a summary of their discussion.

Limitations

Like all research projects, this one also has a number of limitations. The first is the challenges I encountered in recruiting research participants for one of the cases I consider, PS. When I was beginning my fieldwork, I discussed my research plans with the two organizers who were cochairs of PS at the time. My research project was also discussed by the PS Central Committee, which agreed I could use the name of the organization during this research. However, the organizers did not fully embrace my project: they sent an internal email and posted a message in their internal Facebook discussion group on my behalf, but neither the cochairs nor other organizers helped me recruit participants. This was different from my experience with LUMe and the Hungarian activists, and I can only speculate about why that was the case. I had hoped to work around any (perfectly valid) biases against my academic affiliation at the time (the University of Pennsylvania) by highlighting my background as a former activist and my commitment to social justice. I had also hoped to be able to mitigate any surveillance concerns organizers might have had by offering encrypted means of communication and by explicitly mentioning that I would not disclose any of their personal information. As far as I could ascertain, all the interviews that I conducted with the PS members were a positive experience for the participants, who spoke to me at length and seemed to enjoy having the opportunity to talk about their organization. Interviewees also expressed a potential interest in taking part in a VFG. However, given the difficulty of even finding enough interviewees, I could not attempt to schedule a VFG. Regardless of the reasons, about which I can only speculate, and which I in any case respect, the limited number of interviews conducted with PS members, as well as the unfeasibility of conducting VFGs, remain a limitation of this study, which I addressed by supplementing my analysis of the interviews with the examination of other written sources and by observing events and public and semipublic meetings of PS. I also spoke informally about my research with various former and current members of PS, to further validate my findings.

The second limitation is the nature of the qualitative methods that I chose to employ. While I maintain that the multimethod qualitative approach that I laid out provides important insights about the technological imaginaries of the activists I studied, it nevertheless relies on indirect data, that is, participants' post hoc rationalizations of their attitudes and practices. In this sense, the data I work with is different from what I could collect through an ethnographic engagement with these groups, which could allow me to observe how the technological imaginaries of these activists unfold in the moment. For example, while LUMe activists told me that their use of Facebook "sponsored" posts was discussed at length within the movement, I was not able to directly observe any of those discussions. Of course, choosing an ethnographic approach does not guarantee that one will be able to observe all the relevant conversations, but it could provide more occasions to be present should those discussions occur.

Ethics

Throughout my research, I followed the ethics guidelines of the Association of Internet Researchers (AoIR Ethics Working Committee, 2012). My data collection and retention, as well as my consent procedures, also complied with the European General Data Protection Regulation. This research was the object of two different institutional review board (IRB) protocols, one concerning the interviews conducted with the Hungarian activists and one concerning the interviews and focus groups conducted with LUMe and PS. In both cases, the IRB of the University of Pennsylvania determined that the protocols met the criteria for a review exemption (category 2). In chapter 1 I explained in more detail how I think about the ethical issues involved in doing research with/about activists and about my positionality.

I sought the informed consent of the activists I interviewed or included in the VFGs. Hungarian activists gave their consent verbally, after I presented my project to them; interviewees of LUMe and PS signed consent forms. All the participants received a copy of the consent form (or script, in the case of the Hungarian activists), which included detailed information on my project, my data collection procedure, my contact details, and the contact information of the IRB of the University of Pennsylvania, to which they could report any problems with my research. The PS organizers and the Hungarian activists received a consent form/script in English, LUMe received an Italian version.

Activists of LUMe and PS were offered modest compensation for their participation in the interviews and/or the focus groups; activists all elected to give that compensation to their organizations. All participants were made aware of the sources of funding that supported my research.

The interviews and the VFGs offered me spaces to talk to the participants about my preliminary takes on the data I was collecting. VFGs had debriefing moments at the end, after activists had produced their final drawings. At the beginning, as well as at the end, of the individual interviews, I asked participants if they had any questions for me. These moments, especially at the end of the interviews, offered activists an opportunity to inquire about my positionality as a researcher and about my research. I often discussed with them my motivations for doing this research and my tentative takes on my research findings; this often led to more discussions about contemporary activism and the meaning of digital technology. Above all, activists were especially eager to hear about what

movements in other countries were thinking about and doing with digital technologies. In their own rationalizations of what I told them about other activists,
they often commented about how these experiences looked different from their
own, despite reliance on the same digital technologies. Just like me, my participants also wanted to know how different political contexts shaped activists'
experiences with technology.

Notes

1. INTRODUCTION

1. None of the cases that are empirically analyzed in this book can be considered a case of challenge. As I explain in detail in the methodological appendix, this is due to the inductive approach I took for this research, which led me to select my cases based on the characteristics of the social movements, rather than on my expectations of what their technological imaginaries might be. I derived the category of challenge based on my conceptualization of the two other categories of appropriation and negotiation, as well as the literature on contemporary social movements. I could have searched for a "case of challenge" to add to my empirical analysis, but this would have contradicted the spirit of this research and the design choices I made. In fact, one of the core principles that guided this research is that activist technological imaginaries should be reconstructed based on an in-depth empirical analysis of each activist group, without a priori determinations based on the more visible manifestations of their technological practices; selecting another case that would, prior to the analysis, "look like challenge" would not match this principle—and might also result in finding that what "looked like challenge" actually was not a case of challenge at all.

2. TECHNOLOGICAL IMAGINARIES AND THE
UNIVERSAL AMBITIONS OF SILICON VALLEY

1. Parts of this chapter are reproduced from Elisabetta Ferrari, "Technocracy Meets Populism: The Dominant Technological Imaginary of Silicon Valley," *Communication, Culture & Critique* 13, no. 1 (2020): 121–124, by permission of Oxford University Press.

2. Drawing on the same scholarly debates, Emiliano Treré (2018) also connects the notions of social imaginaries and media/sociotechnical imaginaries, explaining the importance of using these concepts to investigate social movements' media practices. His reading of these literatures leads him to focus on the historical recurrence of imaginaries of technological utopia (and dystopia). In particular, he adopts the idea of the "digital sublime," based on Mosco (2004) and Nye (1996), to theorize the existence of "waves of techno-mythification within protest movements" (Treré, 2018, p. 117). For example, he argues that the significance of the technological practices for the Zapatista movement of the 1990s was overemphasized, in what he calls "a clear example of digital sublime 1.0" (Treré, 2018, p. 117). He then examines in detail two (more recent) cases of "digital sublime 2.0," the Italian 5SM and the Spanish Indignados; he demonstrates how these actors reproduce "technological myths" of the digital sublime for different ends. While the 5SM evoked the digital sublime to mask its authoritarian politics (Treré, 2018, p. 124), the Indignados drew on the sublime to support their experimentations with new forms of political participation (Treré, 2018, pp. 152–153). Treré's work is an important contribution to advancing our understanding of the complex relationship between digital technologies and activism. As can be clearly seen in this chapter, this book charts a different theoretical (and methodological) path for the investigation of this issue, which allows us to examine the interplay between dominant and activist technological imaginaries without centering the notion of the "sublime," thus enabling us to examine a wider range of possible activist responses to dominant discourses about technology.

3. The concept of "technopolitics" also shares a focus on nation-states and institutions. While there has been some attention to this concept within social movement research, particularly in the Spanish and Latin American context (see Treré, 2018; Treré & Barranquero Carretero, 2018), the literature on 'technopolitics', drawing on Gabrielle Hecht's work (1998), is mostly concerned with how institutional actors, as opposed to more grassroots collectives, deploy technology for political purposes.

4. The lens of "media practices" has been very significant in the literature on digital media and activism (among others Barassi, 2015; Cammaerts et al., 2013; Clark-Parsons, 2022; Mattoni, 2012) and has contributed an empirically grounded and rich understanding of what activists do with (digital) media. While embracing the insights from this scholarship, in my conceptualization of

technological imaginaries I primarily follow Taylor's (2004) assessment of the relationship between discourses and practices.

5. As I highlight in chapter 3, when talking about how the Hungarian internet tax protests appropriate Silicon Valley's dominant technological imaginary, there is a continuity between the visions of technology articulated in Western modernity and the key tenets of the dominant technological imaginary. Technology and modernity are, in fact, co-constitutive (Misa, 2003); Silicon Valley thus "inherits" some of the modern ways of looking at technology, in particular its association with a promise of progress and liberation.

6. For an exploration of how "colorblindness utopias" informed both the tech industry and internet studies, see Hamilton (2020)

7. Winner (1986) identified five key characteristics of sociotechnical orders: (1) centralization, (2) gigantism, (3) hierarchical authority, (4) elimination of competing activities, and (5) power over politics. These five aspects are also present in the sociotechnical order that Silicon Valley aspires to create. First, while Winner (1986) feared the centralization of technology in the hands of the state, today we can see how the major tech companies have a great deal of centralized power not only over the data they collect, but also over the structure of the everyday activities performed by millions and millions of people, like chatting, moving around, and buying things. And this control is exercised without any form of democratic input by the users of these services. Second, scale is crucial to how Silicon Valley companies justify their power: their global gigantic scale is what allows them to position themselves on the world stage. Third, Winner denounced the authoritarianism that emerged from the need of managing complex technological systems. While anti-authoritarianism is one of the core values of Silicon Valley, there is also tremendous inequality, in terms of the racial and gender discrimination that is prevalent in tech spaces, but also in terms of digital labor (see Andrejevic, 2013) that is required of users. Recent efforts to organize tech workers also speak to this point. While Silicon Valley presents itself as an egalitarian and liberating entity, the reality is very different: there is a disjuncture between the scale and centralization of the current sociotechnical order and Silicon Valley's promise to end all hierarchies. Fourth, Winner (1986) talked about the "tendency of large, centralized, hierarchically arranged sociotechnical entities to crowd out and eliminate other varieties of human activity" (Winner, 1986, p. 48). This is the "network effect": the more people join a platform, the more valuable it becomes, and the more people want to join—thus making alternatives very difficult to establish. Last, Winner highlighted "the various ways that large sociotechnical organizations exercise power to control the social and political influences that ostensibly control them" (Winner, 1986, p. 48). It would be difficult to dispute the power that Silicon Valley giants exercise over social and political institutions (see O'Mara, 2019), a situation that is further complicated by their reach across national borders and legal jurisdictions. Using Winner's (1986)

definition, we can clearly see how Silicon Valley envisions itself as a global socio-technical order, independent from nation-states. This is no longer the independence of "the online" from nation-states declared by John Perry Barlow (1996); that independence is now taken for granted, both because of the scale of these technological corporations and because of the hold of neoliberalism on our ideas concerning the markets and the states. It is an independence rooted in global dominance.

8. For a comprehensive analysis of Zuckerberg's framing of Facebook over time, see Bucher (2021).

9. Much more promising, in terms of challenging the power of the dominant technological imaginary, is the multifaceted organizing work happening among tech workers: from the creation of labor unions to pressure campaigns, such as those directed at stopping tech companies' contracts with US Immigration and Customs Enforcement (ICE). This important pushback has been accompanied by an increased public attention to critical voices, including many women who have told their stories of working in tech, in memoirs such as *Abolish Silicon Valley* (Liu, 2020) and *Uncanny Valley* (Wiener, 2020). The ousting of research scientist Timnit Gebru from Google's AI team over papers that warned about the ethical shortcomings of facial recognition technology generated a wave of outrage toward the company and prompted many discussions on technology and race. What is crucial in this grassroots techlash is that different constituencies are beginning to question the core political underpinnings of the dominant technological imaginary, which I hope will pave the way for a political contestation of Silicon Valley.

10. I chose the concept of technological imaginary, over that of media imaginary, for a few reasons. First, to explicitly connect my work to ongoing discussions in science and technology studies, which focus on the politics of technology. In choosing to think of technological imaginaries I hope to bring these discussions together with the scholarship on social movements and media technologies. Second, I decided to center technology, as opposed to media, in order to explicitly deploy my theoretical framework to critique and denormalize the technologically deterministic assumptions that are so often embedded in how we think about technology. Third, I wanted to allow for the possibility of the emergence of technological imaginaries that are, in fact, not predicated on media and communication technologies; while this is not the task of this book, this framework has the ambition to be applicable to examine how technologies are imagined by actors in different eras. For instance, without the ambition to fully sketch out its meaning, it is worth mentioning that Lenin's proclamation of communism as equivalent to "Soviet power and electrification" (Lenin, 1964) is a technological imaginary: one that is not concerned with media technologies (or digital technologies, for that matter). For these reasons, I choose to speak of a technological imaginary to allow for a broader application of my theoretical framework, beyond contemporary media technologies, and in dialogue with STS approaches.

3. THE SYMBOLIC POWER OF MUNDANE MODERNITY

1. Parts of this chapter first appeared in Elisabetta Ferrari, "'Free Country, Free Internet': The Symbolic Power of Technology in the Hungarian Internet Tax Protests," *Media, Culture & Society* 41, no. 1 (2019): 70–85. Copyright © 2019 (The Author). http://doi.org/10.1177/0163443718799394.

2. As of September 2023, the page is still active and has collected approximately 183,000 likes.

3. The size of the October 28 demonstration was surpassed on April 12, 2017, with one of the demonstrations organized against the ad hoc law against Central European University and the anti-NGO legislation, as recognized by the Twitter account representing the internet tax protests, which stated: "Largest protest in Hungarian history – time to go mr orban #ceu" (NoNetTax_HU, 2017).

4. My research is concerned with anti-Fidesz mobilizations on the left, but the emergence of right-wing protest movements in Hungary is an important phenomenon, addressed for instance by Kaposi and Mátay (2008). The biggest electoral competitor for Fidesz has historically been Jobbik (Jobbik Magyarországért Mozgalom [Movement for a Better Hungary]), originally a far-right, nationalist, and Euroskeptic party (Pirro & Róna, 2019). Jobbik has now morphed into a less extreme formation, which even entered into an electoral coalition with other major opposition parties in the lead-up to the 2022 elections (Popescu & Toka, 2021).

5. Due to the difficult situation of NGOs and civil society actors in the current Hungarian political context, as an added precaution I do not identify any of the organizations whose members were involved in organizing the internet tax protests.

6. The presence of André Goodfriend, then chargé d'affaires at the US Embassy in Budapest (the "ambassador" figure mentioned by Daniel) became the object of controversy when it was denounced by the Hungarian government's spokesperson, Zoltan Kovacs (Lyman, 2014a).

7. While the internet tax spurred some protest in the countryside, too, the political divide between the city and the countryside has been a long-standing issue for the activist opposition to Fidesz (see Wilkin et al., 2015).

8. Budapest is about 50 km from Slovakia and 170 km from Austria.

9. I thank Robert Vámos for this translation.

10. This framing is effective within a national political culture that remembers its past as a string of defeats inflicted by major powers: the Ottomans, the Hapsburgs, Nazi Germany (although not always), and the Soviet Union.

4. FIGHTING THE SYSTEM WITH THE TOOLS OF THE SYSTEM

1. Neofascist activists, such as those of Casa Pound, have also occupied buildings—notably in Rome—to carry out their political activities. These occupations,

however, cannot be considered social centers because of their political orientation and more hierarchical organizational practices (Mudu, 2018).

2. At the time of the research, Brothers of Italy, the extreme right-wing party whose leader Giorgia Meloni would go on to become prime minister in 2022, was still marginal.

3. As I explain in the appendix, each visual focus group began with a questionnaire that the activists completed anonymously. One of the questions, aimed at sparking discussion, asked participants to rate how much they agreed or disagreed with the statement "The internet is a democratic space."

4. While this sentence and other variations of it used by the activists are reminiscent of the essay "The Master's Tools Will Never Dismantle the Master's House" (Lorde, 2007), LUMe interviewees do not appear to be familiar with it; this essay and Lorde's work in general are not well known in Italy, even among activists.

5. This popular vision of supporters of the Five Star Movement as engaging in cringeworthy posting on Facebook does not necessarily match the more complex discursive construction developed by Beppe Grillo and the party, which Natale and Ballatore (2014) and Treré (2018) so eloquently describe. For instance, central to the 5SM's "myth of the web" were more traditional blogs, chiefly Grillo's, and forums such as Meetup, rather than social network sites; later, it was Rousseau, the platform created by the party for internal decision-making (Deseriis, 2017), that became important for the members of the 5SM. While LUMe activists clearly interpret (and respond to) to the technological imaginary of the 5SM as described by Natale and Ballatore (2014) and Treré (2018), as is evident in the paragraphs to follow, this more popular understanding of 5SM sympathizers as particularly active on social media is also present in their minds.

5. ORGANIZING WHERE PEOPLE ARE

1. While the Seattle-based group is the example referenced by PS, there have been several tenant organizing efforts in the United States, rooted in broader struggles for social justice (see Kaun, 2016).

2. On Facebook, a secret group can only be joined after being invited by a group member and cannot be found through Facebook's search function. In contrast, users can find and read the name and description of any closed group; however, only members can see the content posted in the group and its list of members. Users can typically ask to join closed groups through the "Join Group" button.

3. The concept of "activist networking" was also put forward by Jeff Juris in a highly influential article on the global justice movement (Juris, 2005); what PS members were discussing, however, was not the same concept, and they did not appear to be aware of Juris's formulation.

4. As much as possible, I follow their self-characterization and do not refer to them as "activists" in this chapter. However, for the sake of brevity, I do refer to Philly Socialists members with the term *activists* when I consider them together with LUMe and the Hungarian internet tax protests.

6. CONCLUSION

1. Indymedia is the clearest case of an activist attempt to envision and develop a digital alternative to the mainstream. However, I believe it would be a stretch to consider it a case of challenge, as I intend that category in this book, because it was not developed in opposition to Silicon Valley and its technologies, but rather in opposition to mainstream media and their biased coverage of protest (Rucht, 2004). This does not at all diminish its importance for the anti-globalization activists of the 1990s or indeed its legacy for contemporary social movements (see Wolfson, 2014), but it should make us wonder why we haven't yet seen a comparable development of an alternative that challenges the dominance of Silicon Valley.

2. As social movements scholars have shown us, many elements can influence activists' perceptions and decisions: for instance, their interpretation of the political opportunity structure (Tarrow, 2011), their collective identity (Melucci, 1989), their decision-making processes (Polletta, 2002), and emotions (Jasper, 2011) can all play a role in shaping movements' trajectories. By arguing that activist technological imaginaries should also be considered important for a social movement's political choices, I am not disputing the importance of these factors.

3. Similar expectations also emerged very clearly after Elon Musk's acquisition of Twitter in 2022, when many users began to look for an alternative to the platform and public discussions emerged about what service might become "the next Twitter."

METHODOLOGICAL APPENDIX

1. As I described in Ferrari (2022), I conducted two pilot VFGs to test this method before using it with activists.

References

Ágh, A. (2017). Cultural war and reinventing the past in Poland and Hungary: The politics of historical memory in East–Central Europe. *Polish Political Science Yearbook, 45*, 32–44. https://doi.org/10.15804/ppsy2016003

Andersson, L. (2016). No digital "castles in the air": Online non-participation and the radical Left. *Media and Communication, 4*(4). https://doi.org/10.17645/mac.v4i4.694

Andrejevic, M. (2013). Estranged free labor. In T. Scholz (Ed.), *Digital labor: The Internet as playground and factory* (pp. 149–164). Routledge.

AoIR Ethics Working Committee. (2012). *Ethical decision-making and internet research.* https://aoir.org/reports/ethics2.pdf

Appadurai, A. (1996). *Modernity at large: Cultural dimensions of globalization.* University of Minnesota Press.

Atton, C. (2002). *Alternative media.* Sage Publications.

Bagnoli, A. (2009). Beyond the standard interview: The use of graphic elicitation and arts-based methods. *Qualitative Research, 9*(5), 547–570. https://doi.org/10.1177/1468794109343625

Barassi, V. (2015). *Activism on the web: Everyday struggles against digital capitalism.* Routledge.

Barassi, V., & Treré, E. (2012). Does Web 3.0 come after Web 2.0? Deconstructing theoretical assumptions through practice. *New Media & Society, 14*(8), 1269–1285. https://doi.org/10.1177/1461444812445878

Barbrook, R., & Cameron, A. (1996). The Californian ideology. *Science as Culture*, *6*(1), 44–72. https://doi.org/10.1080/09505439609526455

Barlow, J. P. (1996, February 8). *A declaration of the independence of cyberspace*. Electronic Frontier Foundation. https://projects.eff.org/~barlow/Declaration-Final.html

Benjamin, R. (2019). *Race after technology: Abolitionist tools for the New Jim Code*. Polity Press.

Bennett, W. L., & Segerberg, A. (2013). *The logic of connective action: Digital media and the personalization of contentious politics*. Cambridge University Press.

Bienvenu, H. (2016, October 11). Newspaper closes in Hungary, and Hungarians see government's hand. *The New York Times*. https://www.nytimes.com/2016/10/12/world/europe/hungary-newspaper-nepszabadsag.html?nytmobile=0

Bienvenu, H., & Santora, M. (2018, April 14). Thousands of Hungarians protest against newly elected leader. *The New York Times*. https://www.nytimes.com/2018/04/14/world/europe/hungary-protest-orban.html

Bohle, D., & Greskovits, B. (2012). *Capitalist diversity on Europe's periphery*. Cornell University Press.

Boni, F., & Ricci, O. (2015). Dalla dissacrazione all'umiliazione: Nuove forme di satira politica online tra violenza simbolica e distinzione. *Comunicazione Politica*, *1*, 27–42.

Bonilla, Y., & Rosa, J. (2015). #Ferguson: Digital protest, hashtag ethnography, and the racial politics of social media in the United States. *American Ethnologist*, *42*(1), 4–17. https://doi.org/10.1111/amet.12112

Borbáth, E., & Gessler, T. (2020). Different worlds of contention? Protest in Northwestern, Southern and Eastern Europe. *European Journal of Political Research*, *59*(4), 910–935. https://doi.org/10.1111/1475-6765.12379

Bozoki, A. (2015). Broken democracy, predatory state, and nationalist populism. In P. Krasztev & J. van Til (Eds.), *The Hungarian patient: Social opposition to an illiberal democracy* (pp. 3–36). Central European University LLC.

Braun, V., & Clarke, V. (2006). Using thematic analysis in psychology. *Qualitative Research in Psychology*, *3*(2), 77–101. https://doi.org/10.1191/1478088706qp063oa

Brey, J. (2018, July 25). A full-fledged Socialist Party in American politics. Just a dream? These folks beg to differ. *Philadelphia Weekly*. http://www.philadelphiaweekly.com/news/a-full-fledged-socialist-party-in-american-politics-just-a/article_3e08f17c-9085-11e8-b6b3-8f17952cc03d.html

Brouillette, A. (2012). *Hungarian media laws in Europe: An assessment of the consistency of Hungary's media laws with European practices and norms*. Center for Media and Communication Studies, Central European University. http://medialaws.ceu.hu/

Broussard, M. (2018). *Artificial unintelligence: How computers misunderstand the world*. MIT Press.

Bucher, T. (2016). The algorithmic imaginary: Exploring the ordinary affects of Facebook algorithms. *Information, Communication & Society, 20*(1), 30–44. https://doi.org/10.1080/1369118X.2016.1154086

Bucher, T. (2021). *Facebook*. Polity Press.

Bürgerbewegung oder Putschversuch? Die Internetsteuer bringt Ungarn auf Trab. (2014, October 28). *Pester Lloyd*. http://www.pesterlloyd.net/html/1444 antiinternet.html

Burrell, J. (2012). *Invisible users: Youth in the Internet cafés of urban Ghana*. MIT Press.

Buzogány, A., & Varga, M. (2018). The ideational foundations of the illiberal backlash in Central and Eastern Europe: The case of Hungary. *Review of International Political Economy, 25*(6), 811–828. https://doi.org/10.1080 /09692290.2018.1543718

Cadwalladr, C., & Graham-Harrison, E. (2018, March 17). Revealed: 50 million Facebook profiles harvested for Cambridge Analytica in major data breach. *The Guardian*. https://www.theguardian.com/news/2018/mar/17/cambridge -analytica-facebook-influence-us-election

Cammaerts, B., Mattoni, A., & McCurdy, P. (2013). *Mediation and protest movements*. Intellect.

Captain, S. (2011, December 27). Occupy geeks are building a Facebook for the 99%. *Wired*. http://www.wired.com/threatlevel/2011/12/occupy-facebook/

Casaglia, A. (2018). Territories of struggle: Social centres in Northern Italy opposing mega-events. *Antipode, 50*(2), 478–497. https://doi.org/10.1111/anti .12287

Chapman, S. (2018, May 18). Why millennials are drawn to socialism. *Chicago Tribune*. https://www.chicagotribune.com/columns/steve-chapman/ct -perspec-chapman-young-socialism-capitalism-20180520-story.html

Chenou, J. M., & Cepeda-Másmela, C. (2019). #NiUnaMenos: Data Activism from the Global South. *Television and New Media, 20*(4), 396–411. https://doi .org/10.1177/1527476419828995

Christensen, H. S. (2011). Political activities on the Internet: Slacktivism or political participation by other means? *First Monday, 16*(2). https://doi.org /10.5210/fm.v16i2.3336

Clark-Parsons, R. (2022). *Networked feminism: How digital media makers transformed gender justice movements*. University of California Press.

Commission slams Hungary's "internet tax". (2014, October 28). Euractiv. https://www.euractiv.com/section/central-europe/news/commission-slams -hungary-s-internet-tax/

Corbin, J., & Strauss, A. (2008). *Basics of qualitative research: Techniques and procedures for developing grounded theory*. Sage.

Corcione, D., Yeun, J., & Diliberto, A. (2019). Beyond the vote: Base-building for class independence in Philadelphia. In Verso Books (Ed.), *Socialist strategy and electoral politics: A report*. Verso Books.

Cossu, A. (2018). Beyond social media determinism? How artists reshape the organization of social movements. *Social Media and Society*, *4*(1). https://doi .org/10.1177/2056305117750717

Costanza-Chock, S. (2020). *Design justice: Community-led practices to build the worlds we need*. MIT Press.

Csaky, Z. (2017, April 18). Hungary's tipping point. *Perspectives*. https://freedom house.org/blog/hungary-s-tipping-point

De Angelis, M. (2014). Social revolution and the Commons. *South Atlantic Quarterly*, *113*(2), 299–311. https://doi.org/10.1215/00382876-2643630

Deák, A. (2011). Hungarian dances—The origins and the future of Viktor Orbán's revolution. *Lithuanian Annual Strategic Review*, *11*(1), 145–168. https://doi.org/10.2478/v10243-012-0026-z

Dean, J. (2005). Communicative capitalism: Circulation and the foreclosure of politics. *Cultural Politics*, *1*(1), 51–73. https://doi.org/10.2752/174321905778 054845

Della Porta, D., & Tarrow, S. (Eds.). (2005). *Transnational protest and global activism*. Rowman and Littlefield.

Democratic Socialists of America. (n.d.). *Home*. https://www.dsausa.org

Dennis, J. (2019). *Beyond slacktivism: Political participation on social media*. Palgrave Macmillan.

Deseriis, M. (2017). Direct parliamentarianism: An analysis of the political values embedded in Rousseau, the 'operating system' of the Five Star Movement. *JeDEM*, *9*(2), 47–67.

Dessewffy, T., & Nagy, Z. (2016). Born in Facebook: The refugee crisis and grassroots connective action in Hungary. *International Journal of Communication*, *10*, 2872–2894.

Douthat, R., Goldberg, M., & Leonhardt, D. (2019, May 30). The United States of socialism? A debate with Jacobin editor Bhaskar Sunkara. *The New York Times*. https://www.nytimes.com/2019/05/30/opinion/the-argument -socialism-bernie-sanders.html

Downing, J. (2008). Social movement theories and alternative media: An evaluation and critique. *Communication, Culture & Critique*, *1*(1), 40–50. https://doi.org/10.1111/j.1753-9137.2007.00005.x

Dual Power app. (n.d.). Retrieved August 28, 2022, from https://dualpower.app/

Dunai, M. (2014, October 29). *Around 100,000 Hungarians rally for democracy as internet tax hits nerve*. Reuters. http://www.reuters.com/article/us -hungary-internet-protest-idUSKBN0II18N20141029

Dunbar-Hester, C. (2014). *Low power to the people: Pirates, protest, and politics in FM radio activism*. MIT Press.

Earl, J., & Kimport, K. (2011). *Digitally enabled social change: Activism in the Internet Age*. MIT Press.

Eder, M. (2014, October 28). Hungary Internet-tax demonstrations spread as Orban unmoved. *Bloomberg Technology*. http://www.bloomberg.com/news/articles/2014-10-28/hungarians-hold-second-internet-tax-rally-as-cabinet-unmoved

Edwards, P. (2009). *"More work! Less pay!": Rebellion and repression in Italy, 1972–77*. Manchester University Press.

Emmer, P., Rivas, C., Salas Neves, B., & Schweidler, C. (2020). *Technologies for liberation: Towards abolitionist futures*. Astraea Lesbian Foundation for Justice and Research Action Design (RAD). https://www.astraeafoundation.org/FundAbolitionTech/

Eotvos Karoly Policy Institute, Hungarian Helsinki Committee, Hungarian Civil Liberties Union, & Mérték Media Monitor. (2014). *Disrespect for European values in Hungary 2010–2014*. http://www.helsinki.hu/en/disrespect-for-european-values-in-hungary-2010-2014/

Feher, M. (2014a, October 27). Tens of thousands of Hungarians protest against planned internet tax. *The Wall Street Journal*. https://blogs.wsj.com/emergingeurope/2014/10/27/tens-of-thousands-of-hungarians-protest-against-planned-internet-tax/

Feher, M. (2014b, October 28). *Hungary waters down planned tax on internet use*. The Wall Street Journal. http://www.wsj.com/articles/hungary-waters-down-planned-tax-on-internet-use-1414431081

Ferrari, E. (2020a). Bodies that matter, bodies that don't: Selective disembodiment in the early *Wired* magazine (1993–1997). *Internet Histories, 4*(3), 333–348. https://doi.org/10.1080/24701475.2020.1769891

Ferrari, E. (2020b). Technocracy meets populism: The dominant technological imaginary of Silicon Valley. *Communication, Culture & Critique, 13*(1), 121–124. https://doi.org/10.1093/ccc/tcz051

Ferrari, E. (2022, November 22). Visual focus groups: Stimulating reflexive conversations with collective drawing. *New Media & Society, 0*(0). https://doi.org/10.1177/14614448221136082

Fish, A. (2017). Technology retreats and the politics of social media. *TripleC, 15*(1), 355–369.

Fisher, E. (2008). The classless workplace: The digerati and the new spirit of technocapitalism. *WorkingUSA: The Journal of Labor and Society, 11*(2), 181–198. https://doi.org/10.1111/j.1743-4580.2007.00197.x

Fisher, E. (2010). *Media and new capitalism in the digital age: The spirit of networks*. Palgrave Macmillan.

Flichy, P. (1995). *Dynamics of modern communication: The shaping and impact of new communication technologies*. Sage.

Flichy, P. (2007a). *The Internet imaginaire*. MIT Press.

Flichy, P. (2007b). *Understanding technological innovation: A socio-technical approach*. Edward Elgar.

Fotopoulou, A. (2016). Digital and networked by default? Women's organisations and the social imaginary of networked feminism. *New Media & Society*, *18*(6), 989–1005. https://doi.org/10.1177/1461444814552264

Franceschi-Bicchierai, L. (2014, October 27). Thousands swarm Budapest streets to protest unprecedented internet tax. *Mashable*. https://mashable.com/archive/hungary-internet-tax-protest

Freeman, J. (1972). The tyranny of structurelessness. *Berkeley Journal of Sociology*, *17*, 151–164.

Gagyi, A. (2014). Smartphones and the European flag: The new Hungarian demonstrations for democracy. *Studia UBB Sociologia*, *59*(2), 75–86.

Gammage, J., & Irizarry-Aponte, C. (2018a, July 3). Police clash with protesters outside Philly ICE office, arresting 29. *The Philadelphia Inquirer*. https://www.inquirer.com/philly/news/abolish-ice-protest-philadelphia-immigration-berks-20180703.html

Gammage, J., & Irizarry-Aponte, C. (2018b, July 28). Kenney halts data sharing with ICE. *The Philadelphia Inquirer*, 1.

Gehl, R. W. (2015). The case for alternative social media. *Social Media and Society*, *1*(2). https://doi.org/10.1177/2056305115604338

Gerbaudo, P. (2012). *Tweets and the streets: Social media and contemporary activism*. Pluto Press.

Giddens, A., & Pierson, C. (1998). *Conversations with Anthony Giddens: Making sense of modernity*. Polity Press.

Gieseking, J. J. (2013). Where we go from here: The mental sketch mapping method and its analytic components. *Qualitative Inquiry*, *19*(9), 712–724. https://doi.org/10.1177/1077800413500926

Gillet, K. (2017, May 4). Romania drops measure to pardon corrupt officials. *The New York Times*. https://www.nytimes.com/2017/05/04/world/europe/romania-corruption-protests.html

Giuffrida, A. (2018, June 17). Between Italy's cliffs and sea, migrants bid to outwit police. *The Guardian*. https://www.theguardian.com/world/2018/jun/17/italy-ventimiglia-migrants-stuck-at-border-crisis-suffering

Gladwell, M. (2010, October 4). Small change: Why the revolution will not be tweeted. *The New Yorker*. https://www.newyorker.com/magazine/2010/10/04/small-change-malcolm-gladwell

Gladwell, M., & Shirky, C. (2011, January 19). From innovation to revolution: Do social media make protests possible? *Foreign Affairs*, 153–154. https://www.foreignaffairs.com/articles/2011-01-19/innovation-revolution

Glied, V. (2014). From the green movement to a party. The effect of the crisis and democratic movements in Hungary. *Politeja*, *11*(28), 31–61. https://doi.org/10.12797/politeja.11.2014.28.02

Gorondi, P. (2017, April 12). Tens of thousands protest Hungary's education, NGO policies. *Associated Press.* https://www.apnews.com/86ebad08af4f4be799f11ab14492cb1a

Graham-Harrison, E. (2019, January 5). Thousands in Budapest march against "slave law" forcing overtime on workers. *The Guardian.* https://www.theguardian.com/world/2019/jan/05/thousands-in-budapest-march-against-slave-law-forcing-overtime-on-workers

Granville, K. (2019, March 19). Facebook and Cambridge Analytica: What you need to know as fallout widens. *The New York Times.* https://www.nytimes.com/2018/03/19/technology/facebook-cambridge-analytica-explained.html

Greenfield, J. (2019, July 29). Is socialism having its moment in U.S. elections? [Podcast episode]. In *PBS Newshour Weekend.* https://www.pbs.org/newshour/show/will-socialism-ever-have-its-moment-in-u-s-elections

Hamilton, A. M. (2020). A genealogy of critical race and digital studies: Past, present, and future. *Sociology of Race and Ethnicity, 6*(3), 292–301. https://doi.org/10.1177/2332649220922577

Harvey, D. (2007). *A brief history of neoliberalism.* Oxford University Press.

Hecht, G. (1998). *The radiance of France: Nuclear power and national identity after World War II.* MIT Press.

Henwood, D. (2019, May 15). The socialist network: Inside DSA's struggle to move into the political mainstream. *The New Republic.* https://newrepublic.com/article/153768/inside-democratic-socialists-america-struggle-political-mainstream

Hesse, M. (2017, January 26). Thousands demonstrated against Trump in Philly. Is this a new era of perpetual protest? *The Washington Post.* https://www.washingtonpost.com/politics/thousands-demonstrated-against-trump-in-philly-is-this-a-new-era-of-perpetual-protest/2017/01/26/5385dca2-e3ef-11e6-a453-19ec4b3d09ba_story.html?noredirect=on&utm_term=.99b333473062

Hesselberth, P. (2018). Discourses on disconnectivity and the right to disconnect. *New Media & Society, 20*(5), 1994–2010. https://doi.org/10.1177/1461444817711449

Hintz, A., & Milan, S. (2010). Social science is police science: Researching grass-roots activism. *International Journal of Communication, 4,* 837–844.

Hirsch, T. (2011). More than friends: Social and mobile media for activist organizations. In M. Foth, L. Forlano, C. Satchell, & M. Gibbs (Eds.), *From social butterfly to engaged citizen: Urban informatics, social media, ubiquitous computing, and mobile technology to support citizen engagement* (pp. 135–149). MIT Press.

Hobsbawm, E. J. (1952). The machine breakers. *Past and Present, 1*(1), 57–70. https://doi.org/10.1093/past/1.1.57

Horras, T. (2017a, July 20). Base-building: Activist networking or organizing the unorganized? *The Philadelphia Partisan.* https://philadelphiapartisan.com

/2017/07/20/base-building-activist-networking-or-organizing-the
-unorganized-tim-horras/

Horras, T. (2017b, August 23). Where does the march end? Base-building and mass action as discrete moments in a singular process. *The Philadelphia Partisan*. https://philadelphiapartisan.com/2017/08/23/where-does-the -march-end-base-building-and-mass-action-as-discrete-moments-in-a -singular-process/

Horras, T. (2022, January 20). Remarks on dissolution of Marxist Center. *Regeneration*. https://regenerationmag.org/remarks-on-dissolution-of -marxist-center/

Human Rights Watch. (2013). *Wrong direction on rights: Assessing the impact of Hungary's new constitution and laws*. https://www.hrw.org/report/2013 /05/16/wrong-direction-rights/assessing-impact-hungarys-new-constitution -and-laws

Hume, T., & Park, M. (2014, September 30). *Understanding the symbols of Hong Kong's "Umbrella Revolution."* CNN. http://www.cnn.com/2014/09/30/world /asia/objects-hong-kong-protest/index.html

Hungary: Internet tax angers protesters. (2014, October 27). Euronews. http:// www.euronews.com/2014/10/27/hungary-internet-tax-angers-protesters/

Hungary internet tax cancelled after mass protests. (2014, October 31). BBC News. http://www.bbc.com/news/world-europe-29846285

Hungary: Tens of thousands march in Budapest anti-Orban demo. (2018, April 14). BBC News. https://www.bbc.com/news/world-europe-43771392

Jackson, S. J., Bailey, M., & Foucault Welles, B. (2020). *#HashtagActivism: Networks of race and gender justice*. MIT Press.

Jasanoff, S. (2015). Future imperfect: Science, technology and the imaginations of modernity. In S. Jasanoff & S.-H. Kim (Eds.), *Dreamscapes of modernity: Sociotechnical imaginaries and the fabrication of power* (pp. 1–33). University of Chicago Press.

Jasanoff, S., & Kim, S.-H. (2009). Containing the atom: Sociotechnical imagi-naries and nuclear power in the United States and South Korea. *Minerva*, 47(2), 119–146.

Jasanoff, S., & Kim, S.-H. (Eds.). (2015). *Dreamscapes of modernity: Sociotech-nical imaginaries and the fabrication of power*. University of Chicago Press.

Jasper, J. M. (2011). Emotions and social movements: Twenty years of theory and research. *Annual Review of Sociology, 37*(1), 285–303. https://doi.org/10 .1146/annurev-soc-081309-150015

Johnson, B., Jones, E., & Haenfler, R. (2012). Lifestyle movements: Exploring the intersection of lifestyle and social movements. *Social Movement Studies, 11*(1), 1–20. https://doi.org/10.1080/14742837.2012.640535

Juris, J. S. (2005). The new digital media and activist networking within anti–corporate globalization movements. *The ANNALS of the American*

Academy of Political and Social Science, 597(1), 189–208. https://doi.org/10
.1177/0002716204270338

Kallius, A., Monterescu, D., & Rajaram, P. K. (2016). Immobilizing mobility:
Border ethnography, illiberal democracy, and the politics of the "refugee
crisis" in Hungary. *American Ethnologist, 43*(1), 25–37. https://doi.org/10.1111
/amet.12260

Kaposi, I., & Mátay, M. (2008). Radicals online: The Hungarian street protests
of 2006 and the Internet. In K. Jakubowicz & M. Sükösd (Eds.), *Finding the
right place on the map: Central and Eastern European media change in a
global perspective* (pp. 277–296). Intellect.

Kaun, A. (2016). *Crisis and critique: A brief history of media participation in
times of crisis.* Zed Books.

Kaun, A., & Treré, E. (2018). Repression, resistance and lifestyle: Charting
(dis)connection and activism in times of accelerated capitalism. *Social
Movement Studies, 19*(5–6), 697–715. https://doi.org/10.1080/14742837.2018
.1555752

Kavada, A. (2015). Creating the collective: Social media, the Occupy movement
and its constitution as a collective actor. *Information, Communication &
Society, 18*(8), 872–886. https://doi.org/10.1080/1369118X.2015.1043318

Kind-Kovács, F., & Labov, J. (Eds.). (2015). *Samizdat, tamizdat and beyond:
Transnational media during and after socialism.* Berghahn Books.

Kingsley, P. (2018, November 29). Orban and his allies cement control of
Hungary's news media. *The New York Times.* https://www.nytimes.com/2018
/11/29/world/europe/hungary-orban-media.html

Kornai, J. (2015). Hungary's U-turn: Retreating from democracy. *Journal of
Democracy, 26*(3), 34–48. https://doi.org/10.1353/jod.2015.0046

Kraidy, M. (2016). *The naked blogger of Cairo: Creative insurgency in the Arab
World.* Harvard University Press.

Kroes, N. [@NeelieKroesEU]. (2014, October 22). *Proposed internet tax in
#Hungary . . .* [Tweet]. Twitter. https://twitter.com/neeliekroeseu/status
/525057867335081984

Kuo, R. (2018). Racial justice activist hashtags: Counterpublics and discourse
circulation. *New Media & Society, 20*(2), 495–514. https://doi.org/10.1177
/1461444816663485

Large protest in support of Hungary's Soros-backed university. (2017, April 9).
BBC News. https://www.bbc.com/news/world-europe-39549120

Lazzarato, M. (1996). Immaterial labour. In P. Virno & M. Hardt (Eds.), *Radical
thought in Italy* (pp. 132–146). University of Minnesota Press.

Lee, F. L. F., & Chan, J. M. (2018). *Media and protest logics in the digital era:
The Umbrella movement in Hong Kong.* Oxford University Press.

Lenin, V. I. (1964). Communism is Soviet power + electrification of the whole
country. In *Collected works* (Vol. 31, pp. 513–518). Progress Publishers.

http://soviethistory.msu.edu/1921-2/electrification-campaign/communism-is
-soviet-power-electrification-of-the-whole-country/

Levin, S. (2018, July 3). Occupy Ice: Protest camps expand across US amid calls
to shutter agency. *The Guardian.* https://www.theguardian.com/us-news
/2018/jul/03/occupy-ice-protests-immigration-families

Lim, M. (2012). Clicks, cabs, and coffee houses: Social media and oppositional
movements in Egypt, 2004-2011. *Journal of Communication, 62*(2), 231–248.
https://doi.org/10.1111/j.1460-2466.2012.01628.x

Lister, M., Dovey, J., Giddings, S., Grant, I., & Kelly, K. (2009). *New media:
A critical introduction.* Routledge.

Liu, W. (2020). *Abolish Silicon Valley: How to liberate technology from capitalism.* Repeater Books.

Loney-Howes, R., Mendes, K., Fernández Romero, D., Fileborn, B., & Núñez
Puente, S. (2022). Digital footprints of #MeToo. *Feminist Media Studies,
22*(6), 1345–1362. https://doi.org/10.1080/14680777.2021.1886142

Lorde, A. (2007). The Master's tools will never dismantle the Master's house.
In *Sister Outsider: Essays and Speeches* (pp. 110–114). Crossing Press.

LUMe. (2017a). *LUMe non si può spegnere—Appello di solidarietà.* https://www
.change.org/p/città-di-milano-lume-non-si-spegne

LUMe. (2017b, August 13). *Assedio culturale 23 Settembre #lumenonsispegne . . .*
[Status update]. Facebook. https://www.facebook.com/LUMe.occupato
/photos/a.764115920368167/1432908620155557/?type=3

LUMe. (2017c, September 21). *Assedio culturale e artiglieria pensante: Strumenti
di socialità milanese.* Effimera. http://effimera.org/assedio-culturale
-artiglieria-pensante-strumenti-socialita-milanese-lume/

LUMe. (2017d, October 19). *L'ex-Cinema Orchidea e la sua storia.* Milano in
Movimento. https://milanoinmovimento.com/finestre/lex-cinema-orchidea
-e-la-sua-storia-un-dossier-by-lume

LUMe. (2017e, October 25). *Vittoria di LUMe, il cinema sarà restituito ai
milanesi . . .* [Status update]. Facebook. https://www.facebook.com/LUMe
.occupato/posts/vittoria-di-lume-il-cinema-sara-restituito-ai-milanesiil-18
-ottobre-abbiamo-occu/1497107500402335/

LUMe. (2017f, November 3). *Comunicato di rivendicazione . . .* [Status update].
Facebook. https://www.facebook.com/LUMe.occupato/posts/1505757549
537330

LUMe. (2018, October 5). *"Non è reato occupare un edificio se la condotta ha
scopo dimostrativo . . .* [Status update]. Facebook. https://www.facebook
.com/LUMe.occupato/posts/1894030500710031?__tn__=-R

Lyman, R. (2014a, October 29). Proposed internet tax draws Hungarians to
streets in protest. *The New York Times.* http://www.nytimes.com/2014/10/30
/world/europe/hungarians-march-against-proposed-tax-on-internet-use
.html?_r=0

Lyman, R. (2014b, October 31). Hungary drops internet tax plan after public outcry. *The New York Times*. https://www.nytimes.com/2014/11/01/world /europe/hungary-drops-internet-tax-plan-after-surge-of-protests.html

Mansell, R. (2012). *Imagining the internet: Communication, innovation, and governance*. Oxford University Press.

Mao, Z. (1967). Serve the people. In *Selected works of Mao Tse-tung* (Vol. 3, pp. 177–178). Foreign Languages Press.

Marvin, C. (1988). *When old technologies were new: Thinking about electric communication in the late nineteenth century*. Oxford University Press.

Marx, L. (1964). *The machine in the garden: Technology and the pastoral ideal in America*. Oxford University Press.

Mattoni, A. (2012). *Media practices and protest politics: How precarious workers mobilise*. Routledge.

McGreal, C. (2017, September 2). "The S-word": How young Americans fell in love with socialism. *The Guardian*. https://www.theguardian.com/us-news /2017/sep/02/socialism-young-americans-bernie-sanders

McKelvey, F., & Piebiak, J. (2016). Porting the political campaign: The Nation-Builder platform and the global flows of political technology. *New Media & Society*, *20*(3), 901–918. https://doi.org/10.1177/1461444816675439

Mead, J. (2017, January 10). Why millennials aren't afraid of socialism. *The Nation*. https://www.thenation.com/article/archive/why-millennials-arent -afraid-of-the-s-word/

Melucci, A. (1989). *Nomads of the present*. Temple University Press.

Melucci, A. (1996). *Challenging codes: Collective action in the information age*. Cambridge University Press.

Milan, S. (2013). *Social movements and their technologies: Wiring social change*. Palgrave Macmillan.

Milano, studenti e centri sociali occupano il Ministero dei Trasporti. (2019, February 15). *Il Corriere Della Sera, Ed. Milano*. https://milano.corriere.it /foto-gallery/cronaca/19_febbraio_15/milano-studenti-centri-sociali -occupano-ministero-trasporti-cffob18c-3130-11e9-a4dd-63e8165b4075 .shtml

Millennial socialism: The resurgent left. (2019, February 16). *The Economist*. https://www.economist.com/leaders/2019/02/14/millennial-socialism

Misa, T. J. (2003). The compelling tangle of modernity and technology. In T. J. Misa, P. Brey, & A. Feenberg (Eds.), *Modernity and technology* (pp. 1–30). MIT Press.

Montagna, N. (2006). The de-commodification of urban space and the occupied social centres in Italy. *City*, *10*(3), 295–304. https://doi.org/10.1080/13604810 600980663

Morozov, E. (2013). *To save everything, click here: The folly of technological solutionism*. Public Affairs.

Mosco, V. (2004). *The digital sublime: Myth, power, and cyberspace*. MIT Press.

Mudde, C. (2017, April 3). The EU has tolerated Viktor Orbán for too long: It has to take a stand now. *The Guardian*. https://www.theguardian.com/comment isfree/2017/apr/03/eu-tolerated-viktor-orban-hungarian-central-european -university?CMP=share_btn_tw

Mudu, P. (2004). Resisting and challenging neoliberalism: The development of Italian Social Centers. *Antipode, 36*(5), 917–941. https://doi.org/10.1111/j.1467 -8330.2004.00461.x

Mudu, P. (2018). Introduction: Italians do it better? The occupation of spaces for radical struggles in Italy. *Antipode, 50*(2), 447–455. https://doi.org/10.1111/anti .12349

Murru, M. F., & Cossu, A. (2015). Macao prima e oltre i social media: La creazione dell'inatteso come logica di mobilitazione. *Studi Culturali, 12*(3), 353–371. https://doi.org/10.1405/81912

Natale, S., & Ballatore, A. (2014). The web will kill them all: New media, digital utopia, and political struggle in the Italian 5-Star Movement. *Media, Culture & Society, 36*(1), 105–121. https://doi.org/10.1177/0163443713511902

Noble, S. U. (2018). *Algorithms of oppression: How search engines reinforce racism*. New York University Press.

NoNetTax_HU. (2017, April 12). *Largest protest in Hungarian history—time to go mr orban #ceu* [Tweet]. Twitter. https://twitter.com/NoNetTax_HU/status /852235499037216769 (account no longer associated with this organization).

Nowak, J. (2016). The good, the bad, and the Commons: A critical review of popular discourse on piracy and power during anti-ACTA protests. *Journal of Computer-Mediated Communication, 21*(2), 177–194. https://doi.org/10.1111 /jcc4.12149

Nunberg, G. (2019, April 24). *"Socialism" isn't the scare word it once was*. NPR. https://www.npr.org/2019/04/24/716728643/socialism-isn-t-the-scare-word -it-once-was

Nye, D. E. (1996). *American technological sublime*. MIT Press.

"Occupy ICE" activists vacate City Hall after Kenney won't renew PARS agreement. (2018, July 28). CBS Philly. https://philadelphia.cbslocal.com/2018/07 /28/occupy-ice-philadelphia-city-hall-mayor-kenney/

Offe, C., & Adler, P. (1991). Capitalism by democratic design? Democratic theory facing the triple transition in East Central Europe. *Social Research, 58*(4), 865–892.

O'Mara, M. (2019). *The code: Silicon Valley and the remaking of America*. Penguin Press.

Orbán, V. (2014, July 26). *Speech at the 25th Bálványos Summer Free University and Student Camp*. www.kormany.hu/en/the-prime-minister/the-prime -minister-s-speeches/prime-minister-viktor-orban-s-speech-at-the-25th -balvanyos-summer-free-university-and-student-camp

Orso, A., & Feliciano Reyes, J. (2018, July 5). Inside the Philadelphia Occupy ICE camp that police raided Thursday. *The Philadelphia Inquirer.* https://www.inquirer.com/philly/news/occupyicephl-camp-police-raid -philly-socialists-20180705.html

Pállinger, Z. T. (2019). Direct democracy in an increasingly illiberal setting: The case of the Hungarian national referendum. *Contemporary Politics*, *25*(1), 62–77. https://doi.org/10.1080/13569775.2018.1543924

Pap, A. L. (2018). *Democratic decline in Hungary: Law and society in an illiberal democracy.* Routledge.

Philly Socialists. (n.d.). *Joining groups.* Retrieved May 5, 2019, from https://www .phillysocialists.org/joining-groups

Philly Socialists. (2017). *Constitution.* https://static1.squarespace.com/static /59cb1893edaed8670cb27244/t/59f7a88d6c319421a027d291/1509402765969 /Constitution+--+2017+appoved.pdf

Philly Socialists. (2018a). *Philly Socialists* [Pamphlet]. Philly Socialists.

Philly Socialists. (2018b). *Some hot organizing tips we've learned.* https://drive .google.com/file/d/1vOVok_z2Ihocx4e6OI1XdbKTizs3Lsma/view

Philly Socialists. (2018c). *Capital to bring down capitalism: Finances & fundraising workshop.* https://docs.google.com/presentation/d/1IoTSjeJNojtHCi 8buyn5yQrxQW_JQc2Jj8R7WJ_yyeY/edit#slide=id.p3

Philly Socialists. (2018d, July 28). *Cool kids and organizers . . .* [Photo]. Facebook. https://www.facebook.com/PhillySocialists/photos/a.2328488834 23724/2082327778475816/?type=3&theater

Philly Socialists. (2019, March 29). *How to write to incarcerated comrades . . .* [Event]. Facebook. https://www.facebook.com/events/repair-the-world -philadelphia/how-to-write-to-incarcerated-comrades-letter-writing-party /2292967804325181/

Pickard, V. W. (2006). United yet autonomous: Indymedia and the struggle to sustain a radical democratic network. *Media, Culture & Society*, *28*(3), 315–336. https://doi.org/10.1177/0163443706061685

Pirro, A. L. P., & Róna, D. (2019). Far-right activism in Hungary: Youth participation in Jobbik and its network. *European Societies*, *21*(4), 603–626. https:// doi.org/10.1080/14616696.2018.1494292

Polletta, F. (2002). *Freedom is an endless meeting: Democracy in American social movements.* University of Chicago Press.

Popescu, M., & Toka, G. (2021). The Hungarian opposition primaries of fall 2021: Testing the feasible in an authoritarian regime. *Studia Politica: Romanian Political Science Review*, *21*(2), 665–689.

Portwood-Stacer, L. (2013a). *Lifestyle politics and radical activism.* Bloomsbury.

Portwood-Stacer, L. (2013b). Media refusal and conspicuous non-consumption: The performative and political dimensions of Facebook abstention. *New Media & Society*, *15*(7), 1041–1057. https://doi.org/10.1177/1461444812465139

Postill, J. (2014). Freedom technologists and the new protest movements: A theory of protest formulas. *Convergence: The International Journal of Research into New Media Technologies, 20*(4), 402–418. https://doi.org/10.1177/1354856514541350

Prasad, R. (2020). *Infrastructure of a nation: Politics of connectivity in India* [Doctoral dissertation, University of Pennsylvania]. https://www.proquest.com/docview/2572616837/64D3A06542614586PQ/15

Progetto 20k. (2017, December 19). *Our story* [Status update]. Facebook. https://www.facebook.com/progetto20k/

Robin, C. (2018, August 24). The new socialists: Why the pitch from Alexandria Ocasio-Cortez and Bernie Sanders resonates in 2018. *The New York Times.* https://www.nytimes.com/2018/08/24/opinion/sunday/what-socialism-looks-like-in-2018.html

Robins, K. (1996). *Into the image: Culture and politics in the field of vision.* Routledge.

Roos, J. (2011, November 2). The Global Square: An online platform for our movement. *Roar Magazine.* http://roarmag.org/2011/11/the-global-square-an-online-platform-for-our-movement

Roose, K. (2019, March 13). A better way to break up Big Tech. *The New York Times.* https://www.nytimes.com/2019/03/13/technology/elizabeth-warren-tech-companies.html

Rucht, D. (2004). The quadruple "A": Media strategies of protest movements since the 1960s. In W. Van de Donk, B. D. Loader, P. G. Nixon, & D. Rucht (Eds.), *Cyberprotest: New media, citizens and social movement* (pp. 29–56). Routledge.

Russell, A. (2018). Nuit Debout: Representations, affect, and prototyping change—feature. *International Journal of Communication, 12,* 1864–1871. https://ijoc.org/index.php/ijoc/article/view/6422/2336.

Santora, M. (2018, March 17). Young Slovaks buck a trend, protesting to save their democracy. *The New York Times.* https://www.nytimes.com/2018/03/17/world/europe/slovakia-protests-robert-fico-jan-kuciak.html

Sasko, C. (2018, July 6). After police remove ICE encampment, protesters regroup at City Hall. *Philadelphia Magazine.* https://www.phillymag.com/news/2018/07/06/ice-protest-camp-city-hall/

Scheppele, K. L. (2013). The rule of law and the Frankenstate: Why governance checklists do not work. *Governance, 26*(4), 559–562. https://doi.org/10.1111/gove.12049

Schradie, J. (2015). Silicon Valley ideology and class inequality: A virtual poll tax on digital politics. In S. Coleman & D. Freelon (Eds.), *Handbook of digital politics* (pp. 67–84). Edward Elgar Publishing. https://doi.org/10.4337/9781782548768.00012

Schradie, J. (2019). *The revolution that wasn't: How digital activism favors conservatives.* Harvard University Press.

Scott, M., Cerulus, L., & Overly, S. (2019, May 29). *How Silicon Valley gamed the world's toughest privacy rules.* Politico. https://www.politico.com/story/2019 /05/25/how-silicon-valley-gamed-the-worlds-toughest-privacy-rules-1466148

Shirky, C. (2011, January). The political power of social media: Technology, the public sphere, and political change. *Foreign Affairs.* https://www.foreign affairs.com/articles/2010-12-20/political-power-social-media

Stack app. (n.d.). Retrieved August 28, 2022, from https://stackthe.app

Star, S. L. (1999). The ethnography of infrastructure. *American Behavioral Scientist, 43*(3), 377–391. https://doi.org/10.1177/00027649921955326

Stein, J. (2017, August 5). *9 questions about the Democratic Socialists of America you were too embarrassed to ask.* Vox. https://www.vox.com/policy -and-politics/2017/8/5/15930786/dsa-socialists-convention-national

Streeter, T. (2005). The moment of *Wired. Critical Inquiry, 31*(4), 1–17. https://doi.org/10.1086/444514

Százezren az internetadó ellen. (2014, October 25). *Hozd magaddal TE is tönkrement kütyüidet/gépeidet!* [Bring your ruined devices] [Video]. YouTube. https://www.youtube.com/watch?reload=9&v=DzFGMFhSxWM& fbclid=IwARou_NifUmUkBKm89AAeSwkzTsN_sTElxUUqjv67m3IjXIehzo BnO8lkfNo

Tarrow, S. (2011). *Power in movement: Social movements and contentious politics.* Cambridge University Press.

Tavits, M., & Letki, N. (2009). When left is right: Party ideology and policy in post-Communist Europe. *American Political Science Review, 103*(4), 555–569. https://doi.org/10.1017/S0003055409990220

Taylor, A. (2016, March). Against activism. *The Baffler.*

Taylor, B. (2013). From alterglobalization to Occupy Wall Street: Neoanarchism and the new spirit of the left. *City: Analysis of Urban Trends, Culture, Theory, Policy, Action, 17*(6), 729–747. https://doi.org/10.1080/13604813.2013.849127

Taylor, C. (2004). *Modern social imaginaries.* Duke University Press.

Terranova, T. (2000). Free labor: Producing culture for the digital economy. *Social Text, 18*(2 63), 33–58. https://doi.org/10.1215/01642472-18-2_63-33

Terranova, T., & Donovan, J. (2013). Occupy social networks: The paradoxes of corporate social media for networked social movements. In G. Lovink & M. Rasch (Eds.), *Unlike us reader: Social media monopolies and their alternatives* (pp. 296–311). Institute of Network Cultures.

Thompson, D. (2019, January 31). *Before the Philadelphia Tenants Union: Philly Socialists' first tenant fight.* Regeneration. https://regenerationmag.org/an -organizers-history-of-the-philadelphia-tenants-union-part-i/

Thousands of Hungarians protest against sackings at news website. (2020, July 25). France 24. https://www.france24.com/en/20200725-thousands-of -hungarians-protest-against-sackings-at-news-website

Ticona, J. (2022). *Left to our own devices: Coping with insecure work in a digital age.* Oxford University Press.

Tre anni di viaggio nella metropoli. (2018, June 4). Milano in Movimento. https://milanoinmovimento.com/primo-piano/lume-tre-anni-di-viaggio-nella-metropoli

Treré, E. (2018). *Hybrid media activism: Ecologies, imaginaries, algorithms.* Routledge.

Treré, E., & Barranquero Carretero, A. (2018). Tracing the roots of techno-politics: Towards a North-South dialogue. In F. S. Caballero & T. Gravante (Eds.), *Networks, movements and technopolitics in Latin America: Critical analysis and current challenges* (pp. 43–63). Springer International Publishing. https://doi.org/10.1007/978-3-319-65560-4_3

Treré, E., Jeppesen, S., & Mattoni, A. (2017). Comparing digital protest media imaginaries: Anti-austerity movements in Spain, Italy & Greece. *TripleC, 15*(2), 406–424. https://doi.org/10.31269/triplec.v15i2.772

Tufekci, Z. (2017). *Twitter and tear gas: The power and fragility of networked protest.* Yale University Press.

Turner, F. (2006). *From counterculture to cyberculture: Stewart Brand, the Whole Earth Network, and the rise of digital utopianism.* University of Chicago Press.

Valentine, B. (2012, July 27). *Occupy.Here hopes to create a free, open, unregulated community without the internet.* http://hyperallergic.com/54540/dan-phiffers-occupy-here-rhizome-grant/

Vazzana, M. (2017, October 19). Occupato l'ex cinema Orchidea. E scatta la denuncia del Comune. *Il Giorno.* https://www.ilgiorno.it/milano/cronaca/occupazione-orchidea-1.3473553

Venni, F. (2017, October 20). Ex cinema Orchidea fermo da due anni il progetto di recupero. *La Repubblica.* https://ricerca.repubblica.it/repubblica/archivio/repubblica/2017/10/20/ex-cinema-orchidea-fermo-da-due-anni-il-progetto-di-recuperoMilano09.html?ref=search

Wiener, A. (2020). *Uncanny valley: A memoir.* Picador.

Wilkin, P. (2018). The rise of "illiberal" democracy: The Orbánization of Hungarian political culture. *Journal of World-Systems Research, 24*(1), 5–42. https://doi.org/10.5195/jwsr.2018.716

Wilkin, P., Dencik, L., & Bognár, É. (2015). Digital activism and Hungarian media reform: The case of Milla. *European Journal of Communication, 30*(6), 682–697. https://doi.org/10.1177/0267323115595528

Williams, R. (1975). *Television: Technology and cultural form.* Schocken Books.

Winner, L. (1986). *The whale and the reactor: A search for limits in an age of high technology.* University of Chicago Press.

Wolfson, T. (2014). *Digital rebellion: The birth of the cyber Left.* University of Illinois Press.

Yang, G. (2016). Activism. In B. Peters (Ed.), *Digital keywords: A vocabulary of information society and culture* (pp. 1–17). Princeton University Press.

Zayani, M. (2015). *Networked publics and digital contention: The politics of everyday life in Tunisia.* Oxford University Press.

Zerofsky, E. (2019, January 14). Viktor Orbán's far-right vision for Europe. *The New Yorker.* https://www.newyorker.com/magazine/2019/01/14/viktor-orbans-far-right-vision-for-europe

Zontea, A. (2015). The Hungarian student network: A counterculture in the making. In P. Krasztev & J. van Til (Eds.), *The Hungarian patient: Social opposition to an illiberal democracy* (pp. 263–289). Central European University LLC.

Zuckerberg, M. (2017, February 16). *Building global community.* Facebook. https://www.facebook.com/notes/mark-zuckerberg/building-global-community/10154544292806634

Zuckerberg, M. (2019, March 6). *A privacy-focused vision for social networking.* Facebook. https://www.facebook.com/notes/mark-zuckerberg/a-privacy-focused-vision-for-social-networking/10156700570096634/

Index

Ability Caucus, 135

Abolish Silicon Valley (Liu), 37

ACTA. *See* Anti-Counterfeiting Trade Agreement

activism, 1–3, 5–6, 46, 169, 172–74; analyzing activist digital technologies, 11–13; big data approaches to studying, 18; challenge imaginary and, 165; conceptualizing activist digital technologies, 9–11; cultural production and, 93–95; digital technologies being crucial for, 89; internet in radical leftist activism, 111, 113; lifestyle activism, 126, 154, 159; online activism, 155, 157; political activism, 90; searching for alternatives to social media, 109–11; social movements and digital technologies, 6–9

activist networking, 126, 151, 158–59, 164; concept, 202n3; and organizing where people are, 154–57. *See* activist technological imaginaries; organizing where people are

activist opposition, mobilization of, 55–60

activist technological imaginaries, 160–61, 174–75; analyzing, 11–13; case studies of, 13–16; challenge as, 164–68; characteristics of, 31–35; collective imagination and, 28–30; conceptualizing, 9–11; defining, 10, 31; discourses as integral to technologies, 25–28; dominance of, 10–11; exposing social movements to, 4–5, 8; fighting systems with tools of system, 111–21; framework, 44–49; in Hungarian internet tax protests, 50–85; invisibility of, 180–82; LUMe imaginary of negotiation, 86–122; movement politics and, 5; mundane modernity, 66–84; and organizing where people are, 148–59; PS imaginary of negotiation, 123–59; recognizing, 4; reflecting and shaping politics of social movements, 168–73; situating, 24–31; and universal ambition of Silicon Valley, 34–44

Adam, interviewee, 63–64, 66, 68–69, 71–72, 77, 83

Alexander, interviewee, 142, 144

alternative, challenge technological imaginary, 166–67

Amy, interviewee, 129, 138, 146

Anti-Counterfeiting Trade Agreement (ACTA), 179

AoIR. *See* Association of Internet Researchers

Appadurai, A., 81

appropriation, imaginary of, 50–53, 161–62; Hungarian internet tax protests, 53–55; illiberal turn of Hungary, 55–60; mundane modernity of internet, 66–78;

Founded in 1893,
UNIVERSITY OF CALIFORNIA PRESS
publishes bold, progressive books and journals
on topics in the arts, humanities, social sciences,
and natural sciences—with a focus on social
justice issues—that inspire thought and action
among readers worldwide.

The UC PRESS FOUNDATION
raises funds to uphold the press's vital role
as an independent, nonprofit publisher, and
receives philanthropic support from a wide
range of individuals and institutions—and from
committed readers like you. To learn more, visit
ucpress.edu/supportus.